Architecture and Participation

Edited by

Peter Blundell Jones
Doina Petrescu
Jeremy Till

Taylor & Francis
Taylor & Francis Group
LONDON AND NEW YORK

First published 2005 by Taylor & Francis, 2 Park Square,
Milton Park, Abingdon, Oxon OX14 4RN.

Simultaneously published in the USA and Canada by
Taylor & Francis Group . ess, 270 Madison Ave, New York, NY 10016.

Taylor & Francis is an imprint of the Taylor & Francis Group.

Transferred to Digital Printing 2009

Designed and typeset by Ben Weaver.
Typeset in Fedra.

British Library Cataloguing in Publication Data
A catalogue record for this book is available from the
British Library.

Library of Congress Cataloging in Publication Data
A catalog record for this book has been applied for.

ISBN 0-415-31745-2 (Hb.)
ISBN 0-415-31746-0 (Pb.)

Contents

Contributors

Peter Blundell Jones is Professor of Architecture at the University of Sheffield and a frequent contributor to *The Architectural Review*. His books include *Hans Scharoun* (Phaidon 1995), *Dialogues in Time: New Graz Architecture* (HdA Graz 1998), *Hugo Häring* (Menges 1999), *Günter Behnisch* (Birkhäuser 2000) and *Modern Architecture through Case Studies* (Architectural Press 2002). A monograph, *Gunnar Asplund* (Phaidon) is in press.

Jon Broome, after studying at the Architectural Association, worked in the housing department for Lewisham Council. In the 1980s he collaborated with Walter Segal on social self-build groups. From 1984 to 2000 he was director of Architype, which specialised in low-energy design, timber frame construction and sustainable building. He now runs his own consultancy mixing theory and practice. Projects include low environmental impact housing and the Sustainability Works website for the Housing Corporation. His publications include *The Self-Build Book* (1991) and a contribution to *Housing and the Environment*, published by the Chartered Institute of Housing in 1994.

Raoul Bunschoten is director of CHORA-urbanism and architecture and of CHORA-research, the latter a not-for-profit organisation. CHORA-research is involved in a planning project for Peterhead, Aberdeenshire, and in a programming study for the so-called Future Centre of the Rijkswaterstaat (the Netherlands National Department of Water and Infrastructure). CHORA architecture and urbanism is planning two buildings in Ireland, and is a partner in a commission for a masterplan study for Homerton Cross, Hackney, east London. Raoul Bunschoten has taught for 13 years at the Architectural Association in London, most of that time as Diploma Unit Master, and for eight years as thesis tutor at the Berlage Institute in Rotterdam. Currently he is focusing on projects and research.

Giancarlo De Carlo was born in 1919 and studied engineering at Milan polytechnic. During the Second World War, he joined the anti-fascists, met a circle of left-wing intellectuals, and had already produced publications on Le Corbusier, Wright and Morris before he completed his architectural studies in Venice. He started an office in 1950 which has run ever since, and was an editor of *Casabella Continuità* from 1954-56. As a member of CIAM from 1955, he was a key figure in Team Ten, the breakaway group that criticised the shortcomings of the Modern Movement and sought a new direction. His role in academic discourse and criticism led to the foundation in 1976 of ILAUD, the International Laboratory for Architecture and Urban Design, and in 1977 of his own journal *Spazio e Società*. Best known for its penetrating urban studies and sensitive work in historic contexts, his office has a long and distinguished production, including several pioneering works of participation.

Prue Chiles combines teaching with research and pratice. She is a senior lecturer and diploma unit leader at the University of Sheffield School of Architecture. She pioneered the live project programme in the Diploma School. She also directs the School of Architecture's Bureau of Design Research, set up in 2002 to work with both local communities and national groups on research-based design consultancy and heads a small private practice, with recent work including the DfES-funded 'Classroom of the Future'.

Stephen Connelly is a lecturer in the Department of Town and Regional Planning, University of Sheffield. His main research interests are public involvement in governance, sustainable development, and the interrelationship of these in planning in democratic societies.

Fluid are a multidisciplinary organisation composed of architects, urbanists, communications and marketing strategists, who have been heavily involved in community consultation and participatory urban design since their inception in 1996. They have worked on a range of award-winning New Deal For Communities, urban and social renewal projects in London, Liverpool and Derby, spanning consultation, urban masterplanning and architectural design. Most recently they have been working in Kings Cross Central for developers Argent St George on all aspects of community consultation, and on stakeholder and public consultation on the Olympic and non-Olympic regeneration of the Lower Lea Valley as part of the EDAW masterplanning team. Fluid have a long-standing association with London Metropolitan University where they have taught diploma architecture, and helped to set up and run a new MA on Urban Regeneration (Cities; Design and Regeneration) and two research

clusters, the Cities Institute and the Social and Architectural Research Group.

Teresa Hoskyns is a founding member of Taking Place and one of
the organisers of the first London Social Forum. She graduated from
the Royal College of Art in 1999 and is now undertaking a PhD at
the Bartlett School of Architecture, University College London.

Peter Hübner left school early to enter the family business of shoe-
making, then became a joiner before studying architecture in Stuttgart from 1963-68. In the 1970s he was a pioneer in prefabricated
plastics construction, designing portable buildings and bathroom
systems produced in long series. A chair at Stuttgart followed in
1979, teaching alongside Peter Sulzer. Between them they developed
the Bauhäusle student hostel, refounding their practice in participation. Hübner has developed this theme over 20 years, along with
parallel interests in computers and ecological design.

Eilfried Huth was born in Indonesia in 1930 to Austrian parents.
He studied architecture at the Technische Hochschule Graz from
1950-56, and for a few years ran his own office before entering a
partnership with Günther Domenig from 1963-75. This became
internationally known, and was an early focal point of the *Grazer
Schule*. Tension between the expressionistic Domenig and the more
socially-minded Huth eventually broke up the practice, and Huth
has run his own office since 1975, as well as being Professor at the
Hochschule der Künste in Berlin since 1984. He has been the leading
proponent of participation in housing in Graz, and the most prepared to let people decide for themselves.

Lucien Kroll was born in Brussels in 1927 and graduated from the
École Nationale Supérieure d'Architecture de la Cambre in 1951. He
started his own office in 1953, producing modest and sensitive work
in a modernist manner, until the controversial Maison Médicale at
the University of Louvain in 1970 brought him to international
attention. The fuss was caused by its anarchic image, but it was
deeply participative and it exposed in a building political conflicts
that normally remain hidden, as in many later works. Since then,
Kroll's office AUAI (Atelier d'Urbanisme, d'Architecture, et d'Infor-
matique) has built in several countries. He has lectured across the
world, and published several books.

Muf architecture/art were established in London in 1994 with the
then eccentric desire to make work in and for the public realm. They

have been doing so since. **Katherine (Shonfield) Vaughan Williams** wrote taught and speculated on the pleasures and the possibilities of architecture and the city.

Doina Petrescu is a lecturer in architecture at the University of Sheffield and a member of *Atelier d'Architecture Autogérée* in Paris. She has written, lectured and practised individually and collectively on issues of gender, technology, (geo)politics and poetics of space. Atelier d'architecture autogerée (Studio for self-managed architecture) is an associative structure including architects, artists, urban planners, landscape designers, sociologists, students and residents, aiming to develop alternative strategies in architecture and urban planning. They have recently participated at the third Berlin Biennale of contemporary art.

Anne Querrien is a sociologist and urban planner. In May 1968 she was an activist in the 22 March Movement and in the 1970s she worked as researcher at CERFI (Centre d'études, de recherches et de formations institutionnelles) with Félix Guattari. She is an editor of *Les Annales de la Recherche Urbaine* and member of the editorial committee for the magazines *Multitudes* and *Chimères*. In parallel, she is active in different associations such as AITEC (Association Internationale de Techniciens, Experts et Chercheurs) and CLCV (Consommation, Logement et Cadre de Vie).

Tim Richardson is a senior lecturer in the Department of Town and Regional Planning, University of Sheffield. His research explores how discourse theory can contribute to key debates in planning theory and practice. He is currently Visiting Professor in European Spatial Policy at Aalborg University.

Stalker is a collective based in Rome, which engages in actions and research to catalyse creative motions in time and space, to produce self-organised places, environments and situations. It was founded by a group of students during an occupation of Rome University and has been active since 1995. For some years, Stalker has been based at the ex-vet building of Campo Boario (a former slaughterhouse) together with the Kurd community, in order to experiment with a new form of contemporary public space based on reception and hospitality. In the few last years, Stalker has been promoting a network of artists, researchers and organisations named Osservatorio Nomade (ON). ON produces field projects based on social and environmental dynamics. It currently acts as ON/Corviale, ON/Egnatia, ON/Zingari.

Peter Sulzer studied art in Hamburg and attended the Hochschule für Gestaltung in Ulm before being inspired into architecture by an encounter with Konrad Wachsmann. He completed the course at Karlsruhe in 1959, and worked through the 1960s as a specialist in prefabricated construction. This expertise led to a Chair at Stuttgart University in 1969, and a construction course. Influenced by Walter Segal, he started the experiments in self-build with students, and this led his career in a participative direction. Peter Sulzer is also the historian of Jean Prouvé, publishing the French engineer/architect's work in several volumes.

Jeremy Till is Professor of Architecture and Head of the School of Architecture, University of Sheffield. He is also a Director of Sarah Wigglesworth Architects, an award-winning practice best known for their pioneering project, 9 Stock Orchard Street. With degrees in both philosophy and architecture, his writings interrogate the relationship of theory to practice. Over the past years, his work, both written and built, has explored architecture and the everyday; he is now working on a book entitled *Architecture and Contingency*.

Marion von Osten is an artist, curator and writer. She lives in Berlin and Zurich and teaches at the University of Art and Design (HGKZ), Zurich. Between 1996 and 1998 she was a curator at Schedhalle, Zurich, and initiated a number of exhibitions including 'Sex & Space', 'SuperMarket' and 'MoneyNations'. She has edited (with Justin Hoffmann) *Das Phantom sucht seinen Mörder* (Berlin: b_books, 1999) and *Norm der Abweichung* (Voldemeer/Springer, 2003).

Introduction

This book arose out of a lecture series that we jointly coordinated at the School of Architecture, University of Sheffield, in 2002. The three of us shared an interest in the subject of architecture and participation, but had different perspectives on the subject. We hoped that the lecture series would provide a forum for the discussion of ideas, as well as a basis for informing our teaching and research. Our initial aim for the lectures was quite modest; we wanted to introduce our students to an issue that we thought might have a lasting benefit on the way they thought about and went about architecture in the future. We also felt that the time was right for a re-evaluation of participation, particularly given a European political context in which 'participation' had become a buzzword, but with little thought given to what the word actually meant. We decided to keep the word but to question its meaning. To this end we invited speakers from a wide range of backgrounds to explore the general issue of architecture and participation. We were exceptionally fortunate in attracting people who had been at the vanguard of participation in the 1960s, together with some of the contemporary leaders in the field. When we went over the transcripts from the lectures we realised that, viewed together, the contributions presented an important set of insights on the subject. We were also conscious that the literature to date was scant and included little theorising of the subject. We therefore invited our lecturers to develop their contributions for this book, and also asked other people to make contributions where we felt an area had not been covered.

What is immediately striking about the collection of essays is that they offer alternatives to widely accepted approaches to participation. At the level of the lowest common denominator, architectural participation can be defined as the involvement of the user at some stage in the design process. Too often this involvement is token, bringing a degree of worthiness to the architectural process without really transforming it. Recently, government policy in Europe and the USA has made participation a necessary part of public work; it has thus effectively been institutionalised, another box among many to tick in order to get approval and funding.

Participation becomes an organised (and potentially manipulated) part of any regeneration project, in which users are meant to be given a voice, but the process stifles the sounds coming out. The problem is that the term participation is accepted uncritically, and idealised notions which centre on concepts of consensus are implied. Many of the essays in this book present a challenge to that uncritical acceptance of participation and of the role of the user. Instead they open up discussion about the politics of participation, accepting, and in some cases enjoying, the contested conditions of the participatory process, its conflictual possibilities and unpredictable nature. As such, participation is not always regarded as the guarantee of sustainability within a project but as an approach that assumes risks and uncertainty.

Participation needs to differentiate between the demands of the clients and the desires of the users. Architects, needing clients with power and money, are usually on the side of those in power and willing to embrace and express in built terms the ideology and economics of these clients, to the exclusion of the desires of the potential users. There is thus a removal of the general public from the processes of architectural production, which in turn leads to a sense of alienation of the users from their environment. Modernisation has meant the removal of people from decisions, as layers of bureaucracy and specialist procedures compel experts to intervene between the user and the building. These experts bring with them their own value systems that are often at odds with those of the users. A gap thus opens up between the world as built and the world as needed and desired: to see the effects of this gap we need look no further than the mass housing projects of the mid-twentieth century, when a standardised version of living and abstract notions of 'community' were imposed statically by a supposedly benevolent bureaucracy, rather than being allowed to grow more spontaneously according to people's wishes. Participation effectively addresses this gap through involving the user in the early stages of architectural production, leading to an environment that not only has a sense of ownership but is also more responsive to change.

Passing beyond the technical and economic frameworks of architecture, participation inevitably engages with the political, a term often denied by architects in the assessment of their work. In contemporary global politics, where issues of democracy are so contested, true participation in the processes of change is becoming increasingly rare but at the same time is increasingly needed. If people are to feel a sense of belonging to the world in which they live, an involvement in the spaces they inhabit is a good starting point. This is reflected in most of the chapters in the book, and leads to a

reading of architecture as the occupation of space by sensate, politicised beings, not architecture as technically determined process or
rarefied aesthetic. The political dimension is too often avoided by
differentiating between the functional and the aesthetic, treating
the former as a purportedly objective terrain of ergonomics and
efficiency, and seeing the latter as a kind of private language supposedly above the political debate. Many chapters in the book indicate that the functional and the aesthetic are not isolated, neutral
terms but must be placed within a more complex politicised world.
The introduction of politics takes participation beyond the expedient and pragmatic, forcing it to engage with issues that in the long
term will make architecture more responsive and responsible.

It may be argued that with the rise of media coverage of architecture, especially the multitude of populist television programmes,
there is a concomitant rise in public engagement with architecture.
But the media, with its emphasis on image and surface, can lead to
false participation, turning us into passive consumers and not
active doers and makers; the drama on the screen takes over from
the actual lived-in product. By providing snapshots of lifestyles the
media panders to the public's wishes, but in a way that is completely circumscribed by the dominance of taste and consumer technologies – both of which exhibit built-in obsolescence. The public
thus become fixated on a superficial and transient version of architecture, losing sight of the transformative potential of the built
environment and the way in which they might become properly
engaged in the transformation. Architecture needs to be understood
within a broader framework than the surface of image, both in
terms of engaging with context and in terms of engaging with all
the senses, through time and experience of use.

Because true participation concerns real engagement rather
than a grazing of the image, it can provide a counterpoint to the
image-fuelled world of the media. But of course mainstream architectural culture is equally obsessed with the image – we can see how
participation is not merely a means to engage users more fully in
the production of space, but also a means to criticise and redirect
architectural culture. Many contributors to this book demonstrate
that participation, through introducing alternative means of production, leads to alternative aesthetics and spatialities. It is too
easy to dismiss some of these aesthetics as 'crude' or 'dirty', because
that simply reinforces the presumed superiority of the standard
architectural categories of refined and clean. Instead, we should
recognise that the products of participation have their own value
system that stands alongside that of conventional architecture – and
that this value system is perhaps more relevant and appropriate to

the democratic transformation of the built environment. The inclusion throughout the book of artists, planners and curators in inventing creative processes for participation, both individually and collaboratively, is suggestive of the way that participation leads to an expanded field for architectural practice; it is a means of reinvigorating architecture, bringing benefit for users and architects alike.

Indeed, a common theme throughout the book is that participation is not just a catalyst for transformation of the role (and eventual lives) of users, but also for the transformation of architectural practice. It comes as no surprise that many contributors have been consistent irritants to the architectural establishment, in so far as they have consistently highlighted the limits of that establishment. Unfortunately the normal reaction is to marginalise or dismiss the actions of the irritants as perverse behaviour, and with this, participation, by association, is also labelled a marginal activity. Our contention is that, as with all things sitting on the margins, participation is a good means of identifying the strengths and weaknesses of the centre. From this critical view flows a more positive reformulation, in which participation can be seen as a means of making architectural practice more relevant to, and more engaged with, the everyday world.

To accomplish this transformation, we do not present a standard version of participation; we even contest that a standard, unique, version of participation could ever be possible. The danger with a normative technique is that it sees the user (once again) as standard, there to be subjected to common methods. Instead, one has to accept that with multiple users, multiple desires and multiple contexts, multiple forms of participation are necessary. The book covers a wide range of users, situations and methods, reflected to some extent in the differing modes of presenting the work. These range from the informal recording of a lecture, through illustrated essays, to structured texts. We have also consciously mixed up history, theory and practice, in an attempt to see one aspect always informing another. The construction of the book itself was also participative, including different visions and different voices of men and women, of professionals and users, of academics and practitioners, with whom we had many discussions and exchanges. In preparing the bibliography, we were astonished at how little of the available literature on architecture and participation presented any kind of theoretical context. It was our intent to fill this gap, but at the same time to provide useful pointers for future practice. Clearly the book is therefore not a primer, but nor is it a remote academic text. At a time when participation is so played-up by politicians but also greatly misunderstood, we hope that the contributions will inform and inspire future participatory practice in architecture and other fields. Driving all the contributors is a belief that participation can make a difference to the way that we all, users and experts alike, engage with our built environment. If this book makes a small difference to the future quality, and relevance, of that environment, it will have served its purpose. If it succeeds in provoking questions about the procedures and values of standard architectural practice, so much the better.

Politics of participation

Architecture's public

1

As the original translation in *Parametro* was somewhat literal and unclear in places, this version has been re-edited, and includes some improvements added by Benedict Zucchi in the version published in his *Giancarlo De Carlo*, Oxford: Butterworth, 1992.

Editor's note [PBJ]

This milestone in architectural history began life as a lecture given at a conference in Liège in 1969, and was published in extended form with an English translation the following year in the Italian periodical Parametro.[1] *It carries both the optimistic and egalitarian spirit of 1968 and the anger of a younger modernist generation discovering that the social ideals of the Modern Movement had been lost or betrayed. Its strongly political tone recalls a time when the impact of global capitalism was beginning to be felt, and the political implications of the aesthetic were being exposed. Thirty-four years on, much remains relevant, and many of the problems identified are still with us: the tendency for academic architecture to isolate itself in its own discourse, for example, has increased. This remains a key text for anyone concerned with participation.*

The revolt and the frustration of the school of architecture

When the university protest exploded – the most important event since the end of the Second World War – the architecture faculties found themselves immediately in the vanguard. In many universities in Europe and in the wider world, students of architecture were the first to demand a radical renewal of organisational structures and teaching methods.

Why?

Because the faculties of architecture, more than any other faculty, had long been dominated by an academic body interested only in preventing new ideas from penetrating into the school (in architecture new ideas are at least 50 years old). Since the School was the last refuge into which new ideas had to penetrate, the conflict was radical at the beginning. The limits of the conservative position were solid and precise, so the prospects of renewal seemed equally solid and precise. But after an initial period of obstinate resistance, the academic body began to wonder if the new ideas were really so dangerous, especially since they were now accepted by everyone – at all levels of power, even by the state bureaucracy and property speculators. Precisely because of this universal acceptance, the suspicion grew that new ideas and young people had lost their aggressiveness. And so having reasonably accepted this idea, the academic body made an admirable pirouette, changing its previous routine without moving the axis of rotation. By accepting the most innocuous elements of a new language – and possibly by introducing a few new personages chosen from among the most innocuous proponents of these innocuities – it was possible to continue defending something of the old position. The operation promised to be a success, and property speculation – given more time and different circumstances – had already carried it through. But instead it was a total failure. Why?

Because in the meantime the students, matured by their struggle, had changed their outlook. They had realised that it was not just a matter of organisational structures and teaching methods, but a more fundamental question about the purpose of their training and social role. The objective of their struggle could no longer be simply to substitute one symbol for another, or one person for another. It was a question of rediscovering the reasons for being an architect in a world which the academics and power brokers, men of apparently opposing sides, had long accepted and which they, the students, for good reasons had refused. They sought a different way of doing architecture for the edification of a different world (perhaps best defined negatively: not classist, not racist, not violent, not repressive, not alienating, not specialising, not totalising). For architecture to regain a progressive role, it was necessary first to verify how much new material was included in that passed off as new: then to build something truly new, wholly new in content as well as in expressive forms. This has not come about, however, and perhaps it has not even begun. And so the excellent premises which fed the revolt shaded off into a state of confusion which has removed the faculty of architecture from its avant-garde position to a frustrating and inconclusive place at the rear. Why?

Because there was nothing either in the faculty or in architectural practice that could nourish a courageous exploration. There was no line of thought or collection of facts coherent enough with reality to provide a matrix of concrete alternatives for the modification of reality. The field of architecture remained amorphous and impalpable, lacking structure. Not only was it incapable of regenerating itself: it even remained insensitive to the stimuli of its own contradictions.

The ambiguity of the architect's role
Any discussion of the credibility (and of the historical legitimacy) of architecture in the contemporary world must begin with an acknowledgement of this situation, acknowledging it as the origin of any investigation of architecture's future or past. We shall begin

defining the inconsistency between the field of architecture and the facts of reality by examining the behaviour of its protagonist, the architect. No other connotation of a human craft has had such wide and ambiguous meanings. The term has been applied to figures ranging from head-bricklayer to God (supreme 'architect' of the universe), and this unlimited latitude of meaning has weighed enormously on the destiny of those claiming the title, because it has trapped them between the frustrating suspicion of not achieving the minimum and the exalted vanity of arriving at the maximum.

In different historical epochs, depending on the use to which political power put him, the architect has been more a head-bricklayer or more a god. If not exactly head-bricklayer, he was certainly head builder at the end of the Middle Ages and the beginning of the Renaissance. If not exactly God, then he was high priest and custodian of state secrets in ancient Egypt from the First Dynasty to the conquest of Alexander. In all epochs, whatever the importance of his role, the architect has been subject to the world view of those in power. Since money, materials, land and authority to act were necessary, and since the ruling power was the only force capable of furnishing him with these means, the architect by definition had to identify himself with it, even transforming himself into its operative appendage. Bourgeois society, famous for taking care of everything and leaving little room for manifestations of independence to insinuate themselves, also tried to classify the role of the architect, situating it within the more general concept of the profession. As a professional, the architect became a representative of the class in power. His duties were limited to the study and application of building technology (later also urban planning, later still environmental planning). In carrying out his duties he found both his dignity and his payment, as long as he did not worry about motivations or consequences: that is, as long as he did not refer his activity to a more general political condition. So with the rise of bourgeois professionalism, architecture was driven into the realm of specialisation, where only the problems of 'how' are important, because the problems of 'why' are considered solved once and for all. But the subjugation which succeeded so well with most human activities could not succeed with architecture. This was not because architecture had a conceptual and operative structure able to resist instrumentalisation, but precisely the opposite: because it lacked structure. We must not forget that when the sacred programme of specialisation began to succeed in a world shaken by the tremors of the industrial revolution, militant architecture remained obsessed with styles, proposing a mere manipulation of signs when what was really required was a profound subversion of concepts and methods.

But in any case, how and in what could architecture have specialised? The very school for the preparation of architects was born out of an ambiguous coupling of art and technology, destined inevitably to generate a sterile species. Its composition – still almost intact today – was derived from the grafting of a few peripheral branches of the Polytechnical School onto the old trunk of the Academy of Fine Arts, a combination of irreconcilable opposites. The academic artistic background was destined systematically to annul the formation of any concrete proposition connected with technology, while the technical was destined in turn to render commonplace any abstract expressive proposition connected with art. Forced into an inorganic coexistence, both academic art and applied technology retarded the scientific transformation of the architectural discipline and interrupted its contacts with social transformations. Thus the lack of a disciplinary structure saved architecture from specialisation but threw it into the state of vagueness and confusion which persists as the core of its contemporary trouble.

The Modern Movement:
Between commitment and uncommitment

Obviously at this point one could object that there was the Modern Movement, a movement which produced many ideas and many heroes. And it is a pertinent objection: the Modern Movement represented an important chance for cultural renewal in architecture. But we need to question architecture's 'credibility', i.e. its capacity to have a 'public'. And therefore we must start by addressing a fundamental question: what is architecture's public? The architects themselves? The clients who commission the buildings? The people – all the people who use architecture? If the third hypothesis is true – that all the people who use architecture are its public, and today this seems hard to resist – then the presence and the work of the Modern Movement and its heroes must emerge in a different perspective from that allowed by its own publicity machine. We cannot escape the fact that the Modern Movement has preserved substantial defects of the amorphous condition from which it emerged. For example, it preserved the ambiguity of role assumed when it became a bourgeois profession, and it sought to reconcile art and technology by simple qualitative modification of the first of these 'two factors', merely substituting modern art for academic art. Instead, it should have set aside the whole superfluous dilemma, questioning architecture's objectives and methods, both to allow it to become scientific and to allow it a radical expressive renewal.

But this was only the consequence of a more serious failing that the Modern Movement inherited from the amorphous matrix in which it was generated: the deliberate programmatic attitude of an elite. I do not criticise the size of the group – the fact that only small groups can set off processes of real renewal seems unquestionable – but rather the group's choices in defining its field of operation. The field which the Modern Movement intended to conquer (and did in fact conquer) was that already occupied by academic or business architecture; a field restricted to relations between clients and entrepreneurs, land owners, critics, connoisseurs, and architects; a field built on a network of economic and social class interests and held together by the mysterious tension of a cultural and aesthetic class code. This was a field that excluded everything in economic, social, cultural and aesthetic terms that was not shared by the class in power. It is true that a few 'heroes' had intentions and produced works beyond these limits, but always leaning out of their elite positions, never stepping out to stand on the other side: the side of the people – those who use and bear architecture. The ideas and accomplishment of such 'heroes' – for example a Loos or a Le Corbusier or a few others (mostly different, though official criticism bunches them together) – have an inestimable value which architecture cannot do without. Nevertheless they represent only a tiny speck in the great mountain of unsolved problems in the contemporary human environment. By distancing itself from the real context of society and its most concrete environmental needs, the elite attitude of the Modern Movement just accentuated the superfluity of architecture. The old gulf due to an ambiguous professional condition was widened by a further estrangement from reality, isolating architecture in a floating condition. This has favoured the formation of a few great free spirits projecting a daring search for newness, but it has also encouraged the formation of their opposite; a multitude of walk-ons destined to nullify the novelties of the former, reducing them to inert symbols completely commensurate with the requirements of the ruling class.

There is no need to describe these walk-ons in detail: they form the artichoke of cultural activity, layer after layer: philosopher, economist, sociologist, politician, historian, educator, technologist, artist, decorator, designer, builder, city planner, etc. Under the hundredth leaf you find the consultants to those in power – the expert exploiters of floor-space, the manipulators of building codes, the cultural legitimators of the sack of the city, and the territory organised by financiers, politicians and bureaucrats to the detriment of ordinary people. To describe this character further is superfluous, because he is already familiar, if only at the literary level, through novels, comedies, films, and television sketches, which present him as a stereotype of intellectual alienation in our neo-capitalist age. Although this serves to explain why architecture is no longer credible, it is more worthwhile to analyse the phenomenon in its trunk than in its branches, even if the latter are substantial and diversified. The point is that credibility disappeared when modern architecture chose the same public as academic or business architecture; that is, when it took an elite position on the side of the client rather than on the side of the user. Historical experience has taught us that elites, even when claiming neutrality, get caught in fields of force that benevolently concede neutrality because they know that in conceding it they exploit it, simply through the effect of their interest. Conditioning arrives on cue at the very moment when it is expected: for when 'neutrally' dealing with the problems of 'how', the problems of 'why' are forgotten.

Faith in 'how' and ignorance about 'why'
Two examples selected from the history of the Modern Movement will illustrate this failure of memory. The first is the CIAM Frankfurt Congress of 1929 devoted to 'Minimum Housing'; the second the CIAM Hoddesdon Congress of 1951 on the 'Heart of the City'. Certainly the former was more important than the latter in terms of seriousness of commitment, but both were equally important for the prospects they opened up (and closed down). At Frankfurt, the architects addressed the problem of how to manage the great demand for housing that exploded after the First World War in every city of the world. They were right to take up the problem, but wrong to believe that it was their invention. It had already been invented and dramatised by the capitalist system, which having urbanised masses of farmers to generate manpower for industry without providing for their settlement in the city, now found itself in a tight spot, caught in the web of its own contradictions. The alarm expressed itself in the slogan 'more housing or less production' (and in the architects' more strident echo 'architecture or revolution'). The remedy prescribed was the construction, possibly in series, of the cheapest possible housing. It was reduced to the absolute minimum tolerable in terms of floor area, a minimum referred to as 'existential'. The architects of the Congress offered a series of brilliant solutions, competing to see who could most reduce not only the square metres and cubic metres per person, but everything superfluous to an abstract calculation of essential physiological behaviour. Concentrating on the problems of 'how', they played into the hands of the power structure. In neglecting the problems of 'why', they lost track of the most important reasons for their cultural commitment.

Today, forty years later, we find that those proposals have

become houses and neighbourhoods and suburbs and then entire cities, palpable manifestations of an abuse perpetrated first on the poor, and then on the not-so-poor. The proposals became cultural alibis for the most ferocious economic speculation and the most obtuse political inefficiency. Nevertheless, those 'whys' so nonchalantly forgotten at Frankfurt still have trouble coming to the surface. But we have a right to ask 'why' housing should be as cheap as possible and not, for example, rather expensive; 'why' instead of making every effort to reduce it to minimum levels of floor area, space, of thicknesses, of materials, etc, we should not try to make dwellings spacious, protected, insulated, comfortable, well-equipped, rich in opportunities for privacy, communication, exchange, personal creativity, etc. Nobody can be satisfied with an answer that appeals to the scarcity of available resources when we know how much is spent on wars, missiles and anti-missile systems, on moon projects, on research to defoliate forests inhabited by partisans or to paralyse demonstrators emerging from ghettoes, on hidden persuasion, on inventing artificial needs, etc. The priority scale established by the power structures has no sense except that of its own self-preservation, and therefore no one can or should accept the low priority assigned to housing, the city and the landscape. Nor can or should any one go on believing, according to the dogmas established at Frankfurt, that it is a good idea to define spatial limits in order to cook omelettes faster.

Working on 'how' without rigorous control of 'why' inevitably excludes reality from the planning process. Proposals for the solution of problems necessarily stand between the definition of goals and the evaluation of effects. The refusal to correlate one's contribution with the two poles of motivation and control is a typical manifestation of the idiocy of forced specialisation, which also influences the quality of the proposals and their capacity to resist interference. In fact, all the compensation which the Frankfurt architects introduced to counterbalance their minimum dimensions – more air, more light, more sun, more green areas, more formal rigour – were eliminated in practice as useless accessories or frills just like the 'abominable' decoration. These things were not included among those 'concrete goals' which the architects had examined, nor did they appear within the 'concrete controls' which neither the architects nor the users could object to. Not only had the problem been badly defined, but its solutions were destined to cause the disaster with which we are now all familiar. It had been so badly defined that today, forty years later, although it is universally accepted that housing for the poorer classes can be the cheapest and therefore the most squalid product on the market, the demand for housing is still far from satisfied. On the contrary, it represents the most serious scarcity of our time.

At Hoddesdon, as at Frankfurt, but less intelligently
At the Congress of Hoddesdon of 1951 the architects thought they had invented the problem of the rehabilitation of urban centres. Confronted with the squalor of peripheral neighbourhoods and the demoralisation caused by the criteria of functional specialisation which they themselves had proposed with the idea of 'zoning', they conceived the notion that the centre should be given back those opportunities for exchange, communication, choices, and emotions that the city as a whole had lost by now; it should be transformed into a 'heart' capable of pumping blood back into the exhausted and disjointed limbs of the city. At Hoddesdon, as at Frankfurt, but to tell the truth in a weary tone, numerous proposals were made: to concentrate the most important administrative activities in the centre, to place the most attractive leisure activities near the centre, to pedestrianise the centre, to construct huge car parks in the centre, to preserve the historic character of the centre, to concentrate tertiary activities in the centre, to make parks in the centre, etc, etc. But as at Frankfurt, the invention had already been made elsewhere; and in any case, without stopping to investigate motives and consequences, action was decided on superficially. Already at that period landowning capital and state bureaucracy had combined interests, preparing the brutal operation known as 'urban renewal'. In American cities, where the wealthy classes had moved to the suburbs, the excessive commuting distances over congested roads and isolation in an environment that offered nothing but a monotonous repetition of itself began to weigh heavily. In European cities the wealthy classes had remained in the valuable central zones, so it was the obsolete state of the surrounding quarters that began to weigh heavily, increasingly occupied by poorer classes who became ever more numerous. But in both cases the most irresistible attraction was the potential value of the building areas, well located in the centre of the region, the outskirts and the city, and therefore highly profitable once cleared of everything poor and socially unbecoming: negroes or southerners, immigrants or lumpen proletariat, foreign workers, or indeed workers of any kind.

The architectural exercises of Hoddesdon thus once again gave cultural justification to an operation of political and economic plunder. The theories and proposals about the 'heart of the city' gave rise to all that was said and done in the following years to transform urban centres into management centres, commercial centres, recreational centres, or simply historic centres, destined – with mournful rhetoric – to preserve the patrimony of values, together with the privileges of environmental well-being, of the ruling classes. The unconsciousness – or rather congenital irresponsibility – of architecture about motivations and consequences, had contributed decisively to the expansion of social iniquity in its most ferocious and shameful aspect: the segregation of classes in physical space. The centre was reserved for the houses of the rich, for the most profitable economic activities, for bureaucracy and politics. Excluded to the edge in their minimum housing, the poor were cut off from the real life of the city.

Good reasons for the non-credibility of architecture
The two examples of Frankfurt and Hoddesdon are taken from the history of the best architectural movement, and we could easily uncover more serious arguments if we took a look at the history of secondary movements or professional associations. But the point of this analysis is not to accumulate proof but rather to discover the reasons for the crisis of credibility that has hit architecture today, and to demonstrate that they have deep roots to be exposed and eradicated. For the time being it is sufficient to observe and describe, and we can summarise as follows:

1 — The period of the heroes, of the born-again, of the universal solutions is over. Function no longer automatically generates form, 'less' has ceased to be 'more' and there is little probability that 'more' will again become 'less': utility and beauty are no longer two halves of the same apple. But the effort to unite research and action in a coherent whole is also over. On the one hand there is Business, obtuse, repetitive and uncritical; on the other the Academy is regrouping its forces, presumptuous, pompous, and full of phoney ambitions. There are opinions circulating in favour of architecture as pure technology or pure fantasy; of the architect as an industrious functionary of the land registry office or as an inspired creator of monuments. Solutions are awaited from sociologists, economists or geographers; and since they are not forthcoming, in the pathos of an improbable social position, there is much verbal self-negation. But usually those who negate themselves in public, work for property speculation in private, so earning the means to negate themselves without losing their peace of mind. In architecture's ideological sphere, therefore, there is much confusion.

2 — There is just as much confusion in its practical sphere, where planning is as empirical, inspired, intuitive and makeshift as ever, and construction remains as crude, imprecise and inefficient as it was in Roman times. Since the problems of mass production and prefabrication have yet to be solved, a leap has been made

into 'science fiction', and since it has not been possible to deal with the quality/quantity dilemma, the whole problem of planning for the great number has been eluded, simply by slipping into monumentalism or formal utopia, with a great production of 'hypotheses' for mausolea, megastructures, universal systems, futurables etc. designed mostly for art galleries, current events magazines, and in certain cases as ornaments for the demagogical programmes of administrative boards and state bureaucracies. In the meantime, problems of territorial organisation – of urban reorganisation, transport, housing, facilities, the workplace – remain unsolved, and many decision-makers already consider industry the only force capable of dealing with the most pressing demands.

3 — Still more confusion is widespread in the schools, where the students' revolt uncovered once and for all the stupidity and indolence of the academic bodies. The crisis has been profound and serious, but seemingly without decisive consequences. The rapidity with which the professors ran for the lifeboats, leaving the students in the sinking ship, is only equalled by the shrewdness of their return to power on the bridge to resume the voyage for destinations so unknown as to be none of their business.

4 — There is still criticism, and as a vehicle for propaganda the journalism of reviews and weekly magazines. Overfed by the crisis of ideas and action, criticism travels a tangled network of roads (which for the most part, as in a maze, end up at the starting point). But two main lines of development emerge. The first analyses the vicissitudes of architecture through the behaviour of its heroes, and, if lacking heroes, tends to invent them, causing misunderstandings that are troublesome to demythologise. The second creates models of simulation borrowed from the figurative arts, the humanities or literature, sometimes even from the jungle of intellectual paradoxes. This creates even more serious misunderstandings, which not only mystify the cultural content and social responsibility of architecture, but also cause monstrous mutations in the habits of the architect. A symptom is the transformation of the language of architecture, now often incomprehensible and lacking in syntax, and playing on the terroristic effect of its incommunicability to hide the underlying confusion of ideas and purposes.

5 — The decisive function of journalism in estranging architecture from its real context is well-known. There is hardly a magazine or newspaper column that illustrates architecture taking the user into account; that furnishes news about how architecture really functions in its daily existence; that publishes images, photographs or articles in which the people who use, transform, and recompose the three-dimensional physical organism which they have been

given are actually present. It is as if architecture were merely a potential space and not an actual place, concrete, made of real materials, and inhabited by people in a permanent and continually changing relationship.

So why should architecture be credible today? It is not necessary for the user nor even for the client. As in the period of the first industrial transformation, in this new period of obscure forebodings and intense hopes, architects dissertate on trifles and lose themselves in the vacuum of a reassuring lack of commitment.

Architecture is too important to be left to architects

Nevertheless, the world cannot do without architecture. As long as a group of humans in physical space exists, the physical organisation of space will continue not only as a fundamental necessity of existence, but also as the most direct and concrete means of communicating via materialised systems of self-representation. Besides, the main *raison d'être* of human beings in this stage of their evolution is the destiny of making conscious transformations of their environment. It is precisely in dealing with the contradictions as these transformations develop that a role for architecture can emerge. The process, in fact, degenerates in the coils of an intricate paradox. While human activities multiply, becoming diversified and omnipresent, decisions about where and how they should take place are increasingly concentrated in the spheres of economic, bureaucratic and technological power. The role of architecture could be to contribute to the freezing or thawing out of this paradox, according to the stand it chooses to take – on the side of the power structure, or on the side of those overwhelmed and excluded by it. While it is certain that only the second choice can allow a concrete renewal, it is also certain that this choice can never be made by what passes for 'architects' architecture'.

In reality, architecture has become too important to be left to architects. A real metamorphosis is necessary to develop new characteristics in the practice of architecture and new behaviour patterns in its authors: therefore all barriers between builders and users must be abolished, so that building and using become two different parts of the same planning process. Therefore the intrinsic aggressiveness of architecture and the forced passivity of the user must dissolve in a condition of creative and decisional equivalence where each – with a different specific impact – is the architect, and every architectural event – regardless of who conceives it and carries it out – is considered architecture. The metamorphosis, in other words, must coincide with the subversion of the present condition, where to be an architect is the result of power delegated in a repressive fashion, and to be architecture is the result of a reference to class codes which legitimate only the exception, with an emphasis proportional to the degree to which it is cut off from its context. The expedient of 'not reading the surroundings' (used so well by official criticism through the technique of uninhabited, edited, or even trick photographs; or through linguistic analysis excluding all judgement on the use and consumption of the event under analysis) corresponds, in fact, to an ideological, political, social and cultural falsification with no counterpart in other disciplines.

Architecture alters the context in which it is placed

It is improbable that a radical renewal of behaviour and characteristics in architecture will occur quickly, nor can it take place outside a more general renewal of the structures of society. Architecture, a typical superstructural activity, 'depends' on transformations in the structures of society. It is important, however, to clarify the dialectical terms of this dependence, to defend against it being oversimplified and used as an alibi for conservatism or despair. Structural transformations can create space for the renewal of superstructures. But in order for such renewal to become a reality, it must be produced within the superstructures themselves, creating room for yet further structural transformations. The new infrastructural realities feed back into the new structural realities, giving their motivations concrete tangibility. In this respect architecture has an incalculable advantage over other activities, for it produces concrete images of what the physical environment could be like if the structure of society were different. In other words, it allows the wedging of physically perceptible and experienceable facts into the narrow margins of choice (or into the wounds opened up by contradictions) of the structure as it exists today. Nothing new can happen in architecture which has not been first invented and elaborated within architecture and in architecture's own terms. But this new occurrence, if it is really new, really projected toward structural transformation, becomes the 'material cause' of the situation in which it is placed, feeding back into the structure of society and contributing to society's transformation. Therefore we cannot just sit passively in the cave of architecture as-it-exists, waiting for social rebirth to generate architecture as-it-will-be automatically. We must change the whole range of objects and subjects which participate in the architectural process at present. There is no other way to recover architecture's historical legitimacy, or indeed, restore its credibility.

Participation and scientific method

Unlike all proposals for stylistic renewal formulated up to now, to change the whole range of objects and subjects would open a process in architecture which has no prescribed itinerary and no final solutions. Collective participation introduces a plurality of objectives and actions whose outcomes cannot be foreseen. Initially it is possible only to prefigure a line of behaviours and tendencies to set the process on its way. The evolution of society toward abolition of classes, the population explosion, and the continuing development of technology, pose enormous problems in the organisation of the physical environment, and to preserve its role, architecture must clarify its ideological position respecting these issues. The discipline and its ideology are connected by a reciprocal necessity, for just as the vagueness of exploration based on inspiration and taste reflected dependence on the client's whimsical power, so the rigour of scientific method corresponds to an identification of users' real needs. But identifying with the users' needs does not mean planning 'for' them, but planning 'with' them. In other words it means enlarging the field of participation through the definition and use of the plan, introducing into the system a whole set of complex variables which could never be composed into balanced situations except with procedural systems based on a continual alternation of observations, propositions, and evaluations; i.e. the use of scientific method. On this point we must be clear. Therefore we must start by clarifying the basic differences between planning 'for' users and planning 'with' them.

Quality of consensus and quality of plan

The first fundamental difference lies in the quality of consensus on which the architectural event must be based. When we plan 'for' people – even if we overcome the alienation due to deciding and operating externally – we tend, once consensus is reached, to freeze it into permanent fact. Consultation thus influences the conception of the plan but not its subsequent use, in other words the concrete life of the planned event. So unfortunately, the consensus is denied at the very moment when it is received. But if we plan 'with' people, consensus remains permanently open; it is renewed by confrontation with the planned event along the whole arc of its existence and, reciprocally, it renews the planned event by adapting it to the demands of a supporting apparatus which keeps redefining itself. In the case of planning 'for', the act of planning remains forever authoritarian and repressive, however liberal the initial intentions. In the case of planning 'with', the act becomes liberating and democratic, stimulating a multiple and continuous participation. This not only gives the planned event political legitimation: it also makes it resistant to the wear and tear of adverse circumstances and changing times. For example, we know from experience that large-scale planning of cities and regions tends to fail even when drawn up according to the most conscientious analyses and accurate forecasts, and even when collective interests have been carefully considered. This failure is usually attributed to the intervention of forces opposed to the organic development of the collectivity and therefore hostile to the 'wise plans', a credible but not an exhaustive explanation. The 'wise plans' fail, in fact, because the collectivity has no reason to defend them. Since it did not participate in their formulation, it is perfectly within its rights not to consider them 'wise' and therefore not to support them. We all know of neighbourhoods or buildings planned 'for' the users which have suffered a refusal from within which corrupted and disintegrated them in a short period. Usually this refusal is attributed to immaturity or misunderstanding, and once again this is a credible but incomplete explanation. The neighbourhoods and buildings planned 'for' the users decay because the users, not having participated in their planning, are unable to appropriate them and therefore have no reason to defend them.

Following a conventional line of argument, it might be objected that changing one's point of view does not influence the object, that inverting one's view has no effect on what is perceived. But on the contrary, it is precisely the point of view that counts, and the fate of objects changes according to the point from which they are considered. Many recent events show how easily conservative positions can be upset when their hidden mechanisms are exposed, revealing both a condition of abuse and a prospect for progress. When the community becomes conscious of its state, it moves to direct action and takes up arms for change.

The second fundamental difference between planning 'for' and planning 'with' the users, a corollary of the first, lies in the quality of the planning. Here it is perhaps necessary to add that by 'participation of the users' we do not mean that the users should work at the drawing board or that they should dictate while the architects transcribe, transforming aspirations into images. Some people seem to believe in this more literal interpretation of 'participation', or without believing it promote it anyway to turn their frustration into populistic jubilation. But in reality, participation needs to transform architectural planning from the authoritarian act which it has been up to now, into a process. This process begins with the discovery of the users' needs, passing through the formulation of formal and organisational hypotheses before entering the phase of use. Here, instead of reaching its usual full stop, the process must be reopened in a continuous alternation of controls and reformulations, feeding back into the earlier phases. The three phases – discovery of needs, formulation of hypotheses, and actual use – not only follow sequentially but also have a cyclical relationship. Each phase, though, has its specific character, and the possibility of relationships being consequent and well-correlated depends on the ways in which each is carried out.

The discovery of the users' needs

The discovery of the users' needs is not only the prerequisite of the process but also a matter of focusing basic choices. We can opt for an abstract idea of the user: the universal human being, with different symbolic connotations that the purposes and tastes of the dominant cultures of every epoch may attribute to him. In this case the discovery becomes a technical operation which intends to select and classify physiological and perhaps even 'spiritual' needs. An alternative is to opt for a concrete condition of society identifying a particular type of user, for example those belonging to a social underclass, and in this case the discovery becomes a political operation. We know where the first hypothesis, adopted to a large extent by the Modern Movement, takes us: to the illusory formulation of a universal scale intended to include all human needs but which instead, just because of the a priori contraction of reality on which it is based, ends up mirroring the interests, values and codes of the power structure. The four functions of the Charter of Athens provide a good instance of this result. A classification of needs calculated in relation to an imaginary 'average man' opens up no prospects of substantial renewal because it does not take into account the fact that work, dwelling, traffic and leisure, which are completely different activities and in many ways opposed, can be of primary or secondary importance depending on whether they are considered from the point of view of those with power or those without.

The latter viewpoint requires more complex research, for if we want to refer to a concrete social condition – for example, that of the underclass – an identification of needs requires the concrete presence of those who have them. This on the one hand requires a gathering of information and criticism to expose the imposed value system, dissipating the century-old alienation which it has produced, and stimulating a consciousness keen enough to bounce back with fresh information and criticism. On the other hand, it means an acceptance of confrontation: in other words risking the very cultural structures (experiences, values and codes) of those who set off the process. What will emerge in terms of new information and criticism is unforeseeable: it cannot be fed into old models without risking ridiculing the whole process by falling back into mirroring the values of the power structure.

In fact, those excluded from the use of power – and therefore from what is officially recognised as culture, art, architecture – are not larvae waiting for a metamorphosis which will permit them to benefit from the legitimate values of the power structure. They are bearers of new values which already exist potentially, manifested sporadically in the margins not already controlled by institutional power. These are the manifestations of 'disorder' which always leak out into the region, in the city, in neighbourhoods, in buildings, mixing with the pathological dregs of 'order' with which they are usually confused. But while the pathological dregs of 'order' are the result of the exasperation of an authoritarian and repressive condition which outruns its own rules, spreading in a state of amorphous violence, the 'disorder' opposed to it has a complex branching structure of its own which, not being institutionalised, renews itself continually, constantly reinventing images of a reality in transformation.

To discover the real needs of the users therefore means exposing and acknowledging their rights to have things and their rights to express themselves; it means provoking a direct participation and measuring oneself with all the subversive consequences that this implies; it means questioning all the traditional value systems which, since they were built on non-participation, must be revised or replaced when participation becomes part of the process, unleashing energies that have not yet been explored.

The formulation of the hypotheses
The phase of formulating the hypotheses corresponds technically to what is called in authoritarian planning 'the project'. But in authoritarian planning this means translating into organisational and morphological structures, functional and expressive objectives that have been defined once and for all – or which are easily frozen because they follow an institutional, and therefore predictable, logic of behaviour and representation. In process planning, by contrast, the objectives find their definition in the course of the process itself: they are defined through continual interaction between the pressure of real needs and images of spatial configurations. In this process, needs are refined and configurations perfected until they reach a condition of equilibrium, even if some instability remains due to the innate mobility of the process. Thus the function of planning is not to block further interpretation of reality with a permanent and immobile form but, on the contrary, to open up a dialectical process in which reality expands continuously, solicited by images, which in turn become increasingly diversified through

new expansions of reality. In other words, unlike authoritarian planning, which imposes final solutions from the start, process planning formulates a sequence of hypotheses aiming at (and launched by) participation. Each hypothesis enlarges the field of forces already created by the preceding hypothesis, and therefore brings about its own replacement by a successive and yet more appropriate hypothesis. The sequence is suspended when a point of equilibrium is reached which permits the putting into effect – the materialisation in physical space – of the last hypothesis considered satisfactory. Afterwards it starts up again, along a further line of experience, in the phase of use.

The difference between the two ways of planning is so great, both in concept and in practice, that more explanation is necessary. Authoritarian planning cannot question the basic choices of the event it produces because it takes them as read, as already pre-decided by higher authority. In the case of a residential unit, for example, the resources assigned are considered invariable, so the standards corresponding to those resources are considered insurmountable. If designed for a rich social group, it will be planned to high standards, while for a poor social group it will follow low standards – as if the human needs of the two groups were not absolutely identical. The residential unit for the rich will follow high quality urban and building typologies, the unit for the poor low quality and depressing ones.

Observing the phenomenon from an explicitly superstructural point of view, (which deliberately proposes to unhinge the connections between structure and superstructure, finding reasons and leaving room for transformation of the structures) we can disregard the whole series of objections concerning the ineluctable mechanisms of the free market. After all, it is well known that the phenomenon manifests itself in the same fashion even when the market is regulated, where the logic of the capitalistic system is replaced by that of a state bureaucracy. And, in any case, what interests us here is the definition of new procedures for the transformation of the human environment that are based on direct action and therefore independent, by definition, of all the alienating automatisms of the productive system and the power structure. Returning, therefore, to the example of a residential unit for a poor social group, authoritarian planning accepts unhesitatingly the senseless axiom that resources should be scarce and standards poor. At best, technical shrewdness will be applied to the manipulation of the addenda which do not change the balance of the calculation: more green space, but greater construction density, more useful surface, but less subsidiary surface; more service space but less internal refinishing; or vice versa, etc. These manoeuvres are carried out within a supinely accepted cage, and the negotiation of choices between various obligatory paths goes on between client and planner with total disregard for the users.

Process planning instead introduces the user as the fundamental progatonist of the operation and thus questions at the outset the legitimacy of the constraints which are imposed, including those on resources and standards. The job of the planner is to expand the sequence of hypotheses, enlarging the image beyond the margins of the framework imposed by the client: to show what we could (should) achieve if, instead of obeying a condition of preordained subjection, we allowed an objective confrontation with real rights. In the case of an architectural or urbanistic programme involving poor social groups – the most frequent and anyway the most urgent case – the job of the planner must start by re-establishing the clean terms of the class struggle. The sequential hypotheses which he or she has to propose must first reveal to the consciousness of the users the brutality of the authoritarian models which have brought about their present subjugation. This will involve comparison with models we would have a right to, if the economic, scientific and technological means available today were used to satisfy users' real needs. Successive hypotheses should begin to involve the user directly as protagonist in a progressive action of selection and definition of needs which the operation must satisfy, until a precise definition is reached of the architectural or urbanistic image that is to be achieved.

Administration and use

In process planning, the plan does not end with the construction of the architectural object. Instead, from that moment a new line of development begins which is consistent with the preceding one but characterised by different qualities. The client and architect leave the stage and the conflicts are shifted to the relationship between the architectural object and those who use it. For this relationship to be dialectical, it is necessary for each side to possess aptitudes for change through a continuous alternation of reciprocal identification and disassociation. The architectural object changes with the transformations which the user imposes on it as he or she adapts it to varying practical and creative needs; but the user also changes with the stimulation which the intrinsic quality of the architectural object transmits to him or her. In authoritarian planning, only this second line of influence functions, and it does so repressively, because the plan is usually conceived assuming that it is easier, quicker and more profitable to condition people than to condition the environment. Therefore in the phase of use the user must normally adapt him or herself to the architectural object as to an inflexible cage and all tensions are resolved in superficial alterations that contradict the pre-established morphological order, without being able, however, to modify it substantially. At this point, we find manifestations of 'disorder' which originate in the creative pressure of the users and are blocked, deplored and even punished by those who create, support and even guarantee 'order'. The architectural object becomes a material representation of the institutional motivation that has created it, and turns into an institution.

In process planning the carrying out in three-dimensional physical terms of the plan is a tentative hypothesis. Its verification comes about through use and is therefore entrusted to the user who confronts the built environment in experiencing it. This phase which adjusts, subtracts, adds to, or modifies the design is still part of the project: it continues until the point of physical and technical obsolescence, which occurs when the motivation which set it in motion is exhausted or when the building's tissues are exhausted and have lost their regenerative capacity. Through process planning the teleological assumptions which have diverted architecture from its most concrete material causes are exposed.

An architectural work has no sense if dissociated from use, and the way in which it is used, or can be used, is one of the fundamental factors contributing to the definition of its quality. As an empty vessel, it cannot represent itself or establish purposeful relations with nature and history; because its purpose lies in its 'fullness' – in the whole set of relationships established with those for whom it was designed. Following the movement of these relationships, it continues both to modify and to be modified by the user; integrating itself in this way with nature and producing history, becoming itself, through the use that is made of it, part of nature and history.

Following this point of view, some of the subconscious tensions which have agitated recent architectural culture, such as problems of growth and flexibility, take on clearer meaning. Faced with the problem of rapid consumption to which architectural organisms are subjected today because of the change in the circumstances which dictated their initial programmes, an effort has been made to find a solution by contriving their morphological and organisational systems to permit additions and adaptations. But in the framework of authoritarian planning, these devices are immediately blocked at the point at which they contradict a structural and formal order which is by definition pre-established and unalterable. The quality of the object is locked into a tangle of exclusive and private codes which permit exceptions only at the price of enlarging a network of communications which it is precisely their job to restrict. If an authoritarian plan were really flexible and open to growth, it would become possible for everyone to manipulate and understand it: thus it would lose those characteristics of ineffableness and immaculateness which sustain and hide its classist purpose.

Growth and flexibility in an architectural organism are not really possible except under a new conception of architectural quality. This new conception cannot be formulated except through a more attentive exploration of those phenomena of creative participation currently dismissed as 'disorder'. It is in their intricate context, in fact, that we shall find the matrix of an open and self-generating formal organisation which rejects a private and exclusive way of using land, and through this rejection, delineates a new way of using it on a pluralistic and inclusive basis. In giving the user a creative role, we implicitly accept this basis. At the same time, the morphological and structural conceptions and the operative tools which until now governed architectural production are thrown into question. A vast set of variables which institutional culture and practice had suppressed come back into play, and the field of reality in which architecture intervenes becomes macroscopic and complex. Therefore only the assumption of clear ideological positions and the application of rigorously scientific procedure can guarantee a legitimate political and technical framework. Then new objectives can be set and new practical instruments be developed to produce a balanced and stimulating physical environment.

The negotiation of hope

Falling on deaf ears

It is a winter night in 2003. I am attending a consultation session in a church hall in a blighted neighbourhood that has been designated as an NDC area. NDC – *New Deal for Communities* – is the Labour Government's latest attempt at urban regeneration. It is a term that signals both past political failure and future hope. *New*. An acknowledgement that the old systems have not worked. *Deal*. A transaction; we give you money, you give us back improvements. *Communities*. A wishful and wistful hope that fractured territories can be reconsolidated into some semblance of community, without ever specifying what that word may actually mean.

The title NDC also designates that the deal must be struck with the community; consultation and public participation in the process are required. Hence the meeting that I am attending. One year into this particular NDC programme, and the community are showing all the signs that the newness has rubbed off and consultation fatigue has set in. The NDC officer is doing a remarkable job in motivating some response out of the slumped bodies, the dropped shoulders, out of people numbed by years of failed promises.

There is an architect's scheme for a new community centre pinned up at the back, scrawny drawings that no one can really see. A cursory discussion has taken place about the merits of the scheme, and now the community is being asked to vote on it, a procedure statutorily required in this participation process. All but two hands go up. Quite on what grounds approval is being given is hard to tell. Maybe it is late and people want to go home. Maybe they believe that a community hall will actually create a community. Maybe it is the promise of church-hall tea after the vote. Maybe they love the architecture. Maybe the NDC officer has swayed them. Maybe it is like a Mexican wave. Who knows? But this is the very stuff of participation.

The NDC officer is concerned about the hands that have not gone up at and gently coaxes a response out of two old ladies sat at the back of the echoey hall. 'Couldn't hear a word you said,' they shout. 'But it is a lovely building,' the NDC person says. 'Can't hear you, we left our hearing aids at home.' 'IT IS A LOVELY BUILDING.' And so the two hands go up. The deal is done.

Why, you may ask, am I being so sour in my tone? Surely any participation is better than none? Surely the very sensation of feeling ownership is a step towards actually having ownership? Surely, in the time-honoured Olympic platitude, the taking part is as important as the winning? But those Olympic platitudes are normally exhaled through the gritted teeth of the disappointed athlete ('… the crowd were great… I did what I could… I'll be back…'). Or else they are applied by patronising Western journalists to, for example, the doggy-paddling efforts of a swimmer from the developing world ('… didn't he do well, his training to date was in the local park's fishpond'). Olympic participation here signals either defeat or distance, and so did the experience in the church hall: hence my sour tone. Under the guise of inclusion, the same old patterns of power repeat themselves, defeating the expectations of the participant citizens in actually gaining themselves anything better, and distancing them from the real processes of spatial production.

In this case the NDC officer was certainly not a traditional figure of power. She did not impose a particular vote; through a mixture of charm and cajoling she dragged a response from a stultified audience. The triumph was not what the response was, but that there was a response at all. The triumph was necessary because participation could now be deemed to have happened and the political process of regeneration could move on. Of course all the power lay outside this church hall; it resided in the centre, and was inscribed in the targets and procedures that the NDC officer had to meet. The system generated lots of participative noise [1] but it all fell on deaf ears. In effect, everyone had left their hearing aids behind.

We should not be so surprised about this apparent gap between the ideals and reality of participation. The story of participation runs parallel to that of democracy, and one does not have to be a great political theorist to detect that the soothing Hellenic etymology of democracy – *the people's rule* – is disturbed by undercurrents of power, manipulation and disenfranchisement. These undercurrents are equally true in participation. We should be surprised, therefore, that the term participation is so willingly, and uncritically, accepted as being for the common good. It is the unequivocal acceptance of participation as a better way of doing things that is both its strength and its weakness. The strength in so much as it encourages all parties to engage in it, its weakness in so much as this engagement can be uncritical, and thus oblivious as to how to act in the face of the dangerous undercurrents.

[1]
For sources of participative noise, see B. Wisner, 'Participatory and action research', in E. Zube and G. Moore (eds), *Advances in Environment, Behaviour and Design*, New York: Plenum, 1991, p.280.

2

The literature on planning and partici-
pation is very extensive, far more so than
on architecture. Some of the key texts are:
J. Friedmann, *Retracking America; A theory of
transactive planning*, Garden City, NY: Anchor
Press, 1973; J. Forester, *Planning in the Face of
Power*, Berkeley, CA: University of California
Press, 1989 and P. Healey, *Collaborative
Planning: Shaping places in fragmented societies*,
Vancouver: UBC Press, 1997. For a full
bibliography on planning and participation,
see Richardson and Connelly in this book.

3

Taken from a longer table in Wisner,
'Participatory and action research', p.277.

4

S. Arnstein, 'The ladder of citizen participation', *Journal of the Institute of American
Planners*, 34, no.4, 1969, pp.216-24. The
ladder is, from the bottom: manipulation –
therapy – informing – consultation –
placation – partnership – delegated power –
citizen control. See Figure 04.01.

5

C. Pateman, *Participation and Democratic
Theory*, Cambridge: Cambridge University
Press, 1970.

6

Ibid., p.25.

The issues inherent in participation have been traced in other
disciplines, notably planning,[2] but not often in the field of architecture. The supporters of participation are generally fervent – it is all
good. That goodness is often contrasted to the evils of non-partici-
pative architecture, forming a simplistic dialectic: inclusive/exclu-
sive, democratic/authoritarian, bottom up/top down.[3] But this is
too easy, leaving as it does the original terms unscathed and the
new terms unanalysed. Critics of participation are few and far
between; it is seen as politically unpalatable to be seen to challenge
something so eminently sensible. Instead, as will become clear,
mainstream architectural culture is in a state of denial about participation, a denial that is tantamount to rejection but without the
need to be explicit about it.

My aim in this essay is to unravel some of the causes of this
denial. My argument is that participation presents a threat to
normative architectural values. Once this threat is identified, it is
possible to overcome it and see participation not as a challenge to
architecture, but as an opportunity to reformulate, and thus resuscitate, architectural practice. However, before doing this it is necessary to ask what may be meant by the term participation.

Placatory participation

Participation as an unchallenged generic term disguises the fact
that in all participatory processes there are degrees of involvement ranging from token participation to full control of the process
by citizen participants. These degrees are identified in Sherry Arnstein's oft-quoted 'ladder of participation' in which she sets out a
hierarchy of participatory control.[4] At the bottom of the ladder is
'manipulation' and at the top is 'citizen control'. Interestingly the
word 'placation' sits just over halfway up the ladder. This is strange:
that placation should be awarded an above average rating in this
ladder of expectation – that placation is effectively deemed as an
acceptable outcome of participation. To understand this apparent
problem one has to understand that Arnstein's simple diagram is
embedded in a much more complex politics of participation, as set
out in Carole Pateman's classic work *Participation and Democratic
Theory*.[5] Pateman contrasts the position of 'classical' democratic
theory, most notably Rousseau's, with that of contemporary democratic theory. The participation of the individual citizen in political
decision-making is a central tenet of Rousseau's political theory.
Participation serves as a part of an educative process through which
'the individual will eventually come to feel little or no conflict
between the demands of the public and private spheres'.[6] As a result
of participation the decision of the collective is more readily

7
Ibid., p.27.

8
Ibid., p.7.

9
Ibid., p.13.

10
H. Sanoff, 'The application of participatory methods in design and evaluation', *Design Studies*, 6, no.4, 1985, pp.178-234. My italics.

11
E. E. Lozano, *Community Design and the Culture of Cities*, Cambridge: Cambridge University Press, 1990.

accepted by the individual and (importantly) it 'increases the feeling among individual citizens that they belong in their community'.[7] Pateman contrasts this essentially transformative model of participation with the democratic theories of the 1960s. These suggest that wider public participation may present a threat to the stability of the political system. As Pateman notes (but does not approve): 'We arrive at the argument that the amount of participation that actually obtains is just the amount that is required for stable systems of democracy.'[8] A power relationship is clearly established here, with the stable authority of the state paramount. If participation acts as a palliative to ensure that stability, then that is acceptable. If participation acts as an agent in the transformation of the values of the state, then it is not acceptable. In this light, Pateman argues that 'participation, as far as the majority is concerned, is participation in the choice of the decision makers. Thus the function of participation is solely a protective one.'[9] Protecting, placating, participation is really no more than a placebo.

Whilst much of the rhetoric of architectural participation resonates with the Rousseau model of transformative action, the reality is actually closer to the later model, in which architectural participation can be seen as a means to get the presumed support of the citizen user for actions that have already been determined by professional agents. One of the main advocates of architectural participation, Henry Sanoff, argues that: 'participants *have a sense* of influencing the design process... it is not so much the degree to which the individual needs have been met, but the *feeling* of having influenced the decisions'.[10] This is an explicit example of placation, with the authority of the state replaced by the authority of the expert, and the citizen beguiled by the term participation into a sense of feeling good whilst in fact being passive in the face of decisions already made by experts.

Still worse is when this soothing gesture becomes downright manipulation – when the act of participation is in fact one of imposition under the false guise of inclusion. Take this sentiment from another US community designer: 'Community Designers should steer the decision-making process towards desired goals... designers must function in communities both as interpreters and as agents of change who challenge anti-urban values.'[11] Whilst this kind of attitude may appear extreme, one suspects that it may in fact be quite mainstream; the only difference is that Lozano has been honest (or stupid) enough to come clean. Normally the action is more covert, a hidden persuasion. For example, in research as to what was most useful in a participatory process, some architects stated that the 'problem' (sic) of a participative meeting was worth confronting

12
J. Watts and M. Hirst, 'User participation in the early stages of building design', *Design Studies*, 3, no.1, 1982, p.17.

13
Pateman, *Participation and Democratic Theory*, p.68.

14
Ibid., p.71.

15
This term draws on the notion of transformative theory developed by the planning theorist, John Friedmann. See J. Friedmann, *Planning in the Public Domain: From knowledge to action*, Princeton, NJ: Princeton University Press, 1987.

because of the 'increased acceptability of the designer', and that the final usefulness lay in 'educating users'.[12] These architects were prepared to engage in a participatory process simply to increase their acceptability by a sceptical public; this then allowed the architects to sneak their expert values through the back door. The whole process thus left a predetermined outcome unscathed by public opinion.

Carole Pateman labels such types of participation as 'pseudo-participation… (this) covers techniques used to persuade employees to accept decisions that have already been made'.[13] Whilst her analysis is based on participation in the workplace, it is equally relevant to the architectural field, particularly when she describes pseudo-participation as creating a 'feeling' of participation. It may be argued that much of what passes for participation in architecture fits well into the category of pseudo-participation; certainly the evening meeting in the church hall did.

Pateman contrasts pseudo-participation with full and partial participation. Full participation is described as 'where each individual member of a decision-making body has equal power to determine the outcome of the decisions'. Partial participation is when there is not equal power in how the decision is made: 'the final power to decide rests with one party only'.[14] Full participation is an ideal, but an impossible one to achieve in architecture. It depends on each party being in possession of the requisite knowledge *and* in there being transparent channels of communication. Neither of these pertains in architecture, where the expert knowledge of the architect and the tacit knowledge of the participant user remain on different levels, and where the lines of communication are compromised by codes, conventions and authority. Whilst partial participation acknowledges this differential in power, it still assumes that the final power resides with the person with the most knowledge, in this case the architect. This may be a realistic analysis of architectural participation, but not one to aspire to if one believes that the goal of participation is the empowerment of the citizen user and not of the expert. What is needed, therefore, is another form of participation that is realistic enough to acknowledge the imbalances of power and knowledge, but at the same time works with these imbalances in a way that transforms the expectations and futures of the participants. Let us call this type of participation *transformative participation* [15] as an active signal of its opposition to the passive nature of placatory participation.

Transformative participation

How then may transformative participation be achieved in archi-

Apart from the conference grouping which includes Nigel Cross, Bill Mitchell and Nicholas Negroponte, it is also interesting to note that many participation advocates such as Henry Sanoff came from a design methods background.

17
See N. Cross, *The Automated Architect*, London: Pion, 1977, p.123.

18
W. Mitchell, 'Experiments with participation-orientated systems', in N. Cross (ed.), *Design Participation*, London: Academy Editions, 1972, p.75.

19
See Cross, *The Automated Architect*, p.124. It might appear that this grouping were dazzled by the white heat of technology of their 8-bit computers, but these sentiments still pervade. A recent book on the subject opens with: '(Our) new perspective is that technical optimization and social optimization should not be carried out separately, but be integrated into one design process.' The essential skills of urban designers and architects should include skills in numerical computer modelling. However, the real aim of this approach is revealed when the authors refer to 'persuasion by numerical and geometrical modeling'. See L. v. Gunsteren and P.-P. v. Loon, *Open Design: A collaborative approach to architecture*, Delft: Eburon, 2000, p.v.

tecture? One of the problems identified in participation is that the channels of communication between the expert and the non-expert are not transparent, and so participation remains dominated by the experts who initiate the communication on their own terms, circumscribing the process through professionally coded drawings and language. This problem was addressed in the early 1970s with the design methods movement, in which a strange alliance was formed between systems theory, computer programmes and participatory rhetoric.[16] The proponents agreed that one of the barriers to participation in architecture is the obscurity of the design process. They argued that by explicating the process through rational means, and through the use of computers, design will become transparent and the non-expert will be able to engage more fully in the design process. As Nigel Cross notes:

> By making the design process more open and explicit, computers also open the way for a wider range of participants to contribute to the process... in particular the users of the building, who have traditionally been allowed no participation in the design process, could become involved in a computer-aided process.[17]

Key to this was the rise of the computer and numerical modelling which would, in Bill Mitchell's hope, 'result in an opening up of architectural and urban design processes to a wider and truer participation by making it possible for non-specialists to comprehend and directly manipulate quite powerful models of the environment'.[18] In the most extreme version, Nicholas Negroponte's Architecture Machine Group, the architect is supposedly dispensed with altogether as users develop their own building designs by direct interaction with the computer.[19]

In 1970 a group including Nigel Cross, Bill Mitchell and Nicholas Negroponte came together at a conference entitled *Design Participation*. Looking through the papers, it is difficult to identify much of what is now perceived of as participation within the slew of diagrams and technical data. What the diagrams reveal is a clarity of intent on the designers' part, and whilst the stated reason is that such clarity allows others to engage with the process, the engagement is explicitly on the experts' terms and therefore in thrall to them. The strong feeling is that participation, or rather pseudo-participation, is being used as a socially acceptable shield behind which the authors can develop their technically-determined ideologies. Reyner Banham, in his introduction to the conference, suggests as much when he writes:

20
Banham, 'Opening remarks', in N. Cross (ed.), *Design Participation*, London: Academy Editions, 1972.

When one looks down the list of speakers at this conference and the titles of their papers, one wonders whether we have not got the same old Design Conference, but with the new wonder ingredient, 'participation'... some of us are putting our social consciences at work.[20]

Banham, in identifying the expediency of using participation as a screen, also notes the impossibility of keeping politics out of the participative mix. As organiser of the conference, Nigel Cross' original aim was to look 'for examples of new technologies and new techniques which might be sidestepping conventional political controls. That the conference seemingly *had* to come round to discussing politics, suggests this may have been a fallacy.'[21] By the end of the conference political issues had entered into the debate; they could not have been kept out. Participation is inherently political, not in the party political sense of the word, but in the sense that it affects people's lives.

21
N. Cross (ed.), *Design Participation*, London: Academy Editions, 1972, p.14.

The experience of the *Design Participation* conference is indicative of the relationship between architecture and participation; one cannot suppress what needs to be there and yet architectural culture is in a state of denial about many aspects of participation. The reason, as we shall see, is that participation presents a threat to many of the central tenets of architecture and the profession does what it can (either knowingly or by default) to resist that threat. The denial of the political realm is one such mechanism by which that threat is suppressed.

The threat may be explained by the tension that exists between the ideals and the reality of architectural practice. Architects cling to a perfected model of practice, neatly and simplistically summarised in an idealised version of the Vitruvian triad – commodity, firmness and delight. Idealised commodity (solve the 'problem' of function in as efficient a manner as possible). Idealised firmness (advance on technical fronts as a sign of progress). Idealised delight (a polishing of forms in accordance with prevailing aesthetic sensibilities). The problem arises when these ideals meet the reality of the contingent world: a threefold undermining of the values of the ideals takes place. Contingent reality first upsets the carefully laid plans of utility (users can be so annoyingly unpredictable). Second, it ignores many of the values held high by architectural culture (for example, the public hardly share architects' obsession with the refined detail). Third, it brings into play issues that are overlooked by the Vitruvian triad (most notably issues of the social and political world). Disappointment, as Rem Koolhaas resignedly notes,[22] is inevitable in the face of this undermining. And so the architect will do everything possible to delay the fateful moment when reality

22
Koolhaas defines the 3 stages of practice as elation, suspense and disappointment.

bites. Suspension of disbelief is a condition of design practice. One knows in one's heart of hearts that the suspension cannot last, but the state is hypnotic whilst it does – those clean diagrams, those neatly scheduled packages of work that defy all construction practice, those empty photographs taken before the great unwashed (users, dirt, weather, change) move in. And when it all goes wrong afterwards, when reality truly does upset the ideals, one can always resort to the publication of a monograph to resuscitate and perpetuate the mythology of a perfected state of architectural production.

Participation brings forward the moment of reality and in so doing inevitably challenges that suspension of disbelief. The participative process, as a signal of the reality to come, confronts architects with issues that they may otherwise have preferred to either hide from, or else delay dealing with, for as long as possible. Most obviously this happens by bringing forward and prioritising the desires of the users. Where clients are generally concerned with economy, efficiency and longevity – all issues which elide with the Vitruvian triad and thus ones that the architect is comfortable with – users bring other concerns to the table.[23] It is in this way that participation presents a threat to normative architectural values, and so it is not surprising that most architectural participation tends towards the pseudo corner of Pateman's construct, because only there are the values left unscathed behind a veneer of social engagement. The challenge, therefore, is how to move architectural participation from the pseudo to the transformative. To achieve this one has to overcome any notions of participation as a threat and to see it as a process that is transformative for all parties – the architect included. The issues that transformative participation brings forward actually present an opportunity, not a threat; an opportunity to reconsider what is often taken for granted in architectural practice. It is to these issues that we shall now turn in order to see how they individually and collectively suggest a positive transformation of architectural production that benefits architects and users alike.

The expert-citizen/citizen-expert

It is through the agency of the user that participation brings forward issues that the architect has to face up to at an early stage. In normal circumstances there is an immediate imbalance in the initial exchanges. The architect, as possessor of expert knowledge, sets the terms of reference for the participatory engagement. A problem is posited, plans are drawn and a solution negotiated – all framed by the architect's knowledge system and specialised modes of communication. Clearly this establishes a power structure in which the expert architect assumes authority over the inexpert layperson, and

23
Lefebvre is clear in identifying the problem of the word 'user', which tends to denote the user as some kind of functional object, subject to architectural manipulation. See H. Lefebvre, *The Production of Space*, trans. D. Nicholson-Smith, Oxford: Blackwell, 1991. However, user is probably the most commonly employed term in architectural participation and identifies a different category from the client. Real participation must engage the user over and above the client, whose priorities are so often similar to those of the architect.

24
For a critique of this approach, see
M. Crawford, 'Can architects be socially
responsible?' in D.Y. Ghirardo (ed.),
Out of Site: A social criticism of architecture,
Seattle, WA: Bay Press, 1991. For
justification of it: N. Wates and C. Knevitt,
*Community Architecture: How people are creating
their own environment*, London: Penguin, 1987.

25
L. Lerup, *Building the Unfinished: Architecture
and human action*, Beverly Hills, CA: Sage,
1977, p.136.

26
G. Rose, 'Athens and Jerusalem: A tale of
two cities', *Social and Legal Studies*, 3, 1994,
p.337. For a development of this argument
see J. Till, 'Architecture of the impure
community', in J. Hill (ed.), *Occupying
Architecture: Between the architect and the user*,
London: Routledge, 1998.

27
This is Reyner Banham's term to
describe the container that houses the
self-referential world of architecture.
R. Banham, 'A black box: The secret
profession of architecture', in. R. Banham
(ed.), *A Critic Writes*, Berkeley, CA: University
of California Press, 1996.

clearly this imbalance is unacceptable if one aspires to a participatory process that empowers the user. In an attempt to reverse this power relationship, the community activists of the late 1960s and 1970s resolved to strip experts of their authority and reduce them to being technical facilitators, there to deliver the desires of the community without imposing on them.[24] In this model the architect remained an outsider but one acting on the users' behalf. The problem, as Lars Lerup clearly identifies, is that participation becomes largely a 'managerial solution... there is a "symmetry of ignorance" between the dweller and professional – neither knows the dweller's needs'.[25] On the one hand, in the enforced relinquishment of power, the expert professionals also relinquish their knowledge (because in the well-worn formulation reduced from Foucault, knowledge is power). As mere facilitators the architects are unable to re-imagine their knowledge from the perspective of the user; their knowledge is not used transformatively, rather their skills are used instrumentally. On the other hand, the technical know-how of the expert is not enough to help the users to develop new spatial visions; the user is given nothing to enable them to expand on their nascent but unarticulated desires, and so these remain at the level of the lowest common denominator. In Gillian Rose's memorable phrase, 'the architect is demoted; the people do not accede to power'.[26]

This indicates that transformative participation cannot be achieved through the disavowal of expert knowledge. Nor is the solution to make the architect's knowledge more accountable by making it more transparent. This is what the design methods movement proposed through open explication of the design process, but as we have seen, this left the framing of the expert knowledge base unaltered. The non-expert is granted easier access to the expert's domain, the gate to the 'black box'[27] is opened wider but the contents remain untouched. Instead a move towards transformative participation demands a reformulation of expert knowledge and the way it may be enacted.

One of the defining features of any profession is that it has its own knowledge base, and the more specialist the knowledge base the 'stronger' – and more exclusive, better remunerated – the profession. In an attempt to establish the inviolate credentials of the profession the architectural knowledge base, and its inscription in language and drawn codes, become more remote from the needs and comprehension of the users. The participatory process brings the limits of architectural knowledge into sharp focus; in its specialist pursuit of techniques and aesthetics, architectural discourse detaches itself from the everyday desires and needs of the social lifeworld. A gap opens up between the special and the normal. In medicine this gap is actually necessary in defining the profession, because in treating the special (say, a hole in the heart) the expert doctor can return the patient to the world of the normal. Indeed, the wider the gap, the more specialist the knowledge required, the stronger that aspect of the profession, the greater the remuneration: hence the perceived status of the heart surgeon over the general practitioner. In architecture, the participatory process reveals the gap between the special and the normal to be unacceptable, and yet architects will be wary of relinquishing their specialist areas of expertise because they believe this would threaten what sets them apart. There is the nagging doubt that in dealing with the normal, using normal language, one might be seen as normal. Participation thus presents architects with a double bind – the need to reassess what constitutes their knowledge but also the worry that in so doing one may no longer be seen as an architect. Best therefore to avoid the problem altogether, or at least to put it off for as long as possible. Architects thus tend to cling to the certainty of what they know, rather than expose themselves to the uncertainty of what others may know.

The only way to get out of this bind is to reconsider what constitutes the expert. This does not mean the relinquishment of knowledge, but the redeployment of it in another mode. Experts feel most comfortable when the object of their scrutiny is abstracted, because then their specialist knowledge can be applied without disturbance. However, this state of sharp but distanced focus is hard to reconcile with the reality of the spatial, social, world. In another context, the psychologist Roger Barker notes that 'if we want to understand the fullness of baseball, we should not stare ourselves blind at the batter, but blot him out and look at his context'.[28] For architectural participation, this suggests that instead of fixating on the building and user as objects, we transfer our attention to their context. As Lerup says: 'Our old exercise of staring at objects... fixing them in our professional gaze, may be challenged by simply taking the position of the object and seeing how people react to it.'[29]

This suggests that in order to enable transformative participation, architectural knowledge should not be applied as an abstraction from the outside, but developed from within the context of the given situation. This in turn calls for a new type of knowing. The profession is traditionally predicated on a knowing 'how' or a knowing 'that', but at John Shotter argues in his important book, *The Cultural Politics of Everyday Life*, these types of knowledge are 'decontextualised'. Instead Shotter calls for a knowing 'from within', a 'developmental' knowledge that adjusts to and grows out of the social-

28
Roger Barker, *Ecological Psychology*, p.16 as quoted in Lerup, *Building*, p.156.

29
Ibid.

30
J. Shotter, *The Cultural Politics of Everyday Life:
Social constructionism, rhetoric and knowing of the
third kind*, Buckingham: Open University
Press, 1993, p.xiii. The terms 'knowing
how' and 'knowing what' are initially from
G. Ryle, *The Concept of Mind*, New York:
Barnes & Noble, 1962.

31
Lerup, *Building*, p.136.

32
In a parallel discussion of intellectuals and
their relationship to ideologies, Michael
Billig *et al.* make the distinction between
intellectual and lived ideologies, the first of
which is characterised by being formalised
and systematic, the latter of which refers
to a non-formalised notion arising out of
society's way of life. Architects, and other
professionals, tend towards the former
but cannot escape the latter because, as
Billig argues, 'every great theorist has to
confront the conflict between the lived and
intellectual ideologies – because they also
have to live out their lives as citizens'. M.
Billig, *Ideological Dilemmas: A social psychology of
everyday thinking*, London: Sage, 1988, p.32.

33
'Each man, outside his professional life
carries on some form of intellectual activity
… has a conscious line of moral conduct and
this contributes to sustaining a conception
of the world or to modifying it, that is to
bring into being new modes of thought.'
A. Gramsci, *Selections from the Prison Notebooks
of Antonio Gramsci*, trans. Q. Hoare and
G. Nowell-Smith, London: Lawrence &
Wishart, 1971, p.10.

34
C. Boggs, *Gramsci's Marxism*, London: Pluto
Press, 1976, p.77.

35
Gramsci, *Selections from the Prison Notebooks of
Antonio Gramsci*, pp.7-23.

36
See Pateman, *Participation and Democratic
Theory*, p.68.

37
For a development of this, see Friedmann,
*Retracking America: A theory of transactive
planning*, pp.109-11.

cultural surroundings in which it is situated. In Shotter's terms, this is 'knowing of the third kind' (unlike the first two knowing 'how' and 'that').[30] To develop this knowledge from within, the architect must project themselves into the spatial context, physical and social, of the user; the architect becomes 'an activist, working on behalf of and as a dweller'.[31] This is good advice: just as doctors in their brusque bedside manner often seem to forget that they too are potential patients, architects are prone to deny their experience as users, to forget that they too are embodied citizens. What is called for is the ability to move between the world of expert and user, with one set of knowledge and experience informing the other.[32] The architect should, in effect, be an expert-citizen as well as citizen-expert.

The model resonates with Gramsci's notion of the organic intellectual as set out in the *Prison Notebooks*.[33] For Gramsci, intellectuals (and let's be generous and include architects in this category) should be both leading and representative.[34] Crucially, intellectuals should not remain as eloquent outsiders but must become active participators in practical life,[35] without denying their knowledge or relinquishing the opportunity to guide. It is in this oscillation between the expert and citizen, the specialised and the normal, that one avoids the second potential bind of participation, namely the concern that in acting normally one may lose one's professional status. The architect, moving between the worlds of expert and citizen, engages with the world as organic intellectual, a new form of professional.

However, this only gets us halfway towards a transformative participatory process. Whilst the architect as expert-citizen/citizen-expert may be able to engage more actively with the context and concerns of the user, true participation demands that the process is two-way – that the user should have the opportunity to actively transform the knowledge of the architect.[36] This will only happen if the architect first recognises and then respects the knowledge of the user. Because the user's knowledge is often grounded in everyday experience and the commonplace, it is easy to dismiss it as having a lower status than specialised knowledge or else to respond to it at the level of pragmatics.[37] It is common for architects to placate participants through reassuring practical solutions ('yes, we will deal with your rubbish bins') whilst still silently sticking to their own specialised agendas ('… and make sure they are round the back away from our delightful front elevation.'). What is necessary is for the architect to acknowledge the potentially transformative status of the users' knowledge and to provide channels through which it might be articulated. The architect (as citizen-expert) needs to lis-

38
See Sanoff, 'The application of participatory methods in design and evaluation'.

39
In this context it is interesting to note that in Habermas' theory of communicative action, it is his argument for an 'ideal speech situation' that has drawn the most fire. His critics accuse him of seeming naivety in even positing the possibility of authentic speech, his defenders note that people act, and need to act, as if the possibility of ideal speech was achievable.

40
J. Albrecht, 'Towards a theory of participation in architecture', *Journal of Architectural Education*, 42, no.1, 1998, pp.24-31.

41
There is not the space to develop the argument here, but it is neatly summarised by the French architect Jean Renaudie who writes: 'The stubborn refusal of some people to admit to the influence of politics on architecture, and the narrow assertion of others that architecture is politics and nothing else, result in the same thing: inefficiency in practice.' See I. Scalbert, *A Right to Difference: The Architecture of Jean Renaudie*, London: Architectural Association, 2004. The key text in the recent reawakening of the political dimension of space must be Lefebvre, *The Production of Space*.

42
M. Comerio, 'Community design: Idealism and entrepreneurship', *Journal of Architectural and Planning Research*, 1, no.4, 1984, pp.227-43. See Blundell Jones' chapter in this book for the story of the 1960s.

ten to, draw out and be transformed by the knowledge of the user (as expert-citizen). The process becomes two-way and expansive because, as Sanoff notes, 'the knowledge of the user-expert is necessary to state the obvious and the commonplace in order to expand the narrowness of vision often found in highly trained people'.[38] In this light, one can see how participation, through bringing the users' knowledge into the design process at an early stage, far from presenting a threat to architectural production, actually presents an opportunity to reinvigorate it through challenging the very limits and constraints of specialist knowledge.

Negotiating space

As it stands, this notion of transformative participation is too cosy: it suggests idealised conditions of mutual cooperation, uncontested knowledge bases, open communication and eventual consensus. In reality, such ideals do not exist, and it is dangerous to hope blindly that they might. Better instead to accept that no participatory process, no matter how well intentioned, is going to completely dissolve the power structures and inequalities of the various parties.[39] Any theory of participation in architecture must also include the notions of authority [40] and otherness. One aspect of participation makes confrontation with difference inevitable, and this is that the users will bring to the table their personal beliefs. In the negotiation of the personal with the social, the individual with the collective, political space emerges; the participatory process is, as the *Design Participation* conference found out, inherently political. Here it is easier to see how participation presents a threat to mainstream architectural culture, which so often exists in a state of denial about the political implications of the processes and products of practice.[41] Interestingly this denial is echoed in much participatory architecture that has gradually been divested of its initial political impulse. The rise of conservative politics, and the necessity of being seen to be politically 'neutral', have seen a shift in architectural participation from the idealistic stance of the 1960s to the pragmatic expediency of the 1980s and 1990s.[42]

The participatory process brings forward the moment when the political nature of space has to be dealt with: in so doing it disturbs the comfort zone (which architects so often revert to) of a world stripped bare of the messy, complex, lives of users. The functionalist architect attempts to abstract and thus control these lives, whereas participation brings them into unavoidable focus as something that is beyond strict management. However, the attempt to banish politics from architecture is only to delay the inevitable. Just as King Canute was swept away by the waves, social life will find its

43
Koolhaas' pithy reminder is apt here. 'Once
we were making sandcastles. Now we
swim in the sea that swept them away.'
R. Koolhaas and B. Mau, *S, M, L, Xl*,
Rotterdam: 010 Publishers, 1995, p.971.
The problem is his ambivalence in how to
deal with the condition. See J. Till, 'An
incomplete encyclopedia: Rem Koolhaas and
S, M, L, Xl', *Artifice*, March 1996, pp.66-79.

44
Lerup, *Building*, p.30.

45
I take this formulation from the title of
Howell Baum's book *The Organization of Hope*,
which in turn comes from a description
used by a planning student Stephen Blum.
See H. S. Baum, *The Organization of Hope:
Communities planning themselves*, Albany, NY:
State University of New York Press, 1997.
The word 'organisation' is perhaps too
instrumental for participation, hence my
replacement with 'negotiation'.

46
Banham, 'Opening remarks'.

way through the cracks in the wall of architectural denial, eventually overwhelming the hopeless purity of the forms within –
because those forms, conceived in a political vacuum, can put up no
resistance.[43] Better then to take on board these contested territories
earlier rather than be disappointed later. In this light, participation
should occupy a central position in architectural practice, as opposed to sitting on the token margins where it tends to be found. Lars
Lerup is clear about the opportunities that are afforded in the
addressing of the political nature of space at an early stage. 'The fact
remains that if dwellers and their designers take an active part in
the negotiation of political space, new and better vistas will open
up.'[44] The key terms here are 'negotiation' (because that defines the
reality of participation without being idealistic about reaching consensus) and 'new and better' (because that sets the ambition for participation to transcend pragmatics). Lerup goes on to say that if
'negotiation dies, the *hope* for splendid inhabitation dies and most
likely someone else other than dwellers will take over'. This sets
a new context for transformative participation as the *negotiation of
hope* [45] – a potentially contested but ultimately positive process, both
alert to the realities and positing a better future.

The problem of the problem

The idea of the negotiation of hope sits uncomfortably with one of
the normal premises of architecture, namely that it is a problem-
solving exercise; hope projects ambiguously forward, whereas problems look determinedly backwards. In education, the architectural
studio is held up as an exemplar of problem-based learning, the
space where students are set a 'problem' and through the creative,
and reflective, act of design come to a 'solution'. In architectural
practice the 'problem' is what gives the profession something to
act upon in a specialised manner. As Reyner Banham notes, 'a professional is a man with an interest, a continuing interest, in the
existence of problems'.[46] Solving problems is how the profession
legitimates itself; setting problems is how it perpetuates itself.

It is difficult to reconcile the notion of hope with that of problem-solving. The negative connotation of the term 'problem' casts a
gloomy pall over the design process, implying that the best we can
expect from the solution is to make the world a less bad place, as
opposed to the negotiation of hope which is founded on a mutual
aspiration to make the world a better place. John Chris Jones gets it
just right when he says that:

> To think of designing as 'problem-solving' is to use a rather dead
> metaphor for a lively process and to forget that design is not so much

47
J.C. Jones, *Design Methods*, 2nd edn., New
York: Van Nostrand Reinhold, 1992, p.xxix.

a matter of adjusting to the status quo as of realizing new possibilities and discovering our reactions to them.[47]

If one problem with the problem is the way that it closes down the
potential for new possibilities, the other is that the framing and
solving of the problem are an exclusionary act, and thus inappropriate for the terms of transformative participation. Problems, as
Banham indicates, require a certain type of professional, expert,
knowledge to solve them. The identification of the problem thus
inevitably privileges the expert over the user, limiting the possibility of the negotiation of hope as a shared enterprise. We therefore
need to find an alternative paradigm for the design process. In an
eloquent paper, the planner John Forester suggests that we should
replace the normative metaphor of design as the search for a solution with the idea of design as 'sense-making'. 'Sense making is not
simply a matter of instrumental problem-solving, it is a matter of
altering, respecting, acknowledging, and shaping people's lived
worlds.'[48] Central to Forester's argument is that such a move from
the problem to sense-making necessarily brings with it an acknow-
ledgment of the contested social situation in which the design
process is first initiated, and of the contingent social world in
which buildings and their users will eventually be situated. Where
problem-solving, predicated as it is on positivist thinking, tends to
either abstract or exclude the social and the political, sense-making
inevitably engages with them, and in so doing, accords with a model
of participation in which social and political issues are brought to
the fore and then negotiated through spatial discussions.

48
J. Forester, 'Designing: Making sense
together in practical conversations', *Journal
of Architectural Education*, 38, no.3, 1985. See
also Forester, *Planning in the Face of Power*,
pp.119-33.

> If form giving is understood more deeply as an activity of making
> sense together, designing may then be situated in a social world
> where meaning, though often multiple, ambiguous and conflicting,
> is nevertheless a perpetual practical accomplishment.[49]

49
Forester, 'Designing', p.14.

It is Forester's insistence on making sense *together* that resonates so
powerfully with the idea of transformative participation, and so it is
worth following through the implications of this approach. These
are threefold. The first we have already encountered; sense-making
leads to a reconsideration of what constitutes architectural knowledge. As opposed to the instrumentalist knowledge of problem solving, sense-making is developed through knowledge of the third
kind – knowledge from within in which the participatory process is
founded on the will to achieve mutual understanding. The second
implication arises out of the first; in order to achieve this mutual
understanding one needs new models of communication. Third,

sense-making brings with it uncertainty and imprecision that demand the participants face up to the very contingency of architectural practice. It is to these last two issues, communication and contingency, that we now turn.

Urban storytelling

> Doctrines must take their beginnings from that of the matter which they treat. (Vico)

There is always the nagging, but quite serious, concern that conventional methods of architectural communication are describing something that is in fact not architecture. Drawings can never describe the fullness of the future occupation of space; they are, of course, radically reductive. As Robin Evans argues so brilliantly in *The Projective Cast*, this representational reduction is not necessarily a problem as long as one acknowledges the role of the architectural imagination in achieving the translation from drawing to building.[50] The alchemy of imagination is a second means by which the architect achieves professional closure; specialist technical knowledge with indefinable creativity is the combination that establishes architecture apart from other vocations that might have one aspect but not the other. However, in the context of participation the architectural imagination presents a problem, in so much as it is an internalised impulse and thus not available for mutual understanding with the other participants. Drawings, which for the architect may be pregnant with possibilities, remain mute to the outsider. The exclusion is reinforced by the technical nature of so much architectural discourse.[51]

In order to achieve transformative participation, it is therefore necessary to look for a new model of communication. The clue as to what this may be lies in the nature of the knowledge at stake and the make-up of the participants. 'New knowledge neither grows out of a special method, nor the special mind of a genius nor from new theoretical monologues... but from the voices of ordinary people in conversation.'[52] Where professional knowledge tends to reaffirm the status quo, or to incrementally shift it, the knowledge contained in the conversations of ordinary people, of participants, contain the germs of new spatial possibilities. The trick is how to recognise this, how to identify the 'real possibilities present in those fleeting, extraordinary, non-professional moments of indeterminacy, undecidability and ambivalence'.[53] The key lies in recognising the power and validity of ordinary conversation as a starting point for the participatory process. Of course this challenges normative

50
R. Evans, *The Projective Cast: Architecture and its three geometries*, Cambridge, MA: MIT Press, 1995.

51
Having sat on many interview panels to select architects for community-based projects, I am continually astounded at the language that most architects choose to use. Jargon and technical terminology, together with nods to me as the supposed expert, do nothing but alienate, and confuse, the eventual users. These architects do not get the job.

52
Billig, *Ideological Dilemmas*, p.162.

53
Shotter, *Cultural Politics*, p.52.

54
See Ibid., p.141. Much postmodern
academic discourse may be seen to
challenge notions of logic, but still work
out from it as a principle.

55
Ibid., p.39.

56
Ibid., p.128. The same point is made by
John Forester: 'Design as sense-making via
conversation situates the designer's work
in a historical, practical context'. Forester,
'Designing', p.17.

57
G. Vico, *The New Science of Giambattista Vico*,
trans. T. Bergin and M. Fisch, Ithaca, NY:
Cornell University Press, 1948, para 314.

58
Kristin Ross, 'Introduction', in J. Rancière,
The Ignorant Schoolmaster, Stanford, CA:
Stanford University Press, 1991.

patterns of professional and academic legitimacy. Both of these sets of discourse are often predicated on the principles of logic and completeness,[54] against which measures the openness of ordinary conversation is seen as a lower form of communication, and thus one capable of being dismissed. However, this overlooks the potentials to be found in everyday conversation which 'contains more possibilities for our future development than we ever before imagined'.[55]

What is suggested here is the appropriateness of conversation to the architectural participatory process. First, conversation moves the architect from being a detached observer into an engaged participant, enabling him or her to see from within a given situation. Second, it anticipates the future spatial possibilities in terms of time and occupation rather than seeing them as fixed and empty forms. Third, conversations bring into play social relationships because, as Rom Harré notes, the primary human reality is in persons in conversation.[56] Fourth, conversations in their open-ended nature give rise to unexpected consequences; they may lead the participants down paths that they may have never found through logic. In all these four ways conversations can actually describe what architecture may be, namely the temporal, contingent, social occupation of space – a world undiscovered in the reductive drawing. If we follow Vico's urging that 'doctrines must take their beginnings from that of the matter which they treat',[57] then ordinary conversations can form the perfect start to architectural production. What the participatory process does is to provide a context for those conversations to be initiated – and once again participation is here a catalyst for new ways of looking at architectural practice, exposing the limits of normative architectural methods.

'Conversations' is perhaps too vague a term, and also it does not necessarily avoid the imbalance of authority found in most participatory processes. A more equitable and focused conversational mode is found in storytelling. 'The very act of storytelling, an act that presumes in its interlocutor an equality of intelligence rather than an inequality of knowledge, posits equality, just as the act of explication posits inequality.'[58] The authoritative positivist explanation of the expert ('You should have your front door here because it is closest to the road') is replaced by the suggestive and imaginative storyline of the potential dweller ('...we ran through the back door, steaming bodies into air dense with chip fat'). All of us have stories within us, be they descriptive of the past, fictional for the future, anecdotal or practical. Stories have within them elements that are both personal and social, they become a means of describing one's place in the world, of locating the individual within shared spaces. Stories are the place where the imagination finds lines of flight. If one starts a participatory process through a 'what if?' question, and then develops the answers through the forms of stories, two things happen. First the stories arise out of experience of the world and thus have a grounding in reality; second, the 'what if?' allows stories to imagine and to project new spatial visions.[59] Stories thus become conduits for the negotiation of hope, but because of their founding in everyday experience that hope is not impossibly idealistic. Too often hope is associated with unachievable utopias, and participation is founded on idealistic notions of consensus; stories avoid such delusions whilst at the same time not shutting down possibilities and opportunities. The role of the architect becomes that of understanding and drawing out the spatial implications of the urban storytelling. This role requires both knowledge and imagination, but in both cases these attributes are externalised and shared, rather than being internalised and exclusive as happens in non-participatory practice. The architect, as negotiator of hope initiated through urban storytelling, is thus much more than a mere technical facilitator but at the same time is not tarnished with the brush of unfettered power.

Making best sense

If one develops the participatory process out of the strength of story-telling, then these conversations bring with them uncertainty; they bring contingency into the process. So many architectural values are founded on the banishment of contingency,[60] that to be confronted with contingency at the start of the design process represents a serious disturbance to purist architectural production. Again, we see how participation, by bringing forward what is otherwise denied or delayed, presents a 'threat'.

In order to understand how participation, in dealing with contingency, actually offers an opportunity rather than a threat, we need to return to John Forester's notion of design as making-sense-together, and in particular to the ambiguous and complex conditions that such an approach throws up.[61] The question remains, however, as to what type of sense we are making. The most obvious and soothing answer is that we are making common sense – that the process of participation leads to a sense of shared, 'sensible', values. But the notion of common sense is compromised. On the one hand it suggests that solutions will be arrived at in an unthinking, uncontested manner.[62] Small wonder that the Conservative Party used the slogan *Time for Common Sense* as the title of their 2001 election manifesto, as if they could pass off their deeply ideological agenda under the guise of 'straightforward' middle England saloon bar logic. Common sense is also problematic intellectually. The very

59
In a non-participatory context, Sarah Wigglesworth and I initiated the design of our own house, 9 Stock Orchard Street, through telling each other stories. This was to avoid one of us claiming the design first (as would have happened with drawings) but also allowed open-ended, negotiable scenarios to be developed and shared. See J. Till and S. Wigglesworth, 'Table manners', in. J. Till and S. Wigglesworth (eds), *The Everyday and Architecture*, London: Academy Editions, 1998.

60
The suppression of aesthetic disruption through proportional systems; systematised design methodologies; the obsession with cleanliness; the denial of the occupant in media images; Corbusier's 'A boundless depth opens up, effaces the walls, drives away contingent presences'; the Vitruvian triad; fear of time as identified by Karsten Harries. All of these and many more point to architecture's discomfort with contingency. These arguments will be developed in my forthcoming book, *Architecture and Contingency*.

61
Forester notes how this approach recognises design practice as an 'institutionally located, practically constrained, politically contingent, ambiguity resolving, social process'. Forester, 'Designing', p.19.

62
This resonates with one of Vico's less useful, but probably most widely quoted, aphorisms: 'Common sense is judgment without reflection, shared by an entire class, an entire nation, or the entire human race.' Vico, *The New Science of Giambattista Vico*, para 142.

63
As Deleuze notes: 'Philosophy refers to
common sense as its implicit presuppo-
sition… Common sense is thus taken to be a
determination of pure thought… Common
sense shows every day – unfortunately – that
it is capable of producing philosophy in its
own way.' G. Deleuze, *Difference and Repetition*,
New York: Columbia University Press, 1994,
pp.132-35. Deleuze contrasts common sense
(which identifies and recognises) with good
sense (which foresees), but sees them both
as complementary in their attachment to
pure thought. 'Good sense and common
sense complete each other in the image of
thought.' See also G. Deleuze, *The Logic of
Sense*, New York: Columbia University Press,
1990, pp.78-79.

64
'Kant's notion of "*sensus communi*" is
ultimately cognitive and formal rather
than social and cultural.' M. Shapiro,
Cinematic Political Thought, Edinburgh:
University of Edinburgh Press, 1999, p.14.

65
C. Taylor, *Sources of the Self: The making of the
modern identity*, Cambridge, MA: Harvard
University Press, 1989, p.57.

66
As John Shotter notes: 'Joint action… gives
rise to unintended consequences, that is
outcomes which are not intended either by
you or *me*, but which in fact are *our*
outcomes.' Shotter, *Cultural Politics*, p.47.

67
B. Arditi and J. Valentine, *Polemicization: The
contingency of the commonplace*, Edinburgh:
Edinburgh University Press, 1999, p.135.

68
Ibid., p.124.

proposition that sense can be arrived at through commonly agreed
principles presupposes that universal structures of thought can be
erected,[63] and with these universal solutions can be found. In the
context of participation, such universal structures clearly suppress
the development of particular desires. In addition, by identifying
common sense with the realm of the detached intellect, one removes
it from the social world: common sense in this light becomes formal
and prescriptive rather than social and cultural.[64]

Therefore, instead of seeing participation as the move towards
the establishment of common sense, it may be better to posit it in
terms of making best sense. The philosopher Charles Taylor argues
that best sense aims at 'not an absolute best but a partial best… (it
offers) the more realistic orientation about the good, but also allows
us to best understand and make sense of the actions of others'.[65] The
idea of making best sense thus acknowledges three things: first,
that that no one perfect solution exists; second, that others are
involved in the process, it is not the work of the lone intellect or
expert; third, and crucially, it identifies the very contingency of
architectural practice. Architecture is open to forces beyond the
direct control of the architect. In participation, this contingency is
represented first through the desires of the users, and the architect
has to face up to the often conflicting status of these desires. It is
not a matter of attempting to find a consensus among these competing positions, but of using one's judgement to make best sense
of them. The process, whilst potentially leading to unintended consequences, thus still has intentionality.[66] This inevitably leads to
the acceptance of difference rather than the imposition of a false
equality, even if this might grate with accepted liberal norms of participation, in which the search for a solution acceptable to all is
paramount. The spaces arising out of the contingency of participation are thus not necessarily those of static harmony; 'a common
space that is also a fissured space is not an oxymoron'.[67] Instead a
different notion of equality arises, not one based on principles of
absolute universality, but one which 'as a contingent outcome of a
conflicts and strategic calculation is a sedimented moment in a
fluctuating equilibrium'.[68] The hope, therefore, is that a participatory process that is based on the principle of making the best sense
will lead to architecture capable of accepting difference and architecture that is responsive to change over time, since it avoids the
stasis of any universalizing tendency.

The negotiation of hope
In this chapter I have attempted to formulate an approach to participation that moves beyond the token involvement of users towards a

more transformative model. In order for this to happen, architects need to accept changes to the standard methods and values of practice, and in particular to see that the issues that participation brings to the fore present not a threat but an opportunity, leading to a more empowering form of architecture. This is a achieved through an acceptance – or let us hope a welcoming – of the political aspects of space, of the vagaries of the lives of users, of different modes of communication and representation, of an expanded definition of architectural knowledge and of the inescapable contingency of practice. This acceptance leads not only to a revitalised, and more relevant, form of participatory practice, but also to a revitalised, and more relevant, form of architectural practice. For too long architecture has isolated itself in the vain pursuit of the incompatible bedfellows, innovation and timelessness. Participation challenges these values, and brings an awakening of the virtues of engagement: an awakening that might come as a shock to architects more used to a deluded detachment, but one which is necessary if architecture is to have any future relevance.

Participation is not a worthy sop to our political masters; nor is it an excuse for mediocrity; it is not a distraction from supposedly higher values. Participation is the space in which hope is negotiated.[69] What is clear is that this hope refers not just to a better future for the users of the built environment, but also to a better future for architectural practice.

69
I purposely use the word hope to challenge the despair of Manfredo Tafuri who talks of the 'anachronistic "hopes in design"'. Whilst Tafuri's critique of the naivety of architects in the face of capitalist forces is compelling, it behoves us all to suggest alternative methods of architectural production which are politically aware and transformative. See M. Tafuri, *Architecture and Utopia*, Cambridge, MA: MIT Press, 1976.

Losing control, keeping desire

We think any society is defined not so much by its contradictions as by its lines of flight, it flees all over the place, and it's very interesting to try and follow the lines of flight taking shape at any particular moment.

Gilles Deleuze, 1995

Lignes de fuite

The expression *ligne de fuite* – line of flight, of escape, leakage line – is borrowed from Guattari and Deleuze's vocabulary to help us avoid the usual clichés about issues of participation in architecture.[1] Rather than searching for major lines of historic relevance, our text flees away from the central ground towards minor case studies, to a project in progress with which we are directly involved in a small neighbourhood in Paris:

atelier d'architecture autogérée / studio of self-managed architecture (aaa) is a non-profit-making association founded in 2001 whose activity is focused on alternative strategies of urban regeneration in the La Chapelle area, to the North of Paris.[2] It is an interdisciplinary organisation including architects, artists, landscape designers, urban planners, sociologists, students and residents living in the area. Together, we conduct research into participatory urban actions. This collective practice allows for the reappropriation and reinvention of public space through everyday life activities (gardening, cooking, chatting, reading, debating, etc.) understood as creative practices in urban contexts. The aim is to create *a network of self-managed places* by encouraging residents to get access to their neighbourhood and to appropriate and transform temporary available and underused spaces. This strategy valorises a flexible and reversible use of space and aims to preserve urban 'biodiversity' by providing for a wide range of life styles and living practices to coexist.

The starting point was the realisation of a temporary garden made out of recycled materials on one of the derelict sites belonging to the RFF (the French Railway company) located in the area. This garden, called *ECObox*, has been progressively extended into a platform for

[1]
This chapter pays homage to Deleuze and Guattari's thinking. By choosing to follow their schizoanalytic line, we have chosen to move away from the established field known in the Anglo-Saxon world as 'community planning'. We have chosen also to escape a certain French genealogy of the question by taking a line other than Lefebvre's, whose theory has until now been preferred to inform issues of participation and the everyday in architecture. Deleuze and Guattari's thinking has been widely adopted in contemporary architectural theory and practice (especially in the Anglo-Saxon world), but more for its formalism and its direct design application and less for its political critique and practical engagement. In addition to Deleuze and Guattari's reference, this chapter is based on the work of *atelier d'architecture autogérée* (Constantin Petcou, Doina Petrescu, Denis Favret, Giovanni Piovenne, John Roberts) and the contributions of some residents of La Chapelle and external collaborators of ECObox. Their contribution is quoted in the chapter. Some of the authors in this book (Anne Querrien, Teresa Hoskyns, Raoul Bunschoten, Francesco Carreri, Marion von Osten, Liza Fior, Peter Blundell Jones, Jeremy Till) have also inspired this text through discussions and exchange of ideas before and during its making. A number of concepts and quotations have been borrowed from contemporary activist research practices within the *aaa*'s links and network.

2
La Chapelle is one of the areas in Paris with the highest immigration rate (more than 30 per cent of its 30,000 residents are 'foreigners'). Geographically, it is an urban island, bordered by the major train tracks of the Gare du Nord and Gare de l'Est, and the ring road of Paris that isolate the area and constitute a real break within the city. A number of abandoned industrial buildings and left-over spaces (*friches* or *terrain vagues*) are also located in the area. They represent a reserve for potential urban development, but at present, because of their degradation, they are perceived negatively by the residents.

3
The lines of flight are a metaphoric construction issuing from the critical analysis of the capitalist system drawn by analogy with schizophrenic behaviour. It is what Deleuze and Guattari have called schizo-analysis. They consider that 'schizophrenia is undissociable from the capitalist system, itself conceived as primary leakage ('*fuite*') and exclusive malady. The capitalist economy proceeds by decoding and deterritorialization: it has its extreme cases, i.e. schizophrenics, who decode and deterritorialise themselves to the limit; but also it has its extreme consequences – revolutionaries.' 'Capitalism, a very special delirium', in Felix Guattari, *Chaosophy*, New York: Semiotext(e), 1995, pp.72-73.

4
'There is a third type of line, even stranger still, as if something were carrying us away, through our segments but also across our thresholds; toward an unknown destination neither foreseeable nor pre-existent' G. Deleuze and F. Guattari, *On the Line*, New York: Semiotexte, 1998, pp.70-71.

5
G. Deleuze and F. Guattari, *Anti-Oedipus: Capitalism and schizophrenia*, London: Athlone Press, 1984. was written just after the events of 1968 and published in 1972. Guattari was a political activist at that time and was personally involved in the organisation of May 1968 in Paris.

urban creativity curated by the *aaa* members, residents and external collaborators, catalysing activities at the level of the whole neighbourhood. The garden became as such the metonymy of the whole *aaa* project, functioning as social and cultural space, both utopian and real, nomadic and multiple, through a continual process of fabrication and self-redefinition according to its users' desires. The root *eco* is used here in its original Greek sense of *oïkos*, that is 'house, domestic property, habitat, natural milieu'. ECObox is a tool for making the city habitable without domestication and control through official policies or private bodies, but by desiring, claiming, making its memory and its inhabitants' imaginings more intimate.

Guattari and Deleuze's 'lines' challenge the usual designer thinking about lines. They are an abstract and complex enough metaphor to map the entire social field, to trace its shapes, its borders, its becomings. They can map the way 'life always proceeds at several rhythms and at several speeds'. They map individual cracks and collective breaks within the segmentation and heterogeneity of power.[3] The 'line of flight', *ligne de fuite*, is defined not only as a simple line, but as the very force of a tangle of lines flung out, transgressing thresholds of established norms and conventions, towards unexpected manifestations, both in terms of socio-political phenomena and in individual destinies.[4]

By choosing to follow 'lines of flight' rather than mainstream examples, we propose a schizoanalytical reading of this type of approach and take an unusual, abnormal, deterritorialising path that flees from the usual framing of a neo-capitalist architectural practice.

The 'line of flight' occurs in Guattari and Deleuze's work soon after 1968.[5] May 1968 was itself such a line of flight: a non-historical manifestation of a heterogeneous 'Outside'– the eruption of 'a pure becoming', within the social field.[6] It is around 1968 that the participative approach emerges also as a 'line of flight'; not as a historical accumulation, but as a becoming, a 'revolutionary' drive of a critical practice, searching for a new freedom within the architectural profession.[7]

'Ce qui se construit dans la temporalité et n'est pas là pour rester.'[8]

Desire and bricolage

A schizoanalytical approach to 'participation' should start with desire, by considering the participative process as a way of assembling a collective economy of desire, articulating persons, gestures, economic and relational networks, etc.[9] The participation process

6
'Becoming isn't part of history; history amounts only the set of preconditions, however recent, that one leaves behind in order to "become", that is, to create something new. This is precisely what Nietzsche calls the Untimely. May 1968 was a demon-stration, an eruption, of a becoming in its pure state.' G. Deleuze, 'Control and becoming', in *Negotiations*, New York: Columbia University Press, 1995.

7
For more details about the English context of the 1968 events and the emerging of participative approaches in architecture and urban planning, see Peter Blundell Jones's chapter in this book. See also Ben Franks 'New right/new left: An alternative exper-iment in freedom', in S. Sadler and J.R.T. Hughes, *Non-Plan: Essays on freedom, participa-tion and change in modern architecture and urban-ism*, Oxford: Architectural Press, 2000. In France also, there is a link between the 1968 events and participation in architecture, for former revolutionary students were involved in the first participative projects in the 1970s such as the 'auto-rehabilitation' experiences in the Saint Laurent district in Grenoble, the 'ateliers communautaires d'aménagement du cadre de vie' in Cergy Pontoise or the reconstruction of Alma-Gare neighbourhood in Roubaix that is discussed by A. Querrien in Chapter 6 of this book. Nevertheless participation was not the main concern of the French radical practices, who were more concerned after 1968 with the deconstruction of institutions that exerted a centralised control over practice. They sought the introduction of a regulatory competition system in architecture in order to guarantee a democratic access to project commissions, and also the reorganising of the professional education system. Many of these French radical practices were started during a period of research and experiment when, under the Situationist influence, they refused to build; but by the late 1970s and early 1980s they were building a lot, and frequently leaving behind their former interest in working with users. This is the case with Roland Castro, Antoine Stinco, Christian de Portzamparc, Paul Chemetoff, etc. Amongst the few exceptions are Yona Friedman, Paul Virilio and Michel Ragon, who continued in their concern with questions of self-management and partici-pation of users in decision-making in archi-tectural and urban planning processes.

depends on participants' desire.

But if this desire doesn't manifest itself, how can one make it visible? And if it is visible, then how does one welcome it? How could different desires coexist and operate together? And above all, how should we think about desire, about the concept of desire itself, within a participative process?

If we understand participation as a process, as the 'labour of desire', it is because desire itself is processual. There is no desire, says Deleuze, that does not flow into an assemblage of desires, and for him:

> Desire has always been a constructivism, constructing an assem-blage (*agencement*), an aggregate: the aggregate of the skirt, of a sun ray, of a street, of a woman, of a vista, of a colour... constructing an assemblage, constructing a region, assembling.[10]

Desire always relates to the 'multiple', the 'different', and the 'other'. It is:

> A collaging process that seeks to include and to affirm as a way of multiplying possibilities and thus power. It stems not from a lack but on the contrary from an overflowing plenum. Desire is a 'produc-tion'; it 'creates situations'... Desire is an energetic bricolage that uses whatever is at hand in perverse ways: transvaluating the con-text, letting its parts fly free to connect in diverse ways. To desire is to collage one's collage onto another collage.[11]

'Cela me donne une force qui me fait sortir de chez moi...'[12]

Driven by desire, participatory design is a 'collective bricolage' in which individuals (clients, users, designers) are able to interrogate the heterogeneity of a situation, to acknowledge their own position and then go beyond it, to open it up to new meanings, new possibil-ities, to 'collage their own collage onto other collages', in order to discover a common project. As in bricolage,[13] in participative proj-ects, the process is somehow more important than the result, the assemblage more important than the object, the deterritorialisation more important than the construction of territories.

ECObox is a bricolage project resulted from an assemblage of desires. From the very beginning, the collective production of desires has been understood as a process shaping the project. The project started in June 2001 with a consultation on community spaces and a Post-it board where 'gardens of words' were drawn by inhabitants of

8
'That which is constructed in the temporary and is not there to stay', excerpt from a discussion on urban interstices, ECObox, June 2003.

9
'Pleasure' has been a trend in the discourse on participation and non-planning in British (avant-garde) architecture. Even now, it is still a central issue for some creative practices: eg. 'the pleasure of architecture' (Tschumi), 'the pleasure of uselessness' (Jonathan Hill), 'pleasure in public', (The Architectural Fondation) 'pleasure principles: rules for urban design' (Muf), etc. Deleuze articulated his difference with Foucault, precisely by acknowledging his interest in 'desire' versus Foucault's discourse on 'pleasure'. I'll somehow follow Deleuze here, and construct my arguments around participation as driven by 'desire'. I also think that this idea of a productive activity of 'desire' (the uncon-scious as factory) reveals possible parallels between Deleuze and Guattari's project (expressed mainly in *Anti-Oedipus and Thousand Plateaus*) and the Marxist approach of Lefebvre.

10
'D-comme Désir', in Pierre-André Boutang (ed.), *L'Abécédaire de Gilles Deleuze, avec Claire Parnet*, Paris: Vidéo Editions Montparnasse, 1996. In fact, Deleuze and Guattari give 'desire' a central place in their theory. Cf. G. Deleuze, 'Desire and Pleasure', trans. Melissa McMahon. French version 'Désir et Plaisir', in *Deux régimes de fous*, Paris: Les Editions de Minuit, 2003.

11
'Desire', an article submitted by John Landau on 24 October 1997 as a contribution to deleuzeguattarionary. (*http//cs.art.rmit.edu.au/deleuzeguattarionary*)

12
'This gives me the power to step out of my routine…', inhabitant of la Chapelle, speaking about her project at ECObox, January 2004.

different ages and cultural origins. Many people wanted places for children, green spaces, sports fields… Following discussions, a collective garden programme has been negotiated as a tactical start. It is a generous enough metaphor for a transversal practice that includes complex assemblages of activities… Children in La Chapelle call the ECObox 'the gardening' to mark a difference with other gardens in the area. 'The gardening' was perceived as an unfinished garden, a garden-in-progress defined by its very process of fabrication and becoming: a garden-process rather than a garden-object. 'The gardening' was the place where plants were grown, but also cultivated personal and small group projects of all kinds, and with them, relations amongst people; new desires were becoming.

C'est justement peut-être très important, de mon point de vue, qu'ils puissent revenir, même sans leur parents. C'est en tout cas une vérité qui est aussi très belle que de voir venir uniquement des enfants tourner autour de ce jardin qui est aussi comme eux: jeune, sauvage, pas très stable, en devenir. [14]

Molecular revolutions

A participative approach challenges the configuration of power relationships within a project expressed through planning policies, institutions, and design protocols. It should normally question who exerts power and how this power is distributed through the project, aiming to empower both users and clients to play an active role in the decision-making and the creative process.

Deleuze places desire *before* power because, as he says, 'power is an affectation of desire'.[15] In a participative approach, the possibility of expression and evolution of participants' 'desire' is the precondition of their empowerment.

But desire can also play a subversive role within the established power structures of a project. It is always an agent of change, always 'revolutionary' and, according to Guattari, 'all the dramatic social changes will be absolutely un-dissociable from a multitude of molecular revolutions on the level of the economy of desire'.[16]

The participative practices in urban planning and architecture should be driven by such molecular revolutions at the level of economy of desire. The economies of cities should be understood as contiguous with the economies of desire of those that live and work in these cities. A revolutionary reform in urban planning cannot be initiated solely by centralised structures and governmental bodies. It should include these 'microscopic attempts' at the level of collective and individual desires of clients and users in micro-social units: neighbourhood associations, informal teams, squats and other self-managed organisations, experimental institutions, alter-

will promote 'existential values and values of desire' rather than
commercial values.[18]

aaa experiments with a non-centralised, non-specialised type of
planning, starting with a micro-political attempt at taking direct
responsibility for the place where one lives. It suggests the possibility of passing gradually from 'gardens' to other self-managed and collectively created places. Issuing from an idea of 'direct democracy'
rather than 'representative democracy', this transformation affects
both places and people, who start to change their roles from mere
users to citizens, from mere residents to interventionist residents.[19]

Urban actions

… a revolutionary organization must be like a war machine, not like
a state apparatus, it must respond to desire, not just provide an
external synthesis.[20]

The urban protest was a kind of social movement that emerged in
the early 1970s, just after the events of 1968, in the context of dete-
riorating urban conditions and increased control of the public
sphere. At the same time as organised protests, other minor practices emerged based in everyday life: 'urban actions'.[21] These are 'the
precondition of life on the streets', and the activist groups and left-
ist alliances started to consider them in their attempt to establish a
relationship between the street and the academy, the neighbourhood and the political scene.

New urban practices emerged out of this encounter between
forms of activism and urban actions. For example, many of the
community gardens in New York City in the 1980s emerged as a consequence of Green Guerrilla's activist actions in the 1970s. These
actions started with illegal planting, continued with occupation of
land, and then grew into community protest actions to preserve the
created gardens against private or public expansionist policies of
development.[22] In France, such community gardens started in the
late 1990s and their specific status ('jardins partagés') has only
recently been recognised in law.[23] Paradoxically, this happened in
parallel with the decision by the City of Paris to fence off the last
open spaces, small as they are. Collective gardens have become a
means of preserving free public space in the post-capitalist city.

ECObox challenges the role of a community garden and extends its
functions further. The 'lines of flight' initiated by the ECObox strat-

13
We use here the term 'bricolage' in the
sense developed by Lévi-Strauss in his
well-known anthropological study *La
Pensée Sauvage*. Lévi-Strauss argues that
the preferred materials of bricolage are
not concepts (the materials of scientific
theories), but signs – the bricoleur has
the privilege over the scientist of being
able to define a block of wood alternately
as material, support, extension, chopping
board, hammer, and so forth – each
potential use representing a distinct
signification. In this sense, the bricoleur
'interrogates all the heterogeneous objects
of which his treasury is composed to
discover what each of them could "signify"
and so contribute to the definition of a set
which has yet to materialise, but which
will ultimately differ from the instrumental set only in the internal disposition
of parts.'. C. Lévi-Strauss, *The Savage Mind*,
Oxford: Oxford University Press, 1996, p.18.

14
'It is very important, in my view, that they
should feel able to return even without
their parents. It is beautiful to see children
alone enjoying this garden which is like
them: young, wild, not very stable, in
process of becoming.' association (des pas),
collaborator of *aaa*.

15
Deleuze, 'Désir et Plaisir', p.113.

16
F. Guattari, *La Révolution moléculaire*,
Fontenay: Recherches, 1977, p.29.

17
'Although I am against the illusion of a
step-by-step transformation of society –
"small reforms which make up great
transformations" – I believe that microscopic attempts at creating communities –
setting up analytic groups among
militants, organizing a day-care centre
in a university – are crucial.' F. Guattari,
'The best capitalist drug', in *Chaosophy*,
New York: Semiotexte, p.223.

18
F. Guattari and G. Genosko, *The Three
Ecologies*, London: Athlone Press, 2000, p.66.

19
For comments on similar issues, see Teresa
Hoskyns's chapter in this book.

20

F. Guattari and G. Deleuze, 'Capitalism: A
very special delirium', in *Chaosophy*, p.66.

21

The term is introduced by Jocken Becker in
'BIGNESS? Size does matter', in *Image/Politik:
Städtisches Handeln. Kritik der unternehmerischen
Stadt*, Berlin: b_books Verlag, 2001.

22

See *www.greenguerillas.org*

23

As soon as they gained recognition in law,
their definition was reduced to a stereotype. 'The shared garden (jardins partagés),
animated by associations which develop
gardening activities for the public (aiming
for education, insertion, creation of social
relations of proximity: cultural animations,
intergenerational encounters, etc...)'.
Excerpt from 'Main Verte' chart issued by
the City of Paris to supervise and support
the creation of community gardens.

24

For example the urban catalyst project that
explores the role of temporary use in the
contemporary city. See note 53.

25

'DIY was an ethic born in reaction against
a dominant society that considers culture
primarily in terms of a profit-generating,
commercial enterprise... The key in all of
this culture is participation. If you don't
participate, it doesn't happen. Reclaim the
Streets is a protest that only works if everyone participates. This is true not only for
the organisers who create sound systems,
train with tripods, build props and compose
info sheets, but also for those who just
show up on the day of protest in costume,
with radio, drums, or fire-breathing apparatus, and ready to dance. An RTS action is
like a pot-luck dinner. RTS secure the space
and provide the music and the postprotest
support, but what happens at the action
depends on what people bring with them
and what they do once they are there.'
S. Duncombe, 'Stepping off the sidewalk:
Reclaim the Streets/NYC', in B. Shepard and
R. Hayduk, *From Act up to the WTO: Urban
protest and community building in the era of
globalization*, London: Verso, 2002, p.220.

egy organise mobile, multiple presences in different places and connect dispersed desires. Rather than a garden, we should speak about
an agency. This agency started with neither official recognition nor
financial support. It started with desire and no power. It began as a
micro-political attempt to create community-run spaces. As such,
'gardening' became a tactic for both occupying and preserving
spaces, resisting pressure for development and experimenting with
methods of urban management that allow a more democratic access
to decision-making, creation and use. These 'temporary and mobile
gardens' are perhaps the visionary precursors of other self-managed
spaces to come, that will prove to be more and more necessary, to
make our increasingly gentrified cities sustainable.[24]

The bricolage logic of these desiring practices is the driving force
both for participative ethics and for aspirations towards autonomy.
In the Anglo-Saxon context, the DIY activist culture has created new
forms of direct participation, based on principles of self-management and self-production.[25]

'A quoi on participe?' [26]

ECObox is a DIY urban practice. It is 'bricolage' applied to materials,
urban politics and social relations. It creates a new practice that
responds to the needs of the neighbourhood and at the same time
reinvents itself inside the professional context.

It resists pre-existing forms and policies of participation, enabling
inhabitants to participate directly, to decide how they want to organise themselves, knowing that sometimes community desires will
be different from the public or private interests. Community desires
are geared neither to profit-generation nor for urban functionality,
but to something else that is not predictable and constructs itself
every day with everyone participating. How then can we sustain this
long-term participation-in-progress? Defining itself as both a professional structure and an activist group, *aaa* is a new type of architectural practice that has chosen not to work within the model of
an office, an enterprise or a capitalist company but as a non-profit
association, whose economy functions in solidarity with its projects.
Both residents and professionals become equal members in a 'brico-
laged' structure: 'what happens depends upon what people bring
with them and what they do once they are there'. This kind of structure also preserves a certain economic (and political) independence
in the negotiation process with both private and public bodies. But at
the same time, it is a structure which takes risks, because nothing
can be taken for granted when everything depends on the presence

'In what do we participate?' ECObox,
European Social Forum, November 2003.

of all those involved. Sometimes this presence is conflictual, for people's desires change along the way, and one should learn how to deal with tensions, contradictions, oppositions and failures. A heterogeneous participative structure cannot be always consensual. Sometimes it is time to stop and then to start again, in another way.

It was important that beyond being a practice, ECObox defined itself as a place, a laboratory, a 'civic laboratory' an 'agency for urban bricolage'. It plays the role of a symbolic marker in the area and serves as an element of visibility and continuity within the whole process, showing its temporal dynamic.

The small scale enables a certain autonomy within the process. Guattari has stressed the importance of sizing the critical scale of an experiment, like the one in the La Borde clinic, and of exposing the mechanisms that would enable economic, political and social autonomies.[27] ECObox activates at the scale of a neighbourhood, which gives visibility to most of the actors and originators, knowing at the same time that such a neighbourhood, in a metropolis like Paris, is always traversed by regional and global dynamics that exceed the local condition. These broader dynamics constitute the very mechanisms that contribute to a wider integration of a geographically and socially isolated community. The ECObox has developed crossover networks and encouraged participation from outside; thus activists, artists, and specialists from different affiliations and cultures periodically organise events and run activities such as a library, a language workshop, or a series of debates. At the same time, inhabitants such as former immigrants are also operating with cross-connections between their culture of origin and their present culture; they are concerned with economies and networks at a global scale, and these contribute to processes of heterogenesis and connectivity within the neighbourhood.

27
See F. Guattari, 'La Borde, A Clinic unlike any other', in *Chaosophy*, pp.187-208 and *passim*.

Transversal participation

28
'As officials, we discover that conformist desires exist as well...' Excerpt from a discussion on urban interstices, ECObox, June 2003.

'On découvre en tant qu' elu qu' il y a aussi des désirs tres conformistes...'[28]

The existing frameworks of (both governmental and local) participative programmes are always organised in the same way, without taking into account the particularity of each situation. There is a difference between 'organised participation'[29] which is also somehow 'preformed' and under control, inducing the same symptomatic reactions, and a 'transversal participation' (issuing from 'transversality' as a method) which transverses different social strata, which is neither hierarchical (vertical) nor symptomatic (horizontal), and generates unexpected and continually evolving

29
This dates again from 1968, when General de Gaulle asserted that 'From now on the world won't be as before and it will be necessary *to organise* the participation of people in what they are concerned with.'

reactions. How to organise a 'transversal participation' is a real architectural question... 'Faire exister l'espace public en tant que manifestation, prise de parole...'[30] An independently organised participative process does not always tend to achieve agreement with all participants, but it should also retain the possibility of *being in conflict* with the organised nature of 'normal' politics. A participative approach should not seek total efficacy but remain open to unexpected conclusions.

30
'To make the public space to exist as speech manifestation', Excerpt from a discussion on urban interstices, ECObox, June 2003.

ECObox has become a critical observatory of urban politics in the area and as such, has sometimes entered into conflict with the existing programmes (and public bodies) for criticising the formalism of the consultations organised in the area and the manipulation of their results. These consultations, for example the one for ZAC – Zone d'Aménagement Concerté (Area of Concerted Development) in Pajol, have been conducted so as to legitimate pre-existing decisions. Within the programme of renovating Pajol's industrial buildings, the residents contested the ostentatious location of a new office building and asked instead for a garden and community spaces, but the City completely ignored their desires as revealed by the consultation, instead carrying on with their pre-chosen solution, having gained the approval of local officials. In this context, ECObox became a protest site and an information agency where inhabitants could learn about the consultation results and the possibilities of continuing their opposition.

'La concertation officielle est organisée pour figer des espaces.' [31]

31
'The official dialogue is organised in order to solidify spaces.' Excerpt from a discussion on urban interstices, ECObox, June 2003.

Participation is also 'creating space' by creating space for discussion, liberating speech. The problem of the existing consultation procedures is that they are preformed, already oriented towards a certain expected functionality. [32] The way the space of participation is organised has consequences for the results of the discussion. Rigid discussion spaces produce rigid conclusions, and liberated speech can liberate space as well. What would this space be like that does not freeze speech and does not solidify the space produced by it?

32
The few edited 'handbooks' or 'toolkits' for community planning, whilst having many qualities also have the large defect of being too directive and introducing preformed tools and assessment forms, which rather than liberating, tend to control the participative process.

ECObox works with particular enunciative and spatial devices to encourage free speech, creating vacuoles, to use Guattari's term, which are meetings where 'nothing special is expected other than that things just happen and that what is important is said'. [33] ECObox defines itself as a discussion space in which participation is organised along with 'vacuoles'. Urban decisions can be taken during informal meetings, whilst cooking and laughing together.

33
A. Querrien, email exchange with *aaa*.

34
'There are spaces which allow events that
public space does not allow at all'. ECObox,
discussion.

35
'Liberated desire means that desire escapes
the impasse of private fantasy: it is not a
question of adapting it, socializing it,
disciplining it, but of connecting it in a way
that allows its process not be interrupted in
the social body, and its expression to be
collective. What counts is not authoritarian
unification, but rather a sort of infinite
spreading: desire in the schools, the
factories, the neighbourhoods, the nursery
schools, the prisons, etc. It is not a
question of directing, of totalizing, but of
plugging into the same plan of oscillation'.
F. Guattari, 'Capitalism, A very special
delirium', p.62.

36
The first part of the garden was constructed
within the framework of a live project run
conjointly by sixth year architecture
students from the University of Sheffield
and the *aaa* team in October 2002.

37
For more detail on the 'free access' ideology
and a thorough research on alternative and
autonomous economies, see the Tangential
University archive: *http://utangente.free.fr*

38
The memory of the place was marked by
one of the most important political protest
movements in the late 1990s: the *sans-
papiers* movement. Three hundred African
people fought for more than two years to
obtain regular permits and documents from
the French authorities. Their action began
with the occupation of the Church of St
Ambroise in Paris. The current ECObox
location at 22, Rue Pajol, was one of the
places that were occupied for a few months
by a group of *sans-papiers* in 1996.
See *http://bok.net/pajol*

'Il existe des espaces qui permettent ici ce que l'espace public ne permet pas.' [34]

Rather than just a leisure place, this first garden was conceived as a platform, or rather a 'plateau', a zone of articulation of intensities, flows and desires: a place of encounter for different populations, caring for different temporalities, different individual and collective rhythms *'plugged into the same plan of oscillation'*. [35]

The surface of the garden is a platform containing a multiplicity of holes, a 'hollowed surface' like a new habitable ground. It is the floor of a green living-room constructed on the additive principle of horizontal growth. The individual lots are shaped together with the collective surface, so, in order to construct an individual lot, one has to construct a bit of common ground. It is a physical manifestation of the democratic functioning of the ECObox. 'The labour is individual and the fruits are collective', as Mary-Line, one of the residents, says. The garden continues to function while being extended. It changes size and form continually: it is not an established garden but one always becoming, an open-ended process. No social engineering, no urban expectation, but a reversible process in which a minimal welcoming structure is created by people who come to transform the project together.

The surface, made out of recycled pallets, allows for both continuity and diversity within individual and collective actions. It alters its topology in order to host multiple activities and to shape places for flexible use: steps, greenhouses, tool storage, compost bin, water collection – all made from materials that one can get for free. The students who initiated the construction of the garden also made a user guide for its continuation, indicating convenient construction techniques and places where free construction materials (pallets, plastic bottles, gravel, etc.) could be collected in the area. [36] Not only the ecological recycling but also the new economies and politics of the project are supposed to constitute a 'free access' space. [37]

Holes have been made in the outside wall as well, to open the hidden space of the garden to the curiosity of passers-by. Boring pipe-holes in the wall was both a DIY action and a community event, celebrating the visibility of the garden to the public eye. It was also a symbolic gesture of making visible the invisible – i.e. the memory of the place, the garden but also the gardeners – anonymous users, sometimes former immigrants, used to invisibility and confinement. Gardeners have chosen what views of the garden they want to show and realised the pipe-holes by themselves. The garden's breath can now be felt in the street... [38]

Co-produced participation

39
'Collective thinking should construct itself
along with the events.' ECObox discussion,
January 2004.

'La pensée collective doit se construire au fur et à mesure des événements.' [39]

Not all participative processes are liberating experiences. Participation is not a liberating technique in itself. Control can be exerted
through participative approaches as well, and this is one of the
problems with compulsory participative programmes.

In France, the Law of Solidarity and Urban Renewal enacted in
December 2000 imposes compulsory public consultations and transparent procedures for the elaboration of urban planning documents
(SCOT, PLU Cartes de Commune) at all stages. Both the organisation
of public consultation and the final report are left to the local council. According to the SRU law, it is for the local council to decide also
about the method of consultation. Nevertheless, this law, which is
based on a number of democratic principles such as decentralisation, transparency and participation of the residents in the decision-making, creates the political framework of a new form of
urban governance but does not guarantee the real and effective participation of the citizen. In reality, the different urban planning
documents are usually elaborated by experts without any previous
participation, and the consultation goal is somehow to only confirm
and legitimate these documents. In consequence, the consultation
is organised only to record supporting attitudes for the expert proposals and to avoid or calm any opposition. In general, the consultation consists of inviting residents to participate in public debates (in
which they are allocated short time slots to communicate their positions) or to leave suggestions in a mailbox, without being given the
tools and the framework to elaborate and communicate their own
ideas in a pertinent way. The final decision is made by the local
council in most cases without any risk-taking, on the basis of the
supposedly supportive reactions.

As such, the law of participation is formally applied but the
main roles are played by the experts, the state and the administration officials. The residents are only consulted on a carefully prepared documentation in which they can still have their say, but in
fact are not really able to participate in the different structural
stages of the planning process such as diagnosis, expertise, programming, representation, etc. The public consultations are organised to
pay lip-service to the law, rather than to provide critical tools for an
effective community planning process.

The ECObox strategy proposes a different understanding of the participative approach in which residents play the central role: a site-

based planning process involving neighbourhood residents working in self-organised teams (that could eventually include experts of their choice). They are supported in this way to express their own individual and collective desires, to identify priorities and elaborate their own proposals, by being offered planning tools and assistance with information, technical knowledge and representation techniques. These collective proposals, issuing from real consultation and creative work, inventive and well-informed, constitute a real participative contribution and a realistic base for further negotiation with the official partners, aiming for both sustainability and social creativity.

Democratic access to decision-making is not granted by an imposed participation. Participation should be understood as a progressive and evolving process that constructs itself inferentially, by both integrating and adjusting its aims according to the newly created situations. Participation is performative, it is 'to collage one's collage onto another collage', it cannot work through preconceived models. This is also because

> Democracy itself cannot be conceived within an intangible legitimacy; in fact collective thought must be built progressively along with the events and not be the captive of former results or representations. A neighbourhood can change its opinion according to what happens, and it is for 'technicians' to find the means to represent it by incorporating this change as a sign of progress or as a question.[40]

'L'intérêt de la co-production c'est le fait qu'on apprenne...' [41]

Participation is also a formative process. Residents are initiated through dialogue and interventions into becoming an active part of their immediate surroundings. They start to shape their own policies, to articulate their own voices and preferences, to organise themselves independently. By facilitating this process, we might manage to pass on tools that will allow them to re-shape their world. We learn together to 'make do' with the available resources. This energy generated through people acting out in their own environment should lead to a network of support, a critical reading of one's own surroundings and an involvement within the changes taking place.

Une expérience de la négociation entre compétence et incompétence... [42]

ECObox is a learning and doing platform organised through a hetero-

40
A. Querrien, sociologist, collaborator of *aaa*.

41
'The attraction of co-production is the fact that one could learn.' Excerpt from a discussion on urban interstices, ECObox, June 2003.

42
'An experience of negotiation between competency and incompetency...', François Deck, artist, collaborator of *aaa*.

43
Guattari defines heterogenesis as 'processes of continuous resingularisation... Heterogeneity is an expression of desire, of a becoming that is always in the process of adapting, transforming and modifying itself in relation to its environment. Whereas the State works by homogenizing (macro-political consensus), it is always already defeated by heterogenous formations whose singularities cannot be represented (micropolitical disensus).' See Guattari and Genosko. Op. cit.

44
Such programmes have been organised until now in partnership with the University of Sheffield, École d'Architecture Paris Malaquais and École Nationale de Beaux Arts de Grenoble.

genesis of levels of praxis.[43] 'Knowledge' and 'space' are produced at the same time and by different participants: professionals and researchers, users, institutional representatives, teachers, students, children, etc... Pedagogical and research programs are conjointly conducted by the *aaa* team and different institutions (live projects, workshops and participative studios).[44] ECObox became a formative structure that draws co-productions and participatory action research, involving both professionals and users of all ages. It creates a shared learning environment in which forms of personal knowledge co-evolve through group interactions.

Participation in the ECObox is effective not only within the production of spatial objects but within spatial practices as well, within the invention of new tools for multiple and flexible use. For example, a series of modules of mobile furniture have been co-produced by *aaa* members, eco-designers, residents, and students to function as urban catalysts and mobile extensions of the ECObox garden: these include an urban kitchen, a ludotheque, a mobile cinema, a library, a seed bank, a fountain/rainwater-collector, and a drawing office. They generate infrastructure and networks, stimulate desire and pleasure at the scale of proximity. Inhabitants can use them for different activities to appropriate space within the city. They enable a *tactical practice*, in the sense of Michel de Certeau, formalising a type of urban 'resistance' through techniques of infiltration and *détournement*. They empower minor cultures, minor languages and minor urban practices to validate local traditions and personal abilities to resist the dominant forms of knowledge, institutional control and prescriptive ways of living in the city.

Autonomy and subjectivation

A participation process should also enable users to constitute themselves as active-reactive subjects, as subjects in transformation. Participation should concern not only the realisation of sustainable spaces but also what Deleuze and Guattari have called *subjectivation processes*, creative understandings of the subjects themselves in relation to their environment and the ways they inhabit it. The outcome of a subjectivation process cannot be planned, cannot be referred to any pre-existing or projected form of knowledge and power. The subjectivation process is as unpredictable as an event:

There are various ways individuals and groups constitute themselves as subjects through processes of subjectivation: what counts in such processes is the extent to which, as they take shape, they elude both established forms of knowledge and the dominant forms of power. This is of value even if they in turn engender new forms of power or

45
G. Deleuze, 'Control and becoming', in *Negociations*.

become assimilated into new forms of knowledge. For a while, they had a real rebellious spontaneity.[45]

Autonomy within a community will not be realised by disciplinary regulation imposed by power, but by internal displacement, shift-ings, settings and dissolutions that constitute a process of self-composition: the self-regulation of a living society.

The architect-user/the user-architect

Within a *real* participation, which is a self-regulation process driven by the rebellious spontaneity that Deleuze speaks about, the archi-tect is no longer granted the role as master of the project. In partici-pative approaches, the architect should accept losing control. Rather than being a master, the architect should understand him-self/herself as one of the participants.[46]

46
Clara Greed in her article 'Can man plan? Can women plan better?' makes a distinction between public and professional participation within the current regeneration schemes and criticises the current 'public particip-ation' exercises organised on 'hit and run' practices. She speaks about the necessity of a planner acting as 'a broker of ideas, an organiser or advocate, rather than as a "master-planner"'. She asserts a feminist position (that we subscribe to) according to which 'it is better to work for a community within the voluntary sector than to work for local government', becoming a member of the 'planned', better to seek to implement policy by means over and above, or apart from, the mainstream planning system'. See Sadler and Hughes. Op. cit., p.166.

47
J. Hill, *Actions of Architecture: Architects and creative users*, London: Routledge, 2003.

ECObox began with a group of architects who started to work where they lived, in their own neighbourhood. They manifested an immediate political concern and civic engagement with their own surroundings, acknowledged themselves as architect-residents, architect-citizen, architect-users... This position, blurring tradi-tional borders between the architect and the user, also invites its reversal: the user-architect, the citizen-architect, etc... A whole per-mutation of roles is initiated...

Design-action

For an architect-resident or architect-user, 'use' is no longer sepa-rated from the design process. Such a position takes critically Jon-athan Hill's assumption that 'architecture is made by use and by design'.[47] The practice of such an architect-user could be called design-action, by analogy with what we have called urban action. Like urban action, design-action is based on the critical contri-bution of users who start to be considered by activist design groups in their attempt to establish a relationship between the everyday and the academy, the neighbourhood and the political scene. Design-action goes beyond academic disciplines and standardised practices.

In a design-action there is no border between design and use... Creativity is present in use, where one continually has to find ways of adapting and reinventing everyday life contexts... Design-action is inclusive and accessible: it prepares for new aesthetics resulting from a mix of the designer's and the user's aesthetics. Design-action works with the concrete logics of bricolage rather than with abstract concepts, with presentations rather than representations.

Design-action is interventionist design. It takes political positions and catalyses social processes.[48]

Cuisine urbaine is an urban device that articulates the memory of places, individual tastes, cultural backgrounds, personal narratives, know-hows, inventions and lucky finds. Together with the very act of cooking, other informal practices take place around the kitchen: meetings, discussions, testimonials, storytelling, exchange, play. It is a tool for concocting food, the community and the city. The kitchen can be used by one or several persons, adults and children outside and inside of ECObox. Principles of material and energy economy, recycling, self-sufficiency, autonomy, participation and multiculturality have been considered in its construction. The shape and scale of the urban kitchen vary according to its users' desire. Tools and accessories (dishes, carpets, cushions) are collected in the neighbourhood. Beyond its role of urban catalyst, the urban kitchen is an informal economy generator.

This is not so much a bottom-up approach, but one 'in the middle', as Deleuze would say. It is an approach that places the architect and the user in the middle of a creative architectural process. In feminist terms, one could speak of a 'politics of location',[49] the strategic way one places him or herself in the architectural profession, as well as the way one may try to operate with situated knowledge in design and urban planning. In many ways, this is a location in the middle, this 'middle' which, for Deleuze, is the place where lines and politics acquire their speed.

Urban curating

Urban curating is a new planning tool, discussed and experimented with by a number of contemporary architects by analogy with current practices in contemporary art.[50] An architect who acts as 'curator' defines their professional location in the middle, in between institutions, clients, and users. Rather than a master, they are a mediator:

As an independent cultural worker, she escapes what we would call limitations, the 'myth' of the artist-architect whose authority is based on professional judgement and authorship, institutional bureaucracy that is founded on the building law and abstracted knowledge, and economic limits that are determined by the developer and the market. The curator moves in between. Official instruments for urban planning are strict and not especially flexible. There is need for interference, which may take different faces, and which

48
An example of design-action is the Urban Parkfiction project, in Hamburg, a radically participatory planning programme of a self-organised park that developed in reaction against a development project that was blocked by the inhabitants. The Parkfiction project addresses issues of accessibility and inclusion: 'The main issue is to develop strategies for shaping a planning process in such a way that it becomes accessible for people who, due to cultural and social preconditions as well as their experience in life, are usually excluded from actively designing the public sphere', (*www.parkfiction.org*).

49
The 'politics of location' is a trend with the recent feminist project that considers the difference between discursive subjects by taking into consideration various determinations (geographic, ethnic, cultural, libidinal, etc.). R. Braidotti, *Nomadic Subjects: Embodiment and sexual difference in contemporary feminist theory, gender and culture*, New York: Columbia University Press, 1994, p.268.

50
The term belongs to Raoul Bunschoten and has been issued within Chora's methodology. A number of architects and artists have borrowed the 'urban curating' technique and applied it in different ways. (Jeanne van Heeswijk, Meike Shalk, Helena Matson, Kirsten Wilein, etc.).

51
Meike Shalk, 'Urban Curating',
www.soc.nu/urbancurating

52
Meike Shalk, 'Urban Curating', (see also
Raoul Bunschoten's chapter in this book).

53
See Marion von Osten's chapter in this
book.

54
One of the best-known proximity centres is
Centro Sociale Leoncavallo, founded in Milan in
1975, (*www.leoncavallo.org*).

55
A. Membretti, 'Centro Sociale Leoncavallo:
The social construction of a public space of
proximity', *www.republicart.net*

must be constantly redefined. We felt strongly that a curatorial practice could make a difference here.[51]

The curator draws on others' creativity: on that of users or clients who provide frameworks for its fulfilment. He or she is a caretaker and a connector of people, things, desires, stories, opportunities, 'a person who scans and lays out a new field by making new readings of "things", which s/he identifies and contextualises'.[52]

What is changed when 'participation' is part of a curatorial practice, rather than part of the mainstream planning process? This form of participation reinserts principles of connectedness and heterogeneity in urban planning and draws into question existing institutional frameworks by creating new readings and interfaces with creative practices and uses.[53] Before regenerating the city, one needs to regenerate the frameworks within the regeneration programmes, the institutions and the bodies that run these programmes. One needs to reconsider the way the projects are represented, to rework the very mechanisms of participation and of the production of subjectivities.

Public space of proximity
New autonomous, self-managed, institutions, cooperatives including both production, education and collective 'lifespaces', start to emerge. Their value consists in the inventiveness they show outside the established frameworks. An example of such autonomous institutions are the 'proximity centres' in Italy resulting from the radical left activism and the squat culture in the 1970s.[54] These centres survived over the years and evolved into institutions but retained their political agenda about individual rights to self-determination. They are experiments in creating a 'public space of proximity':

> Real public space seems to be distinguished by being territory that is fought for, which is always in danger of being subjugated to privatised or bureaucratic control. A symbolic, identitary and complex territory, where the social sphere overlaps with the political, cultural and the economic sphere. A space in which these elements are newly composed again and again within diverse and fragile communities in permanent dialectic with an increasingly global society. A public space of proximity is, in other words, where the discourse on the collective good is rooted in everyday social practices in a common material space with its multifaceted meanings.[55]

The ECObox garden is a self-managed space. Through a permutation of roles and different levels of praxis, several activities and policies run alternatively: i.e. a participative urban laboratory, a self-managed gallery, a workshop for self-productions, an exchange platform between internal and external actors. Economical, intellectual and emotional productions are managed together. The 'participative urban laboratory' is nested in the garden where discussions, protest meetings, design workshops, object fabrication, gardening and other types of material and immaterial productions are proposed by inhabitants. The usual participation framework is reversed: officials and institutional representatives are invited to participate in what is proposed and elaborated in situ, by inhabitants. The 'laboratory' creates at the same time autonomies and alliances within the framework of a public space of proximity. Design is demystified and the project is co-produced without mastering and control but with a new reading. Nevertheless, the typical modalities of self-organisation, in other words horizontality, and the corresponding absence of formal hierarchies of a vertical type, often end up in conflict, so solutions have to be found.

In his book *The Three Ecologies*, Guattari discusses 'other contracts of citizenship', about ways to enable 'the singular, the exceptional, the rare, to coexist with a State structure that is the least burdensome possible'.[56]

'Other spaces' – leaving space for others

'Un contrat avec l'autre dans un réseau de lieux et de relations.'[57]

The ECObox strategy is based on the temporary appropriation and use of leftover spaces and urban interstices. These spaces are (sometimes) the waste from the real-estate market or due to the temporary neglect of the urban planning policies. They are 'other spaces', the other of what constitutes the plannified city.[58] Studies have demonstrated that in big cities they function as an alternative to conventional forms of public space that nowadays are more and more subject to surveillance and control. The leftovers are spaces of relative freedom where rules and codes could still be redefined. The quality of these leftover spaces consists in their resistance to stable and homogenous appropriation. These 'spaces of uncertainty', to borrow Cupers and Miessen's term, are the very opposite of the functional spaces in the city. They define 'public space' as heterogeneous, fragile, indefinite, fragmented and multiple.

Public space and urbanity have always been connected to disorder, functional heterogeneity and diversity. The most meaningful char-

56
Guattari and Genosko, p.51.

57
'…A contract with the other in a network of places and relations.' Stephane Tonnelat, urban designer, external collaborator of *aaa*.

58
Through a critical approach of Foucault and Lefevbre, Mary McLeod theorised these 'other spaces' in both senses: as 'spaces of others' and as 'other kind of spaces'. Other architectures, and as such other designs and other uses, are the potentials in these 'other spaces'. M. McLeod, 'Everyday and other spaces', in D. Coleman, E. Danze and C. Henderson (eds), *Feminism and Architecture*, Princeton, NJ: Princeton Architectural Press, 1996. Cupers and Miessen in their recent book *Spaces of Uncertainty* define these 'other spaces' as an alternative to the public space, which is more and more structured, programmed and controlled. These 'other spaces' are also spaces of encounter with 'the other': the non-consumer, the old, the poor, the restless, etc. 'Public space – with its mechanisms of control – has its *other*, situated in the fragility and indefiniteness of certain spaces and activities. It is both these atmospheres that influence us in the way we live, the way we communicate, and finally the way we think. How ambiguous are our desires, dreams and projections? Is it only the sterile places with clearly defined use that we can enjoy today? Is it the designer shops, the fancy cafes, or the commercial promenades, that provide our satisfaction? What about the social public spaces in the back of our heads? Do we still consider the possibility of diverse encounters with the non-consumer, the other? What about the young, the restless, the old, the poor, and the ones having been excluded from contemporary public space and therefore removed from society?' K. Cupers and M. Miessen, *Spaces of Uncertainty*, Wuppertal: Verlag Müller, 2002, p.151.

59
Cupers and Miessen, *Spaces of Uncertainity*, pp.151-2.

60
'The temporary is something which relates to life.' Excerpt from a discussion on urban interstices, ECObox June 2003.

61
Among attempts to reopen the debate on strategies and tools of planning, we should mention 'Urban Catalyst', a research project that investigates the potential of temporary uses as a motor of urban change. Coordinated by 'Studio Urban Catalyst' at the Technical University of Berlin, an inter-disciplinary network of 12 partners from five European metropolises – Helsinki, Berlin, Amsterdam, Vienna and Naples – has developed models of action and strategic planning tools by integrating the potential of temporary uses into long-term urban development. They have formed a unique archive which is now available to architects, planners, municipalities, developers, property owners and temporary users. (*www.urbancatalyst.de*). The Italian group Stalker speaks also about 'urban catalysis' in the context of their work with the Kurdish community in Campo Boario in Rome. In their case, 'catalysis' is defined as the transformation issued by differentiated forces working together; professional, social, economic and also geopolitical differences are considered. See Stalker's chapter in this book.

62
'A dynamic which is sustainable by temporary presence.' Excerpt from a discussion on urban interstices, ECObox, June 2003.

63
The term 'definitively temporary zones' has been borrowed from sociologist Federico Rahola. F. Rahola, *Zone definitivamente temporare: I luoghi dell'umanità in ecce homo*, Verona: Ombre Corte, 2002.

64
The Taz is a 'guerrilla operation which liberates an area... and then dissolves itself to re-form elsewhere'. Hakim Bey, T.A.Z: *The temporary autonomous zone, ontological anarchy, poetical terrorism*, Brooklyn, NY: Autonomedia, 1991, p.101.

acter of the metropolis lies in this multiplicity beyond physical borders. The urban public sphere can therefore be based on the model of confrontation and instability, as it is characterised by encounters and confrontations between people.[59]

The status of these spaces inspired the ECObox strategy, whose main aim was to leave space for 'others', others than the usual actors of the urban planning process, visible and less visible users, through a process that would enable them to get involved in the decision-making and take control over spaces in the area where they live. It is a political process. The problem is how to avoid freezing functions in these spaces while conserving their flexibility, their programmatic uncertainty, their fragility and indefiniteness. How can we maintain 'otherness' as a rule within both planning and use?

Urban catalysis

'Le temporaire est quelque chose qui relie à la vie'. [60]

Being based upon temporary use of temporary spaces, the ECObox project is itself 'temporary'. An economy of temporary interstices creates new project paradigms: temporary agencies, nomadic devices, urban catalysts.[61] The ECObox strategy tries to manage the different temporalities, politics of use, ownership status and proposes temporary inhabitations that create new usages and new urban functions in the area. The temporary condition supposes mobility and multiplicity. The mobile furniture modules – that act as urban catalysts in the area – generate temporary agencies and form progressive networks of actors. We can speak about a sustainability of processes rather than objects or places... As the aims are continually evolving according to the new spatial opportunities, participation becomes itself a process-in-progress. Usually, the participative process is solidified as soon as the goals are met: when a contested space is occupied, a project is built, etc. The role of these temporary agencies is to keep the use of space and the process of decision open...

'Une dynamique qui est durable par des présences temporaires'. [62]

The ECObox strategy is an experiment that could be extended into broader planning strategies and politics of use that preserve permanent areas for temporary use in the city. 'Definitively Temporary Zones' [63] – by analogy with Hakim Bey's TAZs [64] – could be imagined

as self-run spaces in which there are no functions but only manage-
ments, agencies, catalysts. The continual participation of users will
be the key element for the existence of such spaces.

Nomadic planning and rhizomatic participation

These moving spatial configurations within a multiplicity of sites
and temporalities, of funding sources, and social actors challenge
the norms of planning. They create lines of flight. Because, as
Deleuze puts it, 'to think multiplicity means to draw escape routes
or "lines of flight" away from closed and fixed structures or codes
that restrict and constrain the movement and connectivity of
thought and action'.[65]

65
G. Deleuze and F. Guattari, *A Thousand
Plateaus: Capitalism and schizophrenia*,
Minneapolis, MN: University of Minnesota
Press, 1987, p.8.

The aim of nomadic, rhizomatic thought is to promote micropolitics, to foster the decoding of codes, the deterritorialisation of
desire, language, thought, and practices, in favour of a 'molecular'
or micropolitical transformation of experience. Micropolitics are
not only local politics but could be rhizomatically extended at a bigger scale to confront with challenges raised by the global order. The
forms taken by the alter-globalisation movements (World and
Continental Social Forums, WTO and G8 parallel summits) based on
global scale assemblages of local groups and civil society organisations from all over the world, are a good example in this sense.[66]

66
See Teresa Hoskyn's chapter in this book.

Participating in the imaginary production

67
'How, when starting with almost nothing,
can populations mobilise themselves into
co-fabrication processes?' Excerpt from
discussion on urban interstices, ECObox,
June 2003.

*'Comment à partir de presque rien, des populations peuvent se mobiliser dans la
co-fabrication?'*[67]

In order to sustain a process without making it repetitive, in order
to avoid homogeneity and recurrence of the same, one needs to reinvent it continually. For a truly creative participation, one needs to
go beyond the pragmatism, and the almost compulsory reflex of
using participation mechanically, of standard regeneration programmes in deprived areas of Western European cities. Instead,
participation is needed everywhere where there is a need for real
public space... Rather than just solving environmental, economical
and social aspects of planning, a sustainable approach should also
sustain a creative way of living. If, according to Appadurai, imagination is 'a collective tool for the transformation of the real, for the
creation of multiple horizons of possibility',[68] then it should be a
tool in planning and design processes as well. Planning is not only
for transforming places but also for transforming the imagination
of those who live in these places. Participation could play the role of
a stimulator of diffused creativity and imaginary production.

68
Arjun Appadurai, 'The right to participate
in the work of the imagination', in
Transurbanism, Rotterdam: V2_Publishing/
NAI Publishers, 2002, p.34.

'The dissemination of self-organised knowledge can create a social framework containing infinite autonomous and self-reliant worlds.'[69]

Because ultimately, the imaginary is the most accessible category of a participation process, anybody of any age and from any place in the world could contribute to it. The aim of a nomadic, rhizomatic participation is to sustain this diffused creativity across boundaries and limitations, 'across thresholds of established norms and conventions, towards unexpected manifestations' within both sociopolitical phenomena and individual destinies, towards autonomous and self-reliant worlds forming multiple and diversified networks.

'Seizing the power of the imaginary, reinvent a taste for freedom...' [70]

[69]
Franco Berari Bifo, 'What is the meaning of autonomy today?', *www.republicart.net*

[70]
B. Holmes, activist theorist, collaborator of *aaa*.

Top row, left to right: 03.01 – *Gardens of words*, consultation Place Torcy, La Chapelle 2001; 03.02 – Children from rue Pajol, and students from the University of Sheffield on the construction site of the Ecobox garden, 2002; 03.03 – Hammocks installed by the group Stalker in the Ecobox garden as part of their project Via Egnatia, 2003.

Second row, left to right: 03.04 – 'A wall is the support for a window', mural poster realised by children, Ecobox, 2003; 03.05 – Mopping up with the residents of La Chapelle, Ecobox, 2003; 03.06 – One of the debates within the community urban observatory hosted by Ecobox, 2003. Third, fourth & bottom row: 03.07– 03.17 – Pipe holes in the enclosure wall, Ecobox, 2003.

Top: 03.18 – The mobile kitchen in the Ecobox garden, 2004. Bottom: 03.19 – Questions translated into the different languages spoken in La Chapelle. These questions are issued in the debates organised at Ecobox and displayed on the enclosure wall of the garden, 2003 (installation by Marie-Charlotte Moreau).

Mass housing cannot be sustained

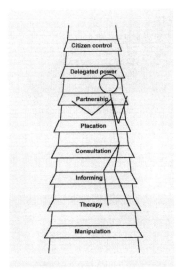

04.01 – Arnstein's 'Ladder of Participation'

1
S. Arnstein, 'The ladder of citizen participation', *Journal of the Institute of American
Planners*, 34, no.4, 1969. The ladder is,
from the bottom: manipulation – therapy –
informing – consultation – placation –
partnership – delegated power – citizen
control.

My experience in the housing field is particular, and lies near the top of the 'Ladder of Participation' devised in 1969 by Sherry Arnstein, a planner in the United States.[1] I write mainly from experience as an architect working in the 1970s and 1980s with housing cooperatives and with groups of people designing and building their own homes with the help of an architect. It has been a small-scale operation, but it goes beyond the lower rungs of manipulation, informing and consultation that generally pass for participation in housing. The self-builders were partners with the local authority and enjoyed a degree of delegated power, but they did not exert full control over the process represented by the top of the ladder.

The current interest in the idea that we should build sustainably brings the role of residents in the housing process back into focus. I say 'back into focus' because participation was widely seen as an important issue in the 1970s but has been displaced since by preoccupations with reducing costs, improving efficiency and moving into prefabrication. In my view, involving people in the housing process is a necessary precondition for a sustainable housing process, and resident participation belongs with energy conservation and low environmental impact construction to make housing developments sustainable in the long term. This is in contrast with the overwhelming preponderance of mass housing in Britain that leaves the occupant in a passive role. Mass housing has been the norm since the Victorian industrial city, where dwellings provided by philanthropists mitigated the worst slums. Local authorities became involved at the end of the nineteenth century followed by speculative developers between the wars, and more recently housing associations. All built without knowledge of the occupant, but having a stake in one's housing has special resonance. We all have an intimate relationship with the place we call home, for as Christopher Alexander wrote in *The Timeless Way of Building* in 1979:

2
C. Alexander and Center for Environmental
Structure, *The Timeless Way of Building*, New
York: Oxford University Press, 1979.

Whoever you are, you may have the dream of one day building the most beautiful house for your family, a garden, a fountain, a pond, a big room with soft light, flowers outside and the smell of new grass.[2]

What do we mean by sustainable development?

According to Brundtland, sustainable development means 'To ensure that the needs of the present are met without compromising the ability of future generations to meet their needs.'[3] I would put it more strongly: 'To pass on to future generations a stock of capital assets that will allow the quality of life to be maintained.' These capital assets are of three kinds:

3
Our Common Future, World Commission on Environment and Development, Oxford: Oxford University Press, 1987. Also known as the *Brundtland Report* after the chair of the commission, the then Norwegian Prime Minister, Gro Harlem Brundtland.

- *Natural capital*. This implies the conservation of natural resources such as fossil fuels, materials and water.
- *Man-made capital*. This includes buildings and implies the need to make our stock of them adaptable to future needs and expectations.
- *Social capital*. This refers to social institutions, implying social inclusion and the need for people to participate.

The role of people in establishing sustainable systems is crucial. For example, I spend much time on technical measures aimed at reducing the use of fossil fuels and consequent emissions of greenhouse gases arising from heating and lighting of houses, but design for energy conservation is of little value if people open windows when they are too warm. Again, fitting a low flush WC and other measures can reduce water consumption by up to 30 per cent, but all this is negated if a tap is left dripping. People need to be aware of the issues and understand how their house operates to keep it working properly. So one might say that achieving a sustainable system is 20 per cent to do with technology and 80 per cent to do with people. In my experience, residents are interested both in saving the planet and reducing environmental impacts. Often they are ahead of the professionals, housing managers, designers and contractors, who are more concerned with perceived costs and risks. Involving residents in the housing process can act as a powerful stimulus to addressing the issue of sustainability, even if only to reduce fuel and water bills. The need for people to be part of the process was stressed at the Rio Summit of 1992. It is also at the core of the Local Agenda 21 process instigated at Rio.

Dweller control

A radical perspective on the theme of participation in housing is that of 'Dweller Control' developed by John Turner in the 1970s. Turner's First Law, taken from the book *Freedom to Build*, states that:

> When dwellers control the major decisions and are free to make their own contribution to the design, construction or management of their

housing, both the process and the environment produced stimulate individual and social well-being. When people have no control over, nor responsibility for key decisions in the housing process, on the other hand, dwelling environments may instead become a barrier to personal fulfilment and a burden on the economy.[4]

4
R. Fichter, J. Turner and P. Grenell, 'The meaning of autonomy', in J.F.C. Turner and R. Fichter, *Freedom to Build: Dweller control of the housing process*, New York: Macmillan, 1972, p.241.

Residents should not only be participants, but should 'control the major decisions' which risk their housing becoming 'a burden on the economy': not sustainable, in other words. Colin Ward, environmental educationalist and author of books on self-help environments, suggested in the Preface to Turner's *Housing by People* a second Turner law:

> The important thing about housing is not what it IS, but what it DOES in people's lives, in other words that dweller satisfaction is not necessarily related to the imposition of standards.[5]

5
J.F.C. Turner, *Housing by People: Towards autonomy in building environments*, London, New York: Marion Boyars, 1991, pp.5-6.

Ward even added a third Turner's law:

> Deficiencies and imperfections in YOUR housing are infinitely more tolerable if they are your responsibility than if they are SOMEBODY ELSE'S.[6]

6
Ibid., p. 6.

Building is almost always a compromise between dream and reality; between brief and budget. A participatory process can lead to far higher levels of satisfaction with the outcome, and satisfied residents are necessary for a sustainable housing system. Colin Ward even argued that the opportunity to participate is a necessary part of a proper democratic way of life when in the 1985 book *When We Build Again* he observed:

> Housing policy assumes that people are helpless and inert consumers and ignores their ability and their yearnings to shape their own environment. We are paying today for confusing paternalistic authoritarianism with social responsibility... let's give people a chance and have housing that works![7]

7
C. Ward, *When We Build Again: Let's have housing that works!*, London: Pluto Press, 1985, p.10.

The current role of participation is not clear
If John Turner in the 1970s saw participation as an economic necessity and Colin Ward added in the 1980s that it is a political one, in the 1990s participation became an element in government policy on social inclusion. It now features in a heady array of political initiatives targeted at neighbourhood renewal, regeneration, employment, childcare and health. Although community involvement is

seen as essential to improving the quality of local life, however, it remains unclear quite what the intention is and how it should be achieved. In 2003 the government also published a plan for housing entitled *Sustainable Communities: Building for the Future* which aims to:

> Transform our communities by reversing the legacy of decades of neglect and underinvestment ... and tackle the challenges of ... serious housing shortages in London and the South East and the impact of housing abandonment in places in the North and Midlands.[8]

8
Office of the Deputy Prime Minister, *Sustainable Communities: Building for the future*, London: Office of the Deputy Prime Minister, 2003, p.3.

Despite the 'sustainable communities' of its title, the report includes only one brief paragraph in its sixty-eight pages referring to participation:

> Effective engagement and participation by local people, groups and businesses, especially in the planning, design and long-term stewardship of their community, and an active voluntary and community sector.[9]

9
Ibid., p.5.

How can participation be achieved?

Interest in participation in the late 1960s and early 1970s led to the development of practical methods for involving residents in decision-making, planning and design. These took the form of meetings, exhibitions, newsletters and workshop sessions. In the early 1980s the Community Architecture movement gained a certain legitimacy through the support of the Prince of Wales and the election of Rod Hackney to the Presidency of the Royal Institute of British Architects.[10] Hackney mobilised a street of residents in Macclesfield to resist the demolition of their homes, which they then refurbished. Other architects had paved the way: as early as the mid-1970s, Ralph Erskine set up a site office in the redevelopment area of Byker in Newcastle. John Thompson had involved council tenants of Lea View, Hackney, in the rehabilitation of their block of flats. Bill Halsall had developed Weller Street and other community-based new build cooperatives in Liverpool, and community centres and play buildings designed and sometimes built by residents were created on many estates. Participation techniques must offer a process that can reconcile opposing points of view to arrive at an acceptable consensus, and achieving this with a large group of people is a complex problem, for if two people disagree, ten people can have a hundred disagreements. A common approach is to concentrate people's minds on matters of fact rather than opinion and get them to agree on those before moving on to more controversial issues. This is the thinking behind the 'Planning for Real' idea devised by Tony Gibson

10
N. Wates and C. Knevitt, *Community Architecture: How people are creating their own environment*, London: Penguin, 1987.

11
The Neighbourhood Initiatives Foundation,
The Poplars, Lightmoor, Telford TF4 3QN.

at the Neighbourhood Initiatives Foundation.[11] Residents place suggestion cards on a large three-dimensional model of a neighbourhood indicating what they would like to happen. These suggestions are then prioritised by participants working in small groups who sort the cards into groups of 'now', 'soon', 'later'. Everyone converges on the model, allowing a practical method of non-threatening communication.

The pattern language

Once introduced into the planning process, people need to become aware of the issues of urban design, site layout, house planning and building construction. I have found the pattern language developed by Christopher Alexander in 1977 a useful concept for introducing people to ideas about what makes good cities, neighbourhoods and dwellings.

> The people can shape buildings for themselves, and have done it for centuries, by using languages which I call pattern languages. A pattern language gives each person who uses it the power to create an infinite variety of new and unique buildings, just as his ordinary language gives him the power to create an infinite variety of sentences.[12]

12
C. Alexander and Center for Environmental Structure, p.167 (see Note 2).

Alexander identifies and describes the attributes of archetypal arrangements of places that work well.

> The world does have a structure, just because these patterns of events which repeat themselves are always anchored in the space. Consider, for example, the pattern of events which we might call 'watching the world go by'. We sit, perhaps slightly raised ... I cannot separate it from the porch where it occurs. The action and the space are indivisible. The action is supported by this kind of space. The space supports this kind of action.[13]

13
Ibid., p.70.

People know what they like, but don't, in the ordinary run of things, think much about why. Alexander makes explicit in his 273 patterns a vocabulary of widely shared features found in cities, neighbourhoods and buildings. A typical example of such a pattern is 'Light on two sides of every room.' This suggests that:

> When they have a choice, people will always gravitate to those rooms which have light on two sides, and leave the rooms which are lit from only one side unused and empty. This pattern, perhaps more than any other single pattern, determines the success or failure of

14
C. Alexander, S. Ishikawa, and
M. Silverstein, *A Pattern Language: Towns,
buildings, construction*, New York: Oxford
University Press, 1977, p.747.

a room. The arrangement of daylight in a room and the presence of windows on two sides, is fundamental.[14]

This pattern language offers a vocabulary of design features which can make people's experience of the towns, neighbourhoods and buildings where they live explicit and easy to understand, thus enabling them to participate in the development of ideas about their environment.

The Segal method

We have a way of manipulating ideas, we now need a way of giving them physical shape; a way of building that offers choices, can accommodate individual needs and wishes, and which can also be adapted as those needs and expectations change in the future.

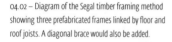

04.02 – Diagram of the Segal timber framing method showing three prefabricated frames linked by floor and roof joists. A diagonal brace would also be added.

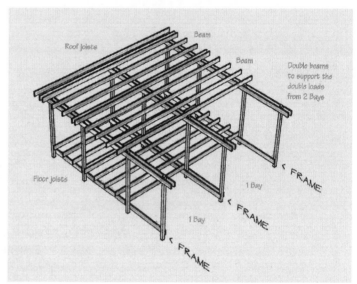

Walter Segal devised a way of building in timber in the mid-1960s by combining readily available components and panels in their standard sizes within a post and beam timber frame (Fig.04.02). The frame is planned on a dimensional grid that is easy for people to understand and use. The construction uses dry jointing techniques such as bolts and screws and there is no wet brick-, concrete- or plaster-work which means that alterations can be carried out easily. Walls and partitions are not load-bearing, and windows and doors can be positioned at will on any floor of the building. This has proved very useful for people not used to reading technical drawings. They can stand in the building under construction and see where the view is, and where the sun comes from, determining the position of windows as they go along. This is in contrast to a con-

ventional building that has to be determined in full detail before you start. In the words of Ken Atkins, chair of the first Lewisham Self Build Group:

> We must be the first council tenants who have been involved with an architect in the design of our own homes. The architect used graph paper to help us represent the modular concept of 2 feet 2 inches, and asked us to draw a house within cash limits. This was about 100 square metres in area. We did this as a group and then went to Walter Segal's house. He took all the ideas and drew up 50 or 60 different house plans and then we went back as individual families to choose and adapt our design ... Every wall is non-load-bearing so it's adaptable and changeable. At any time during the process of building or after I've lived in it, if I feel I want to change it, I can take out any wall and change it.[15]

15
Ken Atkins in *The Bulletin of Environmental Education*, Town & Country Planning Association, London, October 1983.

Atkins reveals a relationship with his home very different to the usual one, and he is already confident in his ability to interact with it. Part of this confidence comes from the fact that he built his house with his own hands and thereby gained a particularly intimate knowledge of how it is constructed. A close relationship was also built up between the members of the self-build group, sowing the seeds for a sustainable community of residents. Walter Segal remarked:

> Help was provided mutually and voluntarily – there were no particular constraints on that, which did mean that the good will of people

could find its way through. The less you tried to control them the more you freed the elements of good will – this was astonishingly clear. Children were of course expected and allowed to play on the site. And the older ones also helped if they wished to help. That way one avoided all forms of friction. Each family were to build at their own speed and within their own capacity. We had quite a number of young people but some that were sixty and over also managed to build their own houses... They were told that I would not interfere with the internal arrangement. I let them make their own decisions, therefore we had no difficulties.[16]

16
W. Segal, 'View from a lifetime',
transcription of lecture in *Transactions of
the RIBA*, vol.1, no.1, 1982, pp.7-14.

04.04 (left) – Walter's Way, Lewisham, interior.
04.05 (right) – Walter's Way, Lewisham, exterior.

The building technology – modular frame and non-load-bearing infill fixed with dry jointing techniques – permits and encourages residents to take an active part in planning and construction. This process has also led to an active collaboration between neighbours who have created a community founded in shared experience. These groups of around a dozen households are surprisingly robust and have embraced new people who moved in and joined the community. One group in Lewisham in South London stages an annual street party to which all their friends with their children are invited. This level of social inclusion is in stark contrast to the alienation experienced by most inhabitants of our inner cities.

Supports

Walter Segal's frame and infill have some things in common with the idea of Support Structures proposed by N. J. Habraken in *Supports: An Alternative to Mass Housing* (published in Dutch in 1961 and translated into English ten years later). Habraken defines a support structure as 'a construction which allows the provision of dwellings which can be built, altered and taken down, independently of the others'. And again, 'A support structure... is built in the knowledge that we cannot predict what is going to happen to it. The more variety housing can assume within the support structure, the better.' [17]

Habraken sees this as a necessary alternative to the mass housing which is so prevalent in the Netherlands and Britain.

> The aspects of (mass housing) which have aroused the resistance of the users are: the denial of involvement and initiative to the inhabitant... It will mean that the mode of operation which has been followed until now has prevented us from providing the kind and quantity of housing we need. The conclusion must be that the return of consultation and involvement on the part of the users, in the most literal sense, must be accepted. [18]

The idea of clearly separating different elements of a building with different timescales of change has been elaborated by Stuart Brand, an American who wrote the book *How Buildings Learn: What Happens After They Are Built* in 1994. [19] He identifies six essential components, each beginning with an S:

1 *The Site*, which is always there.
2 *The Structure or support*. This is difficult and expensive to change. Its life tends to be from 30 to 300 years.
3 *The Skin*: the exterior, which changes every 20 years or so due to fashion, technology or repair.
4 *The Services*, which wear out or become obsolescent after 10 to 15 years. Many buildings are demolished early because their outdated systems are too deeply embedded in the structure to be changed economically.
5 *The Space plan*, involving partitions which may be rearranged in a house every 30 years or so.
6 *The Stuff*: the interior fit-out and furniture which is under the control of the resident.

This approach of dividing the shell and the fit-out is now common in commercial office building. It has been elaborated by Frank Duffy of the firm DEGW who said: 'Our basic argument is that there isn't

17
N. J. Habraken, *Supports: An alternative to mass housing*, London: Architectural Press, 1972, pp.59-61.

18
Ibid., p.61.

19
S. Brand, *How Buildings Learn: What happens after they're built*, New York: Viking, 1994, p.13.

20
F. Duffy, 'Measuring building performance',
in *Facilities*, Bradford: Emerald Publishers,
1990.

such a thing as a building. A building properly conceived is several layers of longevity of built components.'[20] A new interest has arisen in applying this thinking to housing with the move towards 'open building'. This approach separates out each of the sub-systems in a building, permitting a high degree of choice and flexibility. Kendall and Teicher, in *Residential Open Building*, write of 'a varied, fine-grained and sustainable environment and increased individual choice and responsibility within it'.[21] This approach parallels that

21
S. Kendall and J. Teicher, *Residential Open
Buildings*, London: E & FN Spon, 2000.

established in the Netherlands following the work of Habraken, but it has been taken furthest in Japan. Here a housing market has been established that offers customers a choice of features, just as cars come in a range of colours but also with different engines, standard of finish and performance. Houses are adaptable, and purchasers can choose layout, performance and finish. This makes a sorry contrast with the situation in Britain where Michael Ball in *Housing and Construction: A Troubled Relationship?* (1996) blamed mass house builders for offering products which were over-standardised and

22
M. Ball, *Housing and Construction: A troubled
relationship?* Bristol: Policy Press, 1996.

unadaptable.[22]

Participation should be at the heart of housing policy

In my view there is a need to reintegrate ideas of participation and adaptability from the recent past into the current rhetoric of modernisation and efficiency. The Egan Report, *Rethinking Construction* seeks to reduce the cost and improve the quality of construction in Britain through prefabrication amongst other things.[23] Still un-

23
Department of Trade and Industry,
*Rethinking Construction: the Report of the
Construction Task Force*, Office of the Deputy
Prime Minister: London, 1998. Also known
as the *Egan Report* after the chair of the task
force, Sir John Egan.

mentioned, however, are sustainability, adaptability or participation. The danger is that mass-produced solutions – volumetric housing for example – may be imposed without the views of future residents being articulated, and without the residents being given a role in deciding how the housing is used and adapted in the future. When this happened in the 1960s, the housing was so inappropriate in design and standard that much of it had to be demolished long before the end of its design life and before it had been paid for.

The role of residents is still often ignored when sustainable housing developments are planned. This is, I think, the consequence of a cultural climate in Britain that does not recognise ordinary people as trustworthy and responsible. It also reflects the fact that Britain relies overwhelmingly on mass housing provision, in contrast with other economies, which have a substantial self-help housing sector. The term self-help here refers to residents who have control of the process but who will not, for the most part, actually build their house themselves. This sector only takes 8 per cent of the market in Britain, though it is rising as people become more aware of higher standards of performance and choice in other countries.

But the self-help sector occupies more than 50 per cent of the market in Germany and around 30 per cent in the United States.

One could envisage a modern vernacular created by people who shared a way of thinking about building and an accessible method of construction. This might repeat many attributes of traditional vernacular building: human scale, diversity within an overall order; natural, sustainable materials. It could result in charming, low-energy dwellings with a long-term, sustainable future. But most important is what housing does for people, and in my experience those involved in making their houses have grown enormously in self-confidence through working with the authorities, with professionals and with one another. This would fit in well with political rhetoric about social inclusion and the regeneration of urban areas, yet until now effective participation has remained on the margins rather than forming the heart of sustainable housing policy in Britain.

Chapter 05

Tim Richardson and Stephen Connelly [1]

Reinventing public participation: planning in the age of consensus

1

This chapter draws on the authors' individual and collaborative research on planning and policy making in many different contexts: Richardson (2000), Connelly (2002), Richardson and Connelly (2002), Connelly and Richardson (2004).

Introduction

For some, the potential renaissance of planning, in the face of public indifference and distrust and in a climate where the planning system is often characterised as a barrier to development, is to be found in the current turn towards participation. Everywhere planners are being exhorted to engage actively with communities and stakeholders in the planning of urban and rural areas, at scales ranging from regions to cities, neighbourhoods and villages. Participation is now at the heart of plan-making and strategy development, as well as being an inseparable element of individual planning decisions. Planning's core business of 'mediating space and making place' is being redefined as an inclusive endeavour (RTPI 2003). But if planning with participation is to restore trust in public decision-making, hard questions need to be addressed about the nature of the new practices of participation. Are we really seeing the emergence of a new paradigm of participatory planning, where resolving differences of interest over the uses of space, and seeking consensus in the making of places become intrinsically participative activities? Or is public participation just something that planners have to do, part of an increasingly audited system where planners need to show how they have established community support for their plans? Worse, is participation simply being used to create legitimacy for decisions that have already been made? To begin to respond to these types of questions, and to begin to explore whether participatory planning in its positive sense is a feasible project, it becomes critical to focus on what is actually happening on the ground in the name of 'public participation'. Asking uncomfortable, practice-oriented questions like this is crucial if the participative turn is not to hide poor decision-making, continuing public distrust, and social and environmental injustice under a mantle of political worthiness.

Public participation in planning is by no means a new thing. Town and country planning in Britain, for example, is one of the few areas where policy and practical decisions affecting people's quality of life have long been subject to formal public involvement in varying forms. Statutory public involvement in development planning was introduced in the 1968 Town and Country Planning Act, following a crisis of confidence in land use and transportation planning, with fierce battles over slum clearance, housing redevelopment and motorway proposals. In 1969 the Skeffington Committee (MHLG 1969) set a radical agenda for participation, defining public participation as sharing in the formulation of policies and proposals. However, though planning can be seen as a source of ideas and inspiration in the practice of public consultation and participation (which should be seen as quite different things), there remain heated areas of debate. How should participation be conceptualised? What are the benefits of participatory forms of planning against 'scientific' analytically driven, or managerial forms of planning? Can participatory approaches build consensus between competing or incompatible interests? And what claims can be made about the potential of participatory approaches to deliver better outcomes? Such questions lead into difficult and contested theoretical terrain. In this chapter, our aim is to make a short foray into this terrain, to highlight and discuss some of the critical questions which, we feel, are of broader relevance across the built environment professions.

Our focus is a single issue at the centre of much of the debate: the possibility of consensus. The twin beliefs that conflicts between interests are resolvable and that mutual agreement on outcomes may be reached, and moreover that such consensus is a desirable normative principle, lie at the heart of the new participative approach to planning. This marks a distinctive difference from the periodic upsurges of interest in participation since the 1960s (Taylor 2003), largely born out of a tradition which saw conflict as essential for social change (Kenny 2002), where the state's engagement was a response to the public's reaction against top-down decision-making, and consequent demands for more direct involvement. Such demands, and the challenge they posed to the status quo, were largely channelled into safe institutional processes and their radical edge blunted. The more far-reaching proposals in the Skeffington Report were never implemented, and although sporadic experiments with more participative structures and decentralisation of planning continued, the fundamental power balance between state and public was left unchanged (Boaden *et al.* 1980; Leach *et al.* 1994).

The current participative turn is different. It positively embraces and promotes public involvement, and hinges on the central idea of consensus. The origins of this change are complex and unclear, but include: a continued widespread erosion of trust in the traditions of representative democratic government; increasing differentiation of identities and of demands (Healey 1990) which are ill-served by notions of a homogenous 'public interest' or the crudeness of the electoral system; widely held beliefs that consensual decision-making processes are integral to advancing sustainable development (UNCED 1992; Leach *et al.* 2000) and that bringing citizens more actively into governance will both recreate a sense of community, and rebuild the relationship between people and state (e.g. Commission of the European Communities 1992).

This turn in policy and practice is supported by a number of modern intellectuals. In the UK Anthony Giddens is the foremost of these, his 'Third Way' (Giddens 1998) acknowledged as having direct influence on the philosophy and practice of the New Labour Party and government, alongside the communitarian philosophy of Etzioni (1995; 1996) and Putnam (Putnam *et al.* 1993, Putnam 2000). Within this body of thinking, social progress is founded on the possibility of consensus and the non-existence of fundamental, structural differences of interest – conflict is seen as unnecessary and undesirable (Torfing 1999). More pragmatically, mobilising the idea of consensus becomes a powerful rhetorical strategy for a state promoting widespread public participation in the name of social cohesion and non-conflictive progress. Social change carries with it risks of creating dissensus and instability (Renn 1998) – risks which disappear with the construction of consensus as the norm, from which dissensus is a correctable deviation.

In practice, the new vision for planning recognises the difficulty of achieving consensus: 'effective planning cannot always be achieved through consensus. Where hard choices are required, clear and equitable decision-making frameworks are essential' (RTPI 2003). But this is problematic – if consensus is not always possible after all, then what are the options? This is a difficult area for proponents of participatory planning. If participatory planning is not consensual, then does it lead us back to the traditional understanding of public involvement as merely consultation to better inform the decision-makers (exactly the position from which escape is sought) or does it lead to a managed process of neutering conflict, masked by a rhetoric of inclusivity and consensus (Henderson and Salmon 1999), which fails to meet the new ideal?

Debates about participation in planning have usually been framed as conflicts between two paradigms: the polar positions of planning as either expert-led or essentially inclusive and participatory. However, to us this notion of paradigmatic approaches to planning seems problematic. By briefly considering why they are unhelpful as a guide to either understanding planning or practising planning ethically, we move towards an alternative theoretical position, which emphasises the need to understand *pragmatic consensus* – how consensus is built and, importantly, *used*, in political and policy-making processes. We argue that consensus inevitably falls short of the ideal, but we do not see this critical view as cynical in nature, or as calling for a return to top-down decision-making.

Instead, our approach leads to a perspective on public participation in planning as inescapably bound up with the power struggles and conflicts that are the stuff of all planning activity:

> When it comes to portraying planners and planning, the quest of planning theorists could be called the escape from power. But if there is one thing we should have learned today from students of power, it is that there is no escape from it. (Flyvbjerg and Richardson 2002)

If planning operates inescapably in the face of power (Forester 1989), it becomes essential to address challenging ethical and practical implications. If we seek to create emancipatory ways of planning, or if we want to achieve equitable outcomes, then participatory practices become important sites of struggle over questions of empowerment, inclusion and justice. However, there has been a tendency among proponents of communicative approaches to planning to see power as negative and oppressive (see, for example, Healey 1997), and therefore to seek to remove the effects of power from participatory arenas. If we cannot remove power, the alternative is to rethink participation in ways that embrace power as inescapable, essential and productive, rather than as negative and oppressive. This does not lead us to a rejection of public participation, but rather to the suggestion that paying attention to the *quality* of public participation is crucial, rather than uncritically supporting the expansion of this field of activity. We argue that quality means more than developing an exciting toolkit of participation techniques, and engaging ever-increasing numbers of people. It requires reflection over hard issues about power and exclusion, which lead the planner into uncertain and perhaps inhospitable territory. But if such questions are ignored, we see a clear danger that participation will draw heavily on scarce professional time and financial resources, yet result in weak decisions and an increasingly disillusioned public.

If planning is to be inclusive and just, we will argue, it needs to engage critically with participation as a means of working with differences of interest. Crucially, however, this needs to be grounded in a clear understanding that participation does not necessarily lead to consensus. Planners need to be ready to pursue overall aims of social and spatial justice in a milieu of conflict, rather than expect to find consensus every time they launch a participatory process. They need to learn how to work in the face of power, not to step away from it. Here, rather than provide yet more models of good practice, we introduce some hard questions, for critical use by practitioners who are in the daily business of making hard pragmatic judgements about inclusion and for researchers who may be trying to understand how action can be pursued in such challenging contexts. The questions are designed to bring ethical choices to the fore, and to recast participatory work in a more critical light.

It is clear that these arguments are applicable beyond the confines of 'planning' in a narrow sense. The planning system has had to engage with the public for many years, and in consequence planners and planning academics have been led to explore these issues both theoretically and practically. However, similar issues arise in related fields: wherever architects and other built environment professionals come to engage more with the public they will encounter parallel normative debates and face the same ethical and 'political' challenges.

Planning theory: a short history of contingent rationality

Before developing this discussion of pragmatic consensus further, we need to set out more fully the emergence of consensus as a critical idea in planning theory, and to explain why the shortcomings of this consensual approach to planning have led some theorists to seek alternatives which engage more directly with questions of power and conflict. To do this, we need to briefly chart the progression of planning theory's engagement with the idea of *rationality*.

The development of theory in urban and regional planning, and in public policy more broadly, has been marked by a continuing debate over the relationship between rationality and power in policy-making. At the heart of this debate are two issues: how policy is made, and how policy should be made. Competing theories see planning as alternatively taking place: through instrumental rationality, where value-free, scientific processes use the latest technical instruments to analyse and construct solutions; through communicative rationality, where decisions are reached through deliberation and consensus building processes; or in a field of real-life rationality, where political struggles between different interests, competing knowledges and interests contest the 'truths' with which policy is legitimised. Each theoretical position is grounded in an alternative, and incompatible, framing of rationality.

In recent years, communicative theories of planning have gained in popularity, and have been strongly asserted as a reaction against instrumental approaches. At the heart of the communicative turn is an attempt to resolve the 'problem' of power, by creating planning processes grounded in principles of free speech and rational argument. But this movement has triggered a critical response: that these are normative approaches that cannot lead to universal solutions; that there is no escape from power, instead power must be embraced. Wherever this debate leads, it is clear that, as John Friedmann has argued, theorists' ambivalence about power is one of the biggest outstanding problems in theorising planning (Friedmann 1997).

Rational planning

Rationality has been a cornerstone of modern planning, described by Mannheim in 1940 as 'the rational mastery of the irrational' (Mannheim 1940, cited in Healey 1997: 9). Inherent in this approach is the separation of political process from the rational work of policy-making (Davidoff and Reiner 1962; Faludi 1973) and a strong claim to value-free objectivity, supported by a continual development and refinement of scientific and economic instruments for shaping and delivering policy. Thus in the 1960s, the systems approach to planning was typified by new techniques of technical analysis, aided by computer modelling and micro-economic evaluation (see e.g. Faludi 1973; Friedmann 1973, 1987), while more recent developments have seen a reassertion of microeconomics as the basis of policy formulation (Healey 1997) and the post-Rio development of new technical and scientific approaches to environmental planning (Wong 1998; Weston 2000).

Healey has described this as 'a modernist instrumental rationalism' within which 'the planning tradition itself has generally been "trapped"' (1997: 7). Since the 1960s, many critics have pointed to the problems of this approach, highlighting its lack of fit with empirical evidence of how policy-making processes actually work and for its perceived normative shortcomings. As well as ignoring the complexity of policy-making – the presence of actors with competing goals, the impact of institutional rules and values, the inseparability of political decision-making, policy-making and implementation in a continuous, complex, recursive process – it also fails to recognise the values inherent in planning, and so becomes oppressive by excluding non-instrumental human values and reasoning, and ignoring difference. One repeated response within planning theory has been to argue for ways to include more voices in the policy-making process.

The communicative turn

The communicative turn can be broadly seen as an emerging body of theory which is the most recent attempt to break free from

The new paradigm has been given a number of different labels: 'communicative action' (Innes 1995), 'communicative planning' (Forester 1989; Sager 1994), 'argumentative planning' (Fischer and Forester 1993), 'planning through debate' (Healey 1992a), 'collaborative planning' (Healey 1997), 'deliberative planning' (Forester 2000), and 'planning through consensus building' (Innes 1996).

instrumental rationalism.[2] It posits policy-making as argumentation: 'as politicians know only too well, but social scientists too often forget, public policy is made of language. Whether in written or oral form, argumentation is central in all stages of the policy process' (Majone 1989: 1). Power is acknowledged, but regarded as a negative, distorting influence whose effects can be removed by constructing an idealised debate, where all participants have equal status, and where the rationality of argumentation then prevails. The focus on this 'communicative rationality' is the turn's distinctive theoretical element. Informed by Jürgen Habermas' work, theorists of this persuasion (e.g. Fischer and Forester 1993; Innes 1995; Healey 1997) place at its core the notion of reason as intersubjective mutual understanding, historically situated through its development by particular people in particular times and places. Knowledge is negotiated in policy-making, and ways of thinking, valuing and acting are 'actively constructed by participants' (Healey 1997: 29). From this conceptualisation, Healey argues that 'planning and its contents is a way of acting we can choose, after debate' (1992: 157). The resulting collaborative planning process might be characterised as follows:

- Its setting within an ideal pluralist political system
- Its aim of redefining rationality in a new communicative way
- Its pro-modernist theoretical tendency
- The central role of the policy analyst/planner
- Achievement of consensus through unforced reasoning

The last of these points is central to the communicative paradigm:

> Consensus-building approaches are thus assumed as the most mature efforts in proactively addressing the duality of planning as an institutionalised practice and as a factor of institutionalisation through a combination of institutional design and institution-building. (Gualini 2001: 55)

In such approaches:

> Participants seek common ground and collaborate on solutions. These groups can result in both individual and group learning and can change attitudes and commitments. The groups can be most productive when they challenge accepted views and reformulate problems in ways that allow consensual outcomes or creative new directions for action. (Innes 1992: 441)

While there are clear differences between the communicative theorists – in particular over the extent to which their emphasis on consensus is moderated by an appreciation of the ineradicability of conflict – their work is distinctive in its shared foundation in Habermasian thought, and consequent rejection of instrumental rationality as the dominant form of planning. They share the common elements of deliberation, learning, transformation of interests, and consensus as a possible and, in principle, desirable outcome.

The usefulness of communicative theory is widely acknowledged, even by its critics. Its normative positing of a particular style of planning, embracing consensual, deliberative methods is seen as a valuable challenge to the dominance of instrumental rationality, and more analytically it has generated useful microstudies of how planners go about their work. However, the critiques (by, for example, the partnerships of Huxley and Yiftachel, Flyvbjerg and Richardson, Tewdwr-Jones and Allmendinger) are wide-ranging, and are not exhaustively addressed here. At the heart of many of the critiques, though, is the concern that accounts provided from communicative perspectives can provide only part of the story of how planning is actually done, yet they are not explicit about their partiality. The emerging paradigm of communicative rationality, with its focus on the micropolitics of communicative interactions in planning, loses the overview of the policy process in a broader social and political context. Crucially, it is blind to local power outside of communication – a key element of micro-politics – and therefore to the influence of power on policy development, the possibility of distortion of the policy process, and even more fundamentally therefore to the possibility of empowerment.

Furthermore, the analysis of communicative events, driven by the normative perspective of Habermasian theory, seeks to draw attention to 'distortions', which planners can learn from, and therefore presumably avoid in their future work. Yet this relies on a leap of faith which goes beyond the experience and convictions of many practising planners and on what, we argue, is a misconception of the nature of power.

This creates three problems for the communicative approach. First, it is based on the premise that power can be removed from deliberative processes. If, as Healey puts it, planning 'is to contribute to the enterprise of democratic social change' (Friedmann 1987; Forester 1989) then it must seek to challenge the way 'knowledge production and exchange are infused with ideological and political practices that protect the powerful and confuse the powerless' (Healey 1992a) and instead strive to achieve undistorted communication. From our perspective, drawing on Foucault's conceptualisation of power as omnipresent and ineradicable, this premise is simply false, and undermines the whole thrust of the approach's influence on practice. Second, Habermasian analyses of planning processes only tell us about distorted *communications*, and neglect the strategies which interplay through a variety of speech and non-communicative power acts to shape planning policies and decisions (Reuter 1998, 1999). Third, it is difficult for communicative theorists to deal coherently with the issue of empowerment. The aim of empowering disadvantaged interests requires an acknowledgement of power relations and the possibility of power being used in a 'positive' way, yet within this conceptual framework power is theorised as negative, coercive and oppressive.

Ultimately the communicative turn fails to ground itself in what Flyvbjerg has termed *Realrationalität* – 'how knowledge, rationality and power work in real life' – and so fails to capture the role of power in planning (Flyvbjerg 1996: 384). As a result, it is weak in its capacity to serve as a basis for effective action and change. In consequence this approach to theory building is highly problematic for planning.

Given that both instrumental and communicative approaches have theoretical problems, we turn now to an approach which focuses on practice. Sharing with Machiavelli the belief that a 'man who neglects what is actually done for what should be done learns the way to self-destruction' and his intention 'to say something that will be of practical use to the enquirer, [we] have thought it proper to represent things as they are in real truth, rather than as they are imagined' (Machiavelli 2003: 91), we present a deconstructive analysis, as an alternative to modelling what planning should be on the basis of often tendentious norms.

A turn towards the dark side?
This analysis draws on what has been described as the 'dark side' of planning theory, a body of theoretical and empirical work developed over the past few years by Yiftachel (1994), Flyvbjerg (1998) and Huxley (2000), among others, drawing on a long lineage of political theorists including Thucydides and Machiavelli, Nietzsche and Foucault. The work of Michel Foucault (1977, 1979), in particular, provides a useful theoretical foundation for a new understanding of rationality, which potentially unlocks an understanding of the policy process which may more closely fit the messy world of policy than approaches which try to reduce things to an objective level, or prescribe what we think ought to happen in an ideal world. Foucault's critical view turns attention away from both the preoccupation of instrumental rationality with the search for new objective

scientific or economic techniques, and normative communicative rationality, achieved through idealised debate and argument. Instead, he suggests that we live in a society of multiple rationalities which are shaped by discourses, constituted through power/knowledge relations, and made visible in local practices. It is central to his thought that discourse is a complex medium which extends beyond communication to other social practices, within which a complex dynamic between power and knowledge occurs. As a part of this society, policy-making is similarly shaped by discourses, through processes in which claims to knowledge are asserted which may be rational or irrational, reasonable or unreasonable. The relations between power and knowledge shape a contingent rationality as new policy discourses are constructed and institutionalised.

Consequently, power is all-pervasive – it is not a property of individuals but inheres in all relationships, communicative and other social acts. Instead of side-stepping or seeking to remove the traces of power from policy-making, the planning 'darksiders' accept power as unavoidable. However, this is emphatically not an acceptance of oppression: power is to be understood as potentially productive rather than necessarily oppressive, in sharp contrast to the conception espoused within the communicative turn.[3]

3
This is not a universally accepted interpretation of Foucault's work – see for example Giddens (1984).

Within our area of concern, then, this approach encourages an examination of policy as the manifestation of Flyvbjerg's *Realrationalität* (Flyvbjerg 1996), made on a field of power struggles between different interests, where knowledge and truth are contested, and the rationality of policy-making itself is exposed as a focus of conflict. This analysis embraces the idea that 'rationality is penetrated by power', and the dynamic between the two is critical in understanding 'what planning is and what the strategies and tactics are that may help change it for the better' (Flyvbjerg 1996: 393). It therefore 'becomes meaningless, or misleading – for politicians, administrators and researchers alike – to operate with a concept of rationality in which power is absent' (Flyvbjerg 1998: 164-5).

This clearly has radical implications for the understanding of processes which aim to build consensus between different stakeholders. On the one hand it implies that power cannot be removed from such processes, and so that the Habermasian, communicative ideal of unforced rational consensus is theoretically incoherent and practically impossible. On the other hand it does not see this as a problem. Whereas,

Habermas, among others, views conflict in society as dangerous, corrosive and potentially destructive of social order, and therefore in

need of being contained and resolved. In a Foucauldian interpretation, conversely, suppressing conflict is suppressing freedom, because the privilege to engage in conflict is part of freedom.
(Flyvbjerg 1998: 13)

Such analyses are thus heir to a tradition which sees conflict as positive and creative, and which moreover is sceptical about consensus and especially wary of the risk of manufactured consensus becoming a tool of oppression. However, they should not be seen as a new planning paradigm in the making. This approach to theory resists attempts to put forward a single particular view of rationality. Instead of seeking to provide a model of how planning should be done, it seeks to ask how planning is done, to ask difficult questions, to problematise the things planners take for granted. The aim is to encourage planners (and others) to work critically and reflexively within an environment of conflict and difference, but not to provide them with simple solutions.

Consensus in planning in Britain

Having explored these theoretical positions, we turn now to practice. From the debates above, it appears that we should be sceptical about public involvement presented either as consultation to provide a better information base to decision-makers working in a rational planning process, or about public involvement as a central element of a normatively consensual communicative planning process. In practice, both of these putative paradigms coexist and compete, constituting a period of uncertainty and perhaps instability, in which no single planning approach is dominant. It is clear, however, that participatory approaches are in the ascendant, with the necessary concomitant emphasis on consensus as a core value. Furthermore, this is the case not only in the planning system *per se*, but across virtually all fields of policy and practice, including architecture.

Relying on the principle that conflicts between interests are resolvable, and that mutual agreement on outcomes may be reached, citizens and other stakeholders have come together with the traditional institutions of government, engaging with them through a proliferation of innovative forms of public involvement and partnership structures. Within 'planning' in a broad sense, consensual approaches have been promoted in particular for developing strategic plans and managing local areas or sites where complex environmental and social issues are being dealt with, and where many divergent interests are likely to be affected by policy decisions. The possibility of establishing consensus is frequently attempted where more traditional approaches to decision-making have been obstructed by apparently insurmountable conflicts between different interests.

Such 'consensus building' is usually presented as the search for an ideal outcome, an agreement subscribed to by all the stake-holders and arrived at through an open, participative and non-coercive process – a fair procedure which delivers legitimacy, respect, authenticity (in the sense that everyone's views can be expressed, heard and understood), and transparency (O'Riordan and Ward 1997). However, in practice the results are often greater exposure of conflicts and differences of interest and outputs which are either bland vision statements unaccompanied by prescriptions for action (Scott 1999) or which lack legitimacy amongst those not directly involved (O'Riordan and Ward 1997).

We contend that this is not coincidental. Drawing on the theoretical arguments above, it seems clear that the ideal is not only unattainable but not even coherent as an idea. It is thus necessary to draw a clear distinction between *ideal consensus* and what happens in practice, and to examine in detail the inevitable processes of exclusion that result from the myriad conscious and unconscious decisions through which a public involvement process is steered towards what one might term *pragmatic consensus*.

Moreover, such outcomes are often cloaked under the rhetoric of ideal consensus. This is clearly problematic, since such (mis)representation in itself breaks the principle of transparency and so threatens the legitimacy of a process. The use of rhetoric to frame a new rationality of participation is important because it obscures the playing out of a key democratic issue: the extent to which different groups and interests are able to influence policy, or are excluded from its processes.

What is consensus building?

Consensus building is essentially a method of decision-making, and while approaches vary they share certain distinctive characteristics compared with non-consensual decision-making. Sidaway (1998) identifies three specific distinctions: that decisions are reached through mutual consent rather than voting, with each participant given the power of veto; that everyone with an interest and who is prepared to cooperate participates in the process; and that a deliberative process is constructed based on principles of fairness, openness and trust. While consensus-building processes can draw on many of the tools which have been developed for increasing public participation in decision-making (e.g. visioning techniques, environment fora, round tables, and citizens' juries (Williams 1995;

Young 1996)), it should be seen as an *approach* to public participation rather than just as a *method*. It is its norms and rationales which are distinctive, rather than the practical methods adopted, and these are associated with the entire policy process, rather than simply with the public's participation.

Further, the nature of the participants is not the defining characteristic of consensus-building processes. In consequence, similar practices are central to a myriad of hybrid institutional forms which break down the distinction between 'public participation' as involving the state and the public as two separate players, and 'partnerships' as groupings of state agencies. Within these structures consensus can be built between almost any combination of stakeholders, possibly representing different sectors, and including community, state and business actors. It is thus imperative for critical analysis to pay close attention to who is actually involved in such processes, which interests are brought in, and which are reflected in the outcomes.

In the following section we present an analysis showing how practice can stray from the ideal of inclusiveness along differing dimensions of exclusion. In this our focus is on the increasingly frequent processes and structures which are explicitly designed to encourage the development of consensus. However, many of the same arguments apply, often with greater force, to the similarly expanding number of processes in which it is assumed that simply bringing different interest groups together as 'partners' will result in consensual decision-making.[4]

Ideal and pragmatic consensus

The ideal consensus building process delivers a freely reached agreement between all parties with an interest in the issue, to which they all subscribe and from which they all gain. However, where consensus building is used to address difficult complex and/or contested issues, this is obviously a hard or even impossible ideal to attain, given the differing goals, interests, expectations, and levels of trust in each other held by different potential participants, frequently compounded by initial attitudes or histories of antagonism. Furthermore, available resources are inevitably limited and often insufficient.

Moreover, the unforced nature of an ideal consensus-building process can be compromised for other reasons. The simple framing of a process as having consensus as its aim affects its nature (Hooghe and Marks 2001), shaping expectations and norms of behaviour. Such impacts blur with more interested actions, in that actors may have goals beyond the immediate issues which incline

4
Although this chapter deals broadly with the challenges raised by conceptualising *practical* as opposed to *ideal* consensus, in the interests of brevity it has been necessary to leave aside several important and related issues, in particular the crucial micropolitics of relations between participants in consensus-building and the linkage of consensus-building processes to decision-making structures (see Richardson and Connelly 2002).

them towards maintaining the process – for example, to sustaining links with other stakeholders.

So a number of tendencies and temptations exist which moderate the form of consensus aimed at or achieved to something less than the ideal. These are made effective through the choices and decisions made by those initiating, designing and managing a process – a group which can include participants, once the process is underway.

The choices that are made often compromise the ideal of inclusivity along any or all of three dimensions:

- Exclusion of *people*
- Exclusion of *issues*
- Exclusion of *outcomes*

In the following sections we explore each in turn. There are no easy answers to the issues raised, so we have preferred to provide some key questions to assist those designing, analysing or evaluating consensus-building processes, and perhaps to provoke more thought generally.

Exclusion of people
Sidaway's (1998) definition implies that the ideal form of consensus-building is a broad-based participative approach open to all stakeholders, defined as those sharing risks, costs, and benefits (Abbott 1996), and having 'the right to participate in the decision-making process' (Clarke 1996). These descriptions are problematic: in some cases (e.g. major environmental issues) they arguably give *everyone* a right of involvement, and in many cases encompass practically un-

05.01

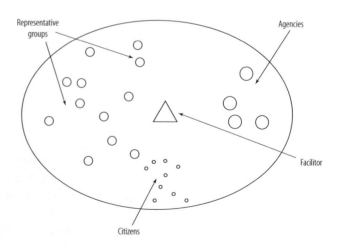

reachable numbers of people. Pragmatic consensus building there-fore usually requires a limited selection of stakeholders to be either identified or invited to participate, and so, conversely, a choice of who to *exclude*. This raises three interrelated issues – the 'location' of consensus, the choice of potentially affected people, and the rela-tionships between those 'inside' and 'outside' the process.

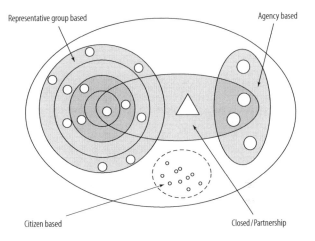

A useful way of analysing the exclusion of stakeholders is by considering the 'location of consensus'. If the possible participants are characterised as citizens, representative groups and agencies, then different patterns of participation can be identified depending on these decisions. Figure 05.01 shows the consensus-building ideal where all interests and stakeholders are fully and unproblematically involved in the process. In practice, however, consensus is more normally developed and located within more restricted groups. This process can take a number of forms, set out here and mapped out in Figure 05.02 in relation to the ideal:

- Closed/partnership – the consensus includes agencies and representative groups from across the categories, but is limited to an exclusive subset of potential stakeholders.
- Agency-based – consensus is developed within a local authority or small group of agencies, often following consultation with other stakeholders.
- Representative group-based – a consensus is genuinely built between different representative groups, but does not include policy-making agencies and so is ineffective.
- Citizen-based – similar to consensus built between representative groups, but open to participation by individual citizens.

These different potential locations for consensus imply qualitatively very different applications of consensus building, each with different rationales. Closed processes tend to be based on an instrumental rationale of pursuing efficiency. Representative- and citizen-based processes can contribute to building social capital, but are structurally restricted in their effectiveness in terms of affecting policies, and so in contributing to democratic goals. More open processes can encompass a wide range of rationales – they can be instrumental, in that in conflict-prone situations it may be necessary to involve people to make solutions stick, but they may well also aim to achieve broader social aims and/or embody the procedural rationale of pursuing democracy for its own sake. However, very inclusive approaches risk diluting the focus and cohesion of the process, resulting in both ineffectiveness and loss of legitimacy and support if they degenerate into 'talking shops' (Wilson and Charlton 1997). Arriving at one of these structures necessarily involves hard decisions which define the inclusivity of the process – decisions which open up the opportunity for deliberate exclusion of stakeholders in order to further the process designers' substantive agendas, or simply to achieve the procedural aim of reaching a consensus through limiting overall numbers and excluding potential participants with known 'difficult' views.

The latter raises the issue of the potential conflict between instrumental aims and democratic and long-term social goals. However, the need for legitimacy also makes these mutually dependent – a successful process needs to be both effective and command support. A balance must always be struck, between selection of participants as a pragmatic decision based on who needs to be present to legitimise or make implementable any outcome, or based on democratic values that involvement should, in principle, be open to all.

Even when manipulation is not intended, identifying appropriate stakeholders is difficult. While it may be fairly obvious which 'agencies' should be involved, there are problems selecting stakeholders from the wider population of citizens and representative groups. It is increasingly recognised that this population is composed of multiple communities, some spatially defined, others interest based (Carley 1995), which are flexible, contested, provisional and precariously-constructed (Massey 1994; Shurmer-Smith and Hannam 1994; Illsley and McCarthy 1998). Despite this, consensus-building practice still tends to assume that 'communities' are homogeneous and place-based, and/or to work with familiar representative groups. Both approaches can be unproductive and exclusionary (Bouriaud 1999; Shucksmith 2000).

It is also clear that the selection of participants is not entirely under the control of process initiators. Despite the assumption often made by policy-makers (e.g. Rural Forum and Rural Research Branch 1997), involvement of 'the public' and other stakeholders cannot be taken for granted. While non-involvement is often (pejoratively) ascribed to apathy, more perceptive observers have noted the occurrence of 'consultation fatigue' (Duncan and Thomas 2000) and the possibility that the intended participants may very rationally consider the potential benefits of involvement not to be worth the effort (Rydin and Pennington 2000). This is likely to be exacerbated by the widespread lack of trust of state institutions and the associated sense that participation is unlikely to affect policy, shared by individuals and groups from the voluntary and community sector (Macnaghten *et al.* 1995; Wilson and Charlton 1997; Duncan and Thomas 2000). The question then becomes whether consensus-building processes can be part of (re)building that trust and sense of agency, implying in turn that processes need to be consciously designed with long-term goals of building social capital (Macnaghten *et al.* 1995; Amdam 2000).

These problems and tensions are often resolved in practice through a combination of restricted consensus building supplemented with a process of *consultation* to involve a wider population. Such an approach is often adopted unproblematically (Roe 2000) and has been proposed as the ideal by Margerum and Born (1995). Nevertheless it is unlikely to be satisfactory. Problems of legitimacy arise where consensus building is intended to be, or is presented as, open and democratic but in practice is set up to be, or becomes, restricted and exclusive (O'Riordan and Ward 1997).

The implication is that if limited partnerships are essential on efficiency grounds, then safeguards in terms of access and public involvement to maintain their legitimacy must be built into them. This raises the issue of linkage, since if some stakeholders are not to participate directly they must be brought into the system in other ways. Gillespie *et al.* (2000) stress the importance of feedback as well as consultation, claiming that this enables stakeholders 'outside' to be involved and maintain ownership, even when the work is done by a smaller group. This approach gives a great deal of power to facilitators and insiders, a potential problem which is perhaps avoided by O'Riordan and Ward's proposal that the consensus-building group should be fluid, composed of 'informal networks of interested parties on a "come and go" basis' (O'Riordan and Ward 1997: 266). This entails a continuous reflexive assessment by the partners of how open they are being, and a preparedness to act on failings which are identified.

An alternative approach is to rely on some form of representation. This is complex and raises issues which are beyond the scope of this chapter. Suffice it to note that 'representation' is itself ambiguous, encompassing both the representation of the views of those groups or interests not present in a consensus-building process and the representation of *commitment* – the extent to which a participant or participating group can commit others considered to be from their community to abide by outcomes or take any agreed actions. Further, it is clear that steps in this direction move away from the consensual ideal of direct stakeholder involvement.

These issues associated with the selection of participants are inevitably present whenever consensus-building is attempted. The most appropriate way to tackle them will depend on the context – on the interactions between a constellation of possible actors, and the purposes of the process. The only constant, in our view, is the need to address these issues of exclusion head-on. This means interrogating a consensus-building process, from inception through to implementation, by asking critical questions such as those set out below:

05.03 – *Critical questions about exclusion of people in consensus building*
- Where is consensus to be located? i.e. which of the possible actors will be involved, and in which arena will consensus building take place?
- What kind of consensus building is being sought – broad-based participative, narrow partnership, or a hybrid?
- What will the relationships be between those 'inside' and 'outside' the process?
- What factors are likely to limit the extent of initiators' control over the process? Is non-participation likely to jeopardise the legitimacy of the process?
- Is prioritisation necessary between aims of inclusivity of participants, holistic policy-making and process goals? If so, what is the order of priority?

Exclusion of issues
Alongside this process of *exclusion of people* is the *exclusion of issues* through focusing attention on selected issues and areas where agreement is most likely. At the broadest level this reflects a choice be-tween two very different 'styles' of consensus building which have not been clearly differentiated in the literature. Usefully labelled 'conflictual' and 'non-conflictual', these are characterised by differing formats and underpinning philosophies and assump-

tions. Both rest on the assumed possibility of agreement, and the construction of participants not as *antagonists* with different, fixed interests but as *stakeholders* who from the beginning recognise that they have a common interest, a stake in something in common (Healey 1998). However, it would be naïve to assume that such an interest is shared from the start – more usually participants come with the expectation of maximising their own interests, as they initially perceive them to be, and perhaps without the goal of reaching a consensus. A necessary corollary is therefore the assumption of a possibility of movement in positions. Such movement relies on the potential for learning, through the acquisition and sharing of information (Margerum and Born 1995), the overcoming of misunderstanding (Sidaway 1998) and through the creation of new ideas (Healey 1998).

The two approaches differ strongly, however, in their understanding of how such movement can be best attained. 'Conflictual' processes draw more or less explicitly on the Habermasian ideal of communicative rationality (Skollerhorn 1998; Forester 1999). They strive to create arenas for debate which come as close as possible to realising this ideal, through such increasingly popular applications as citizens' juries and citizens' panels (Renn *et al*. 1984; Petts 1995) which have been used or advocated for a wide range of issues from local conflict resolution to national, long-term planning (Petts 1995). Differences in initial positions are explicitly sought out and consensus is reached through a process of argumentation – in an ideal situation purely through the force of the better argument, and reflecting the development of opposing positions into shared viewpoints (Healey 1997; Kumar and Paddison 2000). This style is clearly vulnerable to the theoretical and political critiques of collaborative planning outlined above. Critics suggest that these deliberative arenas are inevitably structured by pre-existing power relationships and broader social structures, so that the ideal is not merely hard to attain but the concept itself, of neutral, power-free debate, is theoretically untenable (e.g. Richardson 1996).

In contrast 'non-conflictual' processes explicitly *exclude* initial differences from discussion. They focus instead on a search for areas of common interest and then seek to build shared visions, working typically towards some kind of agreed action plan. This approach offers the clear attraction of facilitating agreement on possible action rather than getting 'bogged down' in argument, and appears to be rapidly gaining ground in Britain. Its conceptual underpinnings are hazy – they clearly do not fit the Habermasian model and perhaps should be looked for in political theories of consensus as a social norm – see, pre-eminently, the work of Talcott Parsons (e.g. 1957). However, by excluding important issues and the full expression of conflicting viewpoints, problems may be suppressed, only to re-emerge later in the policy-making or implementation process. Furthermore, critics suggest that avoiding conflict undermines and disables consensus building, arguing that the mutual learning and 'transformation' which are fundamental to changing initial positions may *require* conflict rather than an illusion of common ground (Driver and Kravatsky 2000).

As before, choices have to be made over which approach to adopt, and which issues will be tackled within a consensus-building process. The approaches have complementary advantages and disadvantages, providing different trade-offs between likelihood of success and quality of outcome. In box 05.04 is a series of questions which, when asked critically, help to open up these dimensions of a consensus building process.

05.04 – *Critical questions about exclusion of issues in consensus building*
- What issues will and will not be covered?
- What principles underlie the process (will a conflictual or non-conflictual approach be adopted)?
- Who decides this – all the participants or just the process designers and managers?

Exclusion of outcomes and actions
The third dimension of exclusion is *exclusion of outcomes* and actions. This dimension has elements that are both internal and external to a consensus-building process. Within such a process, there can be a drift away from substantive action-oriented outcomes towards an acceptance of generalised statements which can be agreed by all. For example, Selman (1998) suggests that this has occurred generally within Local Agenda 21 processes in Britain, where a trade-off developed between broadening participation and the delivery of blander outputs through attempts to reach consensus. Possible outcomes can also be constrained by structures or events outside a process – by the nature of the linkage (if any) between the process and other policy-making and delivery mechanism, or by the prior definition of what outcomes would be acceptable to powerful players in the wider policy-making process. Thus it becomes important to ask a further set of critical questions to keep check on the ways in which consensus building deliberately or accidentally avoids certain (perhaps more radical or controversial) outcomes in favour of others (perhaps more anodyne).

- Is the process managed to deliver meaningful outcomes? Or is it allowed (or encouraged) to drift towards a 'lowest common denominator' consensual agreement?
- Do structures exist to link consensus-building processes with decision-making and implementation within the policy process?
- What level of influence will consensus-building process outputs have on policy-making more generally?
- Has discussion been foreclosed by taking the decision before consensus building has commenced?

Conclusion

As in many other fields, public participation in planning is on the increase. Within planning theory this has been presented as a paradigm shift, from a rational planning paradigm to one of 'communicative' or 'collaborative planning'. We see this as neither a theoretically satisfying nor an empirically accurate presentation. Both so-called paradigms have theoretical weaknesses, and what is observed in practice is a continuous coexistence of, and conflict between, approaches embodying instrumental and communicative (and other) rationalities. Consequently we have explored a different approach, analysing practice whilst being critically aware of the power relations and policy processes within which public participation is set. This approach pays dividends in unpacking the core values which underlie the new consensual practices of participatory planning.

Consensus-based approaches are usually presented as the search for an ideal outcome, an agreement on a position – and often on action – subscribed to by all stakeholders and arrived at through an open, participative and non-coercive process. Within this conception the role of the initiators and facilitators, by implication, is to establish and steer a process which will generate consensus: they become guarantors of openness and inclusivity, remaining neutral over outcomes. While this is variously seen as being unproblematic or requiring hard, conscious work, there is an underlying assumption that such ways of working and outcomes are both feasible and desirable. However, we suggest that this ideal form of consensus building is not practical, and actors (planners, participants, facilitators, politicians, and others) necessarily make decisions and choices in order to achieve *pragmatic consensus* – an agreement between limited numbers of stakeholders which commands both their support and their commitment, and (hopefully) legitimacy in the eyes of the wider world. These choices are inherently exclusionary in their nature, involving the exclusion of certain ('difficult') stakeholders, of certain ('difficult') issues, and/or exclusion of ('wrong') outcomes, possibly in favour of bland statements which can be agreed by all, or decisive actions agreed among a few.

Since this exclusion results from actors' choices, a great deal of power is wielded by the designers and initiators of a consensus-building process, and these issues of power and politics cannot be ignored, or 'wished away' in the name of consensuality. Actors are therefore likely to find themselves exposed in difficult territory if they rely too much on normative, ideal theories – or if they reject these in favour of the tried and tested 'rational' planning approach. Despite the importance of power relations *within* consensus-building processes having been increasingly recognised in the literature, and political scientists acknowledging for many years the power of those controlling the agenda and effectiveness of a decision-making arena, the point here is that the design of a consensus-building process is an expression of the power of the initiators and a select group of stakeholders able to exert influence over process design and management, and that exclusion is at the heart of these particular power relations. We stress that this is not inherently 'bad', but that it *is* inherent in consensus-building.

Moreover, exclusion does clearly carry risks. While consensus-building processes may create situations which rebalance power relations between actors and are arguably elements in the development of a more pluralistic and direct democracy, they also potentially create and reinforce non-accountable systems and raise concerns about the 'quangocracy' and the 'new managerialism' (Duffy and Hutchinson 1997: 359). The latter situation is perhaps the more likely, given that the dynamics of policy-making, reinforced by normative pressure to arrive at a consensus, tend to lead towards exclusion as a 'natural' act and the blunting of consensus building's transformative potential. Such acts of exclusion are, however, often masked by a rhetoric which implies that decisions are made in a way which delivers at least an approximation to the 'ideal consensus'.

So what should an aware and committed practitioner or researcher do? There is clearly no blueprint for acting 'correctly' – every situation is too different for this. In this chapter our aim has been to highlight the importance for those involved of recognising and engaging reflexively with the often-obscured effects of practices which institutionalise exclusion in consensus-building processes. The 'key questions' can act as a guide to such engagement, but the emphasis is on the planner as reflexive practitioner. And not just 'the planner' – the argument is equally valid for all the professions where engagement with the built environment requires collaboration.

Finally, then, the potential for participation making a difference in the pursuit of spatial and social justice relies on individuals exercising situated judgement (Campbell 2002) rather than the unnuanced deployment of generic models or toolkits. Those involved in mediating space therefore need to be critically aware of the existence of power and the treatment of exclusion in consensus-building, rather than maintaining or believing in a rhetoric of ideal consensus where this is not justified in practice. Sometimes they may advise that exclusion of one form or another is necessary, but they will make these decisions in an accountable way. In other cases they may argue that consensus is not a realistic aim. Living and working on the edges of conflict, planners and others must resist the temptation to gloss over difference, to believe that consensus is always a desirable outcome. Nor should they abdicate responsibility:

> Planners cannot be absolved of their individual responsibility for ethical judgment – it is deeply problematic for planners to accept as just that which emerges from communicative process. (Harrison 2002)

This is an inescapable dimension of professional honesty, accountability, and reflexivity.

References

Abbott, J. (1996) *Sharing the City: Community participation in urban management*, London: Earthscan.

Amdam, J. (2000) 'Confidence building in local planning and development, some experience from Norway', *European Planning Studies 8* (5), 581-600.

Boaden, N., Goldsmith, M., Hampton, W. and Stringer, P. (1980) 'Planning and participation in practice', *Progress in Planning* 13(1), 1-102.

Bouriaud, L. (1999) 'Linking social needs and interests in regional forest planning: a case in France', paper presented at Regional Forest Programmes: a participatory approach to support forest-based regional development. Proceedings of the Nordic Research Course on Regional Forest Strategies, Mekrijärvi, Finland, 17-24 June 1999.

Campbell, H. (2002) 'Planning: an idea of value', *Town Planning Review 73* (3), 271-88.

Carley, M. (1995) *A Community Participation Strategy in Urban Regeneration*, working paper, Edinburgh: Scottish Homes.

Clarke, P. B. (1996) *Deep Citizenship*, London: Pluto Press.

Commission of the European Communities (1992) *Towards Sustainability: A European Community programme of policy and action in relation to the environment and sustainable development. The EC Fifth Environmental Action Plan*, Brussels: CEC.

Connelly, S. (2002) Public involvement in Local Agenda 21: the impact of local authority policy processes, PhD thesis, Dept. of Town and Regional Planning, University of Sheffield, Sheffield.

Connelly, S. and Richardson, T. (2004) 'Exclusion: The necessary difference between ideal and practical consensus', *Journal of Environmental Planning and Management* 47(1), 3-17.

Davidoff, P. and Reiner. T. (1962) 'A choice theory of planning', *Journal of the American Institute of Planning* 28, 331-8.

Driver, T. and Kravatsky, A. (2000) 'Participatory learning and action or participatory acting?' in L. Greenwood (ed.) *Participatory Processes in the North*, PLA Notes 38, London: IIED, 3-5.

Duffy, K. and Hutchinson, J. (1997) 'Urban policy and the turn to community', *Town Planning Review* 68(3), 347-62.

Duncan, P. and Thomas, S. (2000) *Neighbourhood Regeneration: Resourcing community involvement*, Bristol: The Policy Press.

Etzioni, A. (1995) *New Communitarian Thinking: Persons, virtues, institutions, and communities*, Charlottesville, VA: University Press of Virginia.

Etzioni, A. (1996) *The New Golden Rule: Community and morality in a democratic society*, New York: Basic Books.

Faludi, A. (1973) *Planning Theory*, Oxford: Pergamon Press.

Fischer, F. and Forester, J. E. (1993) *The Argumentative Turn in Policy Analysis and Planning*, London: UCL Press Ltd.

Flyvbjerg, B. (1996) 'The dark side of planning: rationality and "realrationalität"', in R. Burchell (ed.) *Explorations in Planning Theory*, New Jersey: Rutgers, Center for Urban Policy Research, 383-94.

Flyvbjerg, B. (1998) *Rationality and Power: Democracy in practice*, Chicago: University of Chicago Press.

Flyvbjerg, B. and Richardson, T. (2002) 'In search of the dark side of planning theory', in M. Tewdwr-Jones (ed.) *Planning Futures: New directions for planning theory*, London: Routledge, 44-62.

Forester, J. (1989) *Planning in the Face of Power*, Berkeley, CA: University of California Press.

Forester, J. (1999) *The Deliberative Practitioner*, Cambridge, MA: MIT Press.

Foucault, M. (1977) *Discipline and Punish: The birth of the prison*, New York: Pantheon.

Foucault, M. (1979) *The History of Sexuality*, London: Penguin.

Friedmann, J. (1973) 'The public interest and community participation: towards a reconstruction of public philosophy', *Journal of the American Institute of Planners* 39 (1), 2-12.

Friedmann, J. (1987) *Planning in the Public Domain: From knowledge to action*, Princeton, NJ: Princeton University Press.

Friedmann, J. (1997) 'Planning theory revisited', paper presented at AESOP Congress, University of Nijmegen.

Giddens, A. (1984) *The Constitution of Society: Outline of the theory of structuration*, Cambridge: Polity.

Giddens, A. (1998) *The Third Way: The renewal of social democracy*, Cambridge: Polity Press.

Gillespie, S., Telfer, M., Halhead V. and o. b. o. t. D. team (2000) 'Sowing seeds of sustainability with Duthchas', in L. Greenwood (ed.) *Participatory Processes in the North*, PLA Notes 38, London: IIED, 64-7.

Gualini, E. (2001) *Planning and the Intelligence of Institutions: Interactive approaches to territorial policy-making between institutional design and institution-building*, Aldershot: Ashgate.

Harrison, P. (2002) '"On the Edge of Reason": Planning and the futures of Southern African cities', Inaugural lecture, University of the Witwatersrand, October, 2002.

Healey, P. (1990) 'Places, people and policies', *Town and Country Planning*, 59 (1), 9-10.

Healey, P. (1992a) 'A planner's day: knowledge and action in communicative practice', *Journal of the American Planning Association* 58 (1), 9-20.

Healey, P. (1992b) 'Planning through debate: the communicative turn in planning theory', *Town Planning Review* 63 (2), 143-62.

Healey, P. (1997) *Collaborative Planning: Shaping places in fragmented societies*, Basingstoke: Macmillan.

Healey, P. (1998) 'Building institutional capacity through collaborative approaches to urban planning', *Environment and Planning (A)* 30, 1531-46.

Henderson, P. and Salmon, H. (1999) 'A community development perspective on local governance', *Local Governance* 25 (2), 77-86.

Hooghe, L. and Marks, G. (2001) *Multi-level Governance and European Integration*, Lanham, MD: Rowman & Littlefield.

Huxley, M. (2000) 'The limits to communicative planning', *Journal of Planning Education and Research* 19, 369-77.

Illsley, B. and McCarthy, J. (1998) 'Community-led planning? The case of Dundee', *Scottish Geographical Magazine* 114 (2), 103-08.

Innes, J. (1992) 'Group processes and the social construction of growth management: Florida, Vermont and New Jersey', *Journal of the American Planning Association* 58(4), 440-53.

Innes, J. (1995) 'Planning theory's emerging paradigm: communicative action and interactive practice', *Journal of Planning Education and Research* 14 (3), 183-90.

Innes, J. (1996) 'Planning through consensus building: a new view of the comprehensive planning ideal'. *Journal of the Amercian Planning Association* 58 (4), 440-54.

Kenny, S. (2002) 'Tensions and dilemmas in community development: new discourses, new Trojans?' *Community Development Journal* 37 (4), 284-99.

Kumar, A. and Paddison, R. (2000) 'Trust and collaborative planning theory: The case of the Scottish planning system', *International Planning Studies* 5 (2), 205-23.

Leach, M., Mearns, R. and Scoones, I. (2000) *Consensus or Conflict? Time for a reality check on community-based sustainable development'*, id21 Research Highlights Bulletin, Brighton: University of Sussex, IDS.

Leach, S., Stewart, J. and Walsh, K. (1994) *The Changing Organisation and Management of Local Government*, Basingstoke: Macmillan.

Machiavelli, N. (2003) *The Prince*, London: Penguin.

Macnaghten, P., Grove-White, R., Jacobs, M. and Wynne, B. (1995) *Public Perceptions and Sustainability in Lancashire*, Preston: Lancashire County Council.

Majone, G. (1989) *Evidence, Argument and Persuasion in the Policy Process*, New Haven, CT: Yale University Press.

Mannheim, K. (1940) *Man and Society in an Age of Reason: Studies in modern social structure*, London: Paul, Trench, Trusner and Co. Ltd.

Margerum, R. D. and Born, S. M. (1995) 'Integrated environmental management: moving from theory to practice', *Journal of Environmental Planning and Management* 38 (3), 371-91.

Massey, D. (1994) *Space, Place and Gender*, Oxford: Blackwell.

MHLG (Ministry of Housing and Local Government) (1969) *Report of the Committee on Public Participation in Planning* (The Skeffington Report), London: HMSO.

Morgan, R. K. (1998) *Environmental Impact Assessment: A methodological perspective*, London: Kluwer.

O'Riordan, T. and Ward, R. (1997) 'Building trust in shoreline management: creating participatory consultation in shoreline management plans', *Land Use Policy* 14 (4), 257-76.

Parsons, T. (1957) 'The distribution of power in American society', *World Politics* 10 (1), 123-43.

Petts, J. (1995) 'Waste management strategy development: a case study of community involvement and consensus-building in Hampshire', *Journal of Environmental Planning and Management* 38 (4), 519-36.

Putnam, R. D. (2000) *Bowling Alone: The collapse and revival of American community*, New York: Simon & Schuster.

Putnam, R. D., Leonardi, R. and Nanetti, R. (1993) *Making Democracy Work: Civic traditions in modern Italy*, Princeton, NJ: Princeton University Press.

Renn, O. (1998) 'The role of risk communication and public dialogue for improving risk management', *Risk Decision and Policy* 3 (1), 5-30.

Renn, O., Stegelmann, G., Albrecht, U. K. and Peters, H. P. (1984) 'An empirical investigation of citizens' preferences among four energy scenarios', *Technological Forecasting and Social Change* 26, 11-46.

Reuter, W. (1998) 'Pragmatistic acts – discourse and power in planning', paper presented at Oxford, 1998.

Reuter, W. (1999) 'On the complementarity of discourse and power in planning', paper presented at Bergen, 1999.

Richardson, T. (1996) 'Foucauldian discourse: power and truth in the policy process', *European Planning Studies* 4 (3), 279-92.

Richardson, T. (2000) 'Environmental integration in infrastructure planning: a Foucauldian discourse analysis of the trans-European transport network', PhD thesis, Urban & Regional Studies, Sheffield Hallam University, Sheffield.

Richardson, T. and Connelly, S. (2002) *Building Consensus for Rural Development and Planning in Scotland: A review of best practice*, Edinburgh: Scottish Executive Central Research Unit.

Roe, M. (2000) 'Landscape planning for sustainability: community participation in Estuary Management Plans', *Landscape Research* 25 (2), 157-81.

RTPI (2003) *A new vision for planning: delivering sustainable communities settlements and places. Mediating space – creating place: the need for action*, Royal Town Planning Institute: *www.rtpi.org.uk/about-the-rtpi/vision.pdf*, accessed 14/09/2003.

Rural Forum and Rural Research Branch (1997) *Community Involvement in Rural Development Initiatives: Good Practice in Rural Development No. 2*, Edinburgh: Scottish Office CRU.

Rydin, Y. and Pennington, M. (2000) 'Public participation and local environmental planning: the collective action problem and the potential of social capital', *Local Environment* 5 (2), 153-69.

Sager, T. (1994) *Communicative Planning Theory*, Aldershot: Avebury.

Scott, A. (1999) 'Whose futures? A comparative study of Local Agenda 21 in mid-Wales', *Planning Practice and Research* 14 (4), 401-21.

Selman, P. (1998) 'Local Agenda 21: substance or spin?', *Journal of Environmental Planning and Management* 41 (5), 533-53.

Shucksmith, M. (2000) 'Endogenous development – social capital and social inclusion: perspectives from LEADER in the UK', *Sociologia Ruralis* 40 (2), 208-18.

Shurmer-Smith, P. and Hannam, K. (1994) *Worlds of Desire, Realms of Power: A cultural geography*, London: Edward Arnold.

Sidaway, R. (1998) *Consensus Building: Good practice in rural development No. 5*, Edinburgh: Scottish National Rural Partnership.

Skollerhorn, E. (1998) 'Habermas and nature: the theory of communicative action for studying environmental policy', *Journal of Environmental Planning and Management* 41 (5), 555-73.

Taylor, M. (2003) *Public Policy in the Community*, Basingstoke: Palgrave Macmillan.

Torfing, J. (1999) *New Theories of Discourse: Laclau, Mouffe and Žižek*, Oxford: Blackwell.

UNCED (1992) *Agenda 21*, New York: UN Division for Sustainable Development.

Weston, J. (2000) 'EIA, decision-making theory and screening and scoping in UK practice', *Journal of Environmental Planning and Management* 43 (2), 185-203.

Williams, L. (1995) 'Resolving planning conflicts', *Town and Country Planning*.

Wilson, A. and Charlton, K. (1997) *Making Partnerships Work: A practical guide for the public, private, voluntary and community sectors*, York: Joseph Rowntree Foundation.

Wong, C. (1998) 'Old wine in a new bottle? Planning methods and techniques in the 1990s', *Planning, Practice and Research* 13 (3), 221-36.

Yiftachel, O. (1994) 'Planning and social control: exploring the dark side', *Journal of Planning Literature* 12 (2), 395-406.

Young, S. (1996) *Promoting Participation and Community-based Partnerships in the Context of Local Agenda 21: a report for practitioners*, Manchester: University of Manchester.

How inhabitants can become collective developers: France 1968 – 2000 [1]

[1]
This text is based on the transcription of a lecture given by Anne Querrien at the University of Sheffield in the Forum Series 2002.

Participative problems before 1968

Participative theories have been evident in France for some time but they are still viewed cautiously, because architecture is still in many ways controlled through the rules of the *Ordre des Architectes*, a corporation established during the Second World War by a very right-wing government. Architecture has remained a tool of domination by the powerful and wealthy, and this makes participation a minefield of political complexity. Architecture has become more important with the transition from an industrial to a service economy.[2] Housing for the old industrial economy was not convenient for incoming service workers, as the role of the home had changed. For example, the working class found that collective local communities were very important to them, whilst middle and upper middle-class residents wanted anonymous collective living combined with more comfortable accommodation. Attempts by the state to put people into large concrete blocks of flats in the early 1960s led to financial and social splits between the two social classes who were being forced to live together. In light of this, by 1960-65 new solutions to housing problems were being sought. Workers from foreign countries were employed without any consideration of how they might be integrated: ethnicisation of social divisions and a rise of racism were the results.

[2]
In 1962 the Department of Architectural Heritage moved from the Ministry of Education to the Ministry of Culture, to become Department of Architectural Creation, Education and Heritage. At that time, modern architecture, and more specifically the architecture of social housing, became a governmental matter.

Prior to 1968 Henri Lefebvre and the less well-known Paul-Henry Chombart de Lauwe had used their sociological literature and teaching to call for sweeping changes, but they were now listened to in architectural schools. At that time, architecture in France was studied only at the Beaux-Arts in Paris. Studies concentrated on designing over-scaled public buildings and competition to be one of the small number of prestigious architects in charge of such a project was fierce, due to the gap in status between those few in charge of monuments and public buildings and the others. Revolt inside the school began around 1965 and some reform was undertaken before 1968 in discussions to alter the school's syllabus. In 1966, exterior workshops were created where students were allowed to study social housing and modern problems. Focus groups of intellectuals throughout France were asked by the Department of Culture what should be included in architectural courses. De Gaulle authorised new Beaux-Arts schools at locations across France as a way of precipitating change in the education of France's architects. This was not as radical as many reformers wished: they wanted architecture to become a university subject, part of the general culture.

By 2002 participation had become compulsory by law for regeneration projects throughout France. The law on Solidarity and Urban Renewal was passed on 13 December 2000, which necessitates seeking approval from residents for any work in their neighbourhood. Debate and close collaboration with key skilled individuals are needed to obtain acceptance, and large teams are employed to win the public over, but this does not yet amount to open participation for the inhabitants.

Two examples of participation

1 — *La Courneuve, les 4000*, a film by Patrick Laroche – 1999
La Courneuve, les 4000 is a social housing development built in the late 1960s to house those expelled by urban renewal in the 13th district of Paris, an area which is woefully poor (the average income is half of the SMIG (*salaire minimum interprofessionel garanti*) – a minimum interprofessional income which is guaranteed by the State). The housing is inhabited by a large immigrant population, who get poorer with time. The city plans to demolish some blocks, to create some green areas, and to add cosmetic architecture to attract middle-class residents.

There are a few key figures featured in the film: a spokesperson (linking town hall, state and inhabitants), the architects, mayor, and inhabitants.

The architects were asked by the city and the state to demolish some blocks to allow more green space, and this was explained sympathetically and carefully to resident groups. The design team is shown in discussion with the social housing management team explaining how the demolition of the main blocks will take place. Occupants stress the need to make pleasant spaces for children to play, but it seems to me that the ideas are poor and do not fulfil these requirements. The design proposes a quasi-gentrified appearance, more colourful than the concrete monolith that preceded it, but it does not take any account of the different groups of inhabitants and of the multiplicity of their desires. It just tries to obtain a consensus.

The inhabitants are primarily concerned with playground facilities, with one such area for each block. They do not wish to mix with other blocks, as there is a territorial attitude, and the reluctance to integrate with neighbouring blocks is due to a perceived difference in social status. The mayor insists that they do indeed have a problem of territory.

The process reveals a disparity between idea and design, with the architects relying more on explosives than on ingenuity. Several years of work is needed in a neighbourhood like this to establish a working relationship with the inhabitants, and this work is not funded, even though according to the policy for towns all actions for developing poor neighbourhoods are supposed to be decided and realised with the 'active participation of inhabitants'. The criteria in evaluating this participation are formal: the signature of associations, signs of consensus.

2 — *Quand les habitants prennent l'initiative* (When the inhabitants take the initiative): *l'Alma Gare à Roubaix* – an extract from *La ville est à nous*, a film by Yvonne Mignot-Lefevbre, produced by Société coopérative ouvrière de production – 1979

This film depicts the struggle for urban renewal in a neighbourhood near Lille. The area was to be demolished because of poor living conditions, for example, the lack of running water except in the main square. Since 1968 this has been a place in which the united front put up by inhabitants and students of architecture has succeeded in resisting demolition. CERFI (*Centre d'études, de recherches et de formations institutionnelles*) negotiated with the State the provision of research funds to work on planning alternative projects, and managed to obtain money to pay the architects and my research colleagues to help the project by producing an alternative design.

This is a special case. The municipality started demolishing the locality in the early 1960s with the intention of placing new offices and housing. Unfortunately, the State then decided to concentrate this typology in a new town on the opposite side of Lille: the area was left largely derelict with little land value, and left the municipality with the considerable problem of finding a solution.

The area was a working-class quarter which did not want to be 'upgraded' into the then fashionable social blocks. People wanted to remain in familiar street configurations but with a participative regeneration process. The lack of space available in the established architecture proved instrumental in forging a community spirit, with residents gathering in the streets.

It was one person's job to coordinate the use of a collective washing machine, a key meeting place for the residents. Even now, despite the availability of washing machines, a strong demand still exists for collective washing places in social housing, just to be able to meet and talk while doing the washing. The collective life that has developed in poor housing is impossible in new blocks based on a bourgeois model, in which nothing must be revealed to the outside world.

Residents achieved partial victory when it was decided that 40 per cent of the housing stock should remain as an historical reference. The new neighbourhood was designed by architects, chosen by the inhabitants, and has social facilities and services as defined by the inhabitants. For instance, they created facilities for adult education in the school, and institutions to help the inhabitants look after everyday life, the green areas, the cleaning.

A union of tenants existed in the town to help people who needed their rent reduced: it also offered an open forum of ideas. Consequently, a popular workshop for urbanism was created, inviting architects and other interested parties to be educated in the requirements for a successful regeneration. Such groups allowed individuals to become more professional through their roles as mediators between the inhabitants, the mayor and the State. This made them act differently, as they became isolated from the natural collective and became instigators of change. No longer were neighbourhood leaders simply militants of the old town, irritants in a kind of negative politics. The official and accepted status of such groups allowed them a dexterity and confidence not previously found in such people and projects.

The students of 1968 wanted, above all, to be linked with the working classes. Many went to work with the 'common people' across France and they were present at this development. The students helped in the decisions about how State money should be spent, and also in translating the inhabitants' ideas into plans. The State allowed the residents to choose architects for new buildings to house the poor and elderly, and a grant was made to allow their representatives to visit new housing sites in France and Belgium so that they could decide whom to employ in taking the participatory process further.

They decided that the whole neighbourhood should have rooms – a kind of collective cheap hotel – for visiting relatives or friends, shared between families. A school had a restaurant at its base where family members were allowed to have subsidised meals with their children. Kids were also supplied with breakfast within this canteen. A home for older people was sited nearby so that they could help students with their homework. The school was clearly used as a social centre that could direct family and community activities.

The professionals and the municipality told local people that they should share their newly completed facilities with new inhabitants because of their quality and location. Whereas old houses only had two floors, the new ones had four – the extra two set aside for incoming inhabitants. A large number of immigrants arrived mostly from Algeria and Morocco. Unfortunately, the regular evening policy meetings could not be attended by the arriving minorities due to a clash with the women's cultural duties. As a result the participatory processes were disrupted, and sections of the community threatened the very root of the community's renewal. A research action to get the communities to know each other better began, but after municipal elections and many votes in favour of the extreme-right, the mayor was persuaded to stop the experiment.

Jealousy over the disproportionate spending on this project caused revolt by a neighbouring quarter, which in contrast had received little help. At a time when the whole town was in economic depression, Alma Gare became a ghetto for very poor families. Extremely low-income families moved in, the neighbourhood declined and a quarter of the housing created by this test of participation had to be demolished, because only very poor people would agree to live there. The main leader of the struggle has made her career since in the housing department of the municipality, trying to arrange that poor immigrants disperse across the town, rather than concentrating in the same neighbourhoods.

Participation and mental illness

French national student union: Participation for health [3]
Prior to 1968, the first concern for participation at the university was not in the field of architecture but was in mental health. The student union had discovered that students from rural areas, who in 1965 only numbered 500 at a national level (the French population was then about 50 million, with 500,000 students), had a suicide rate 10 times that of students from urban areas. Because of these statistics the student union decided to begin a programme of action research, and as the students from rural areas were so few, it was decided to involve them all in the study.

The students were asked to attend workshops in towns all around France and the programme was overseen from a base in Rennes – this was the area with the largest proportion of students from rural areas. Correspondence was carried out by post. The students worked to create football teams and cultural activities in their area, and for this and the following two years there were no suicides amongst the rural student population. This study highlighted the

3
Editor's note: A. Querrien was a student activist in the 1960s and was involved in the organisation of May 1968 events. She worked in the 1970s with Félix Guattari at CERFI (*Centre d'études, de recherches et de formations institutionnelles*), and was an editor of the *Recherches* journal. 'CERFI developed a new way of questioning urban space and the function of institutions in that space. They studied the encoding of the normal and the "deviant" in modern societies, focusing above all on the function of the hospital and mental asylum, but also on the role of schools, factories, working life, and so on. In this way they initiated an analysis of modernity that would have many successors' (profile issue on CERFI, *SITE magazine* 2/2002, Stockholm).

importance of participation within social transformation and indicated that participation could have a positive effect both on suicide rates and mental health problems.

Following this experiment, the students sought contact with psychiatrists, who shared the view that mental health has a great deal to do with collective living conditions. This was how the individuals who made up the Institutional Psychotherapy movement came together with students like me around 1965. French students have a special institution to manage their health problems, MNEF (*Mutuelle Nationale des Etudiants de France*) which made innovations in the care of mental health and tuberculosis.

Participation, mental health and resistance

During the Second World War, due to the shortage of food, there was an order from Paris that the inhabitants of mental hospitals should be given less food than other people in France. At that time, the Saint Alban mental hospital in the Cevennes, a central mountain area, was under the direction of a Spanish psychiatrist called Tosquelles who was living there as a political refugee. The hospital began to grow its own food, and with a history of local independence and a relatively low German presence, the hospital became a centre of wartime resistance.

Through this they discovered that the mentally ill of the area benefited from their inclusion in the activities of the local community. At the end of the war one of the young psychiatrists founded La Borde at Cour-Chevenry, near Blois, a project in which Félix Guattari collaborated. At La Borde they cared for the mentally ill using methods involving local organisations and everyday life. Through minimising the difference between trained medical staff and unskilled workers, everyone worked together as a community. With the 100 beds available, they looked after two thousand people, whereas in a traditional hospital those people would have lived in the institution all their life. In La Borde clinic, mentally ill people learned how to live with others and their families, who also learned how to welcome the mentally ill into ordinary life: where this was not possible, other solutions were found. La Borde was conceived as a collective organisation in which the patients were the equals of those taking care of them.

In the national student union, those managing student welfare tried to foster links with people thinking and working in this manner, and to make moves within their own institution, including measures such as free psychoanalysis for students. This fostered a collective discussion on the topic.

At the same time the French government decided that due to

the collapse of the French iron industry they would industrialise the construction of schools and psychiatric hospitals which were in short supply across the country. A competition was set up for architects to produce plans for mass-constructed psychiatric hospitals.

The changing nature of treatment for the mentally ill and the research that had been already done made it clear that large institutional psychiatric hospitals were not what were required. The new methods of treatment called for smaller hospitals within cities with offices and links to psychoanalysts. It was put to the French government that this endeavour would fail for these reasons. Given the lower cost of these urban hospitals, the French government agreed to carry the idea forward.

To further the scheme, the government then sent doctors and architects to La Borde clinic to see how the new smaller psychiatric hospitals could work. At the same time a workshop was set up for all interested parties including doctors, students and architects. These were people who were not just interested in hospitals but in the idea of a collective process, and the idea that by working with a broad spectrum of people, a new programme for participation could begin.

The findings were published in a profile issue of the journal *Recherches* entitled 'Architecture, programme, psychiatrie' ('Architecture, programming, psychiatry') in 1967. The basic idea behind this publication was the awareness that the State could not know the true social needs of the people. This was due to the fact that the State was taking its understanding of social demands simply by asking what people wanted. From the first film (*La Courneuve, les 4000*), it is evident that if you ask the people what they want, the answer can only be what they know already. If the answer already exists, then the new building becomes obsolete quite quickly.

Any collaboration between interested parties has to go further than what already exists. The traditional form of determining demand is not a good one, and it also raises a political problem. In France the trade unions are small but very strong, and they represent the masses in elections and representative systems. In the case of the mental hospitals, the doctors' union asked for more hospitals due to a shortfall of places. The State said that there were already too many places and some other solution must be sought. The problem with the participative processes at the time was a perception that they allowed the State to ignore the demands of the unions. The State halted the process of industrialising the production of psychiatric hospitals, but the real needs and desires of the mentally ill and of mental health workers were still mostly ignored, except in rare cases like La Borde.

Participation and the built environment

The collapse of the State in 1968 was due to a realisation by the French government that in any given field they did not know how to tackle the problems that faced them, as in the proposed industrialisation of the production of psychiatric hospitals.

Until its collapse in 1968, members of the French government were under the impression that their social housing schemes were a success. The unions had asked for social housing schemes, and the State believed that they allowed people to be rehoused in more comfortable conditions. When they discovered that the housing schemes were not a success and that the public believed the slogan 'Renovation is Deportation', they could not understand the problem. At this time the university, like the school of architecture, was very conservative and after 1968 the attempt to understand what had happened needed new researchers from outside the university and the CNRS (*Conseil National de la Recherché Scientifique*).

On 13 May 1968 there were 13 million workers on strike out of 20 million in total. The whole country was in revolt: however, the revolution only lasted a few days. The State recovered through elections in which the vote of the population reflected the fear of social movements and the desire for law and order, and it decided to undertake research in all social fields by asking intellectuals from all left-wing movements, including communists, socialists, situationists and others to develop their ideas with research money. It became clear that development since the war had created too many tensions, and that new ways of managing society had to be found. The first voices for the environment could be heard.

With this money work began in the French new towns, which were used to develop new ideas up until 1975. Alongside the emergence of participative processes, the idea that there should be collective developers including professionals, state representatives, inhabitants and any other parties concerned was promoted, with no limits as to who could become involved. Within the new towns, work was done on mental health institutions, and on schools. There was also research into the impact of the State on local policies in different regions and departments, and on how the collective process could be opened up, taking into account differences, autonomies and self-organisation processes.

It was clear that it was necessary to establish an alternative method of participation in order to sustain the development of the collaborative process. The problem with the State at the time was that once a model has been suggested, that model tended to be applied without taking into account the local, the specific space. The collaborative process elaborated in, for example, the La Borde clinic, was not one that could easily be transferred: it was an historical project that came about due to a particular set of circumstances, and to reproduce it would be to force a solution. The State, however, did not attempt to understand this kind of discourse.

The problem of language often affects the participative process, especially when the process seeks to create spaces, and when architects are involved. The general method of participation is by producing consensus. The thinking of Deleuze and Guattari suggests that when things come together, a split always opens up, and it is this split that allows ideas to be furthered. The State system stabilises things by bridging across, denying the split and producing community through a common image and language.

The parties involved, however, do not start from the same background or knowledge base: such a system allows the domination of the party with the most knowledge over all the others. It is ethically important not to use cooperation as a learning process to climb the social ladder in your own field: for example, the technicians in the community in Roubaix from 1973 until 1983 used their knowledge of the process of participation to gain promotion in the State, and were allowed to head a regeneration organisation at a national level in 1982. In doing this they left real, local, participation behind.

This local regeneration organisation (i.e. a collective assemblage of inhabitants, developers, city administration, researchers) worked at first, but eventually failed because it masked the conflict between the old French population and the immigrant community. It is always assumed that in working-class organisations in France there is no racism, but if the participative process is not organised so that all parties can be involved, even if there is no intention to ignore any parties, their needs cannot be accounted for and they are effectively excluded. The regeneration organisation used their past experiences for new projects, and as a result the individual circumstances of a regeneration project in a particular quarter were overlooked. The specific conditions of that place were not brought under the control of the project.

At present, participation is compulsory in France, but it is organised in such a way that true participation, if there can be any, has become more difficult to obtain, because the field is already occupied by the official organisations. This is bad for the promotion of local projects.

'Participative control' is a provocative idea, but in participation you must take a stance which is almost the opposite of the one normal for architects, researchers and sociologists. Disciplines are supposed to know the state of their art, and you are contracted as a professional who knows the state of the art and will apply this to the problem at hand. In participation, you must act as if the state of the art were unknown and could not be taken for granted. To deal with a problem you must explore the plurality of solutions given by participants to solve this problem: then a spatial representation can be given by the architect. The difficulty for all groups who try to deal with a common problem is the question of how to represent the problem in order to start a discussion and decide between the different ideas.

Participation and architecture

4
See Teresa Hoskyn's chapter in this book.

The participative political process in Porto Alegre[4] in Brazil is one of the most famous examples of participative processes: however, nobody really knows what constitutes a participative process. It is about changing representation: both political and the representation of the urban fabric through participation. The second representation is the realm of the architect, spatial representation. Architects have the ability to show that space is also movement, and that you can create liberty within space, can be useful in participatory processes. However, such involvement can lead to monetary problems as in France, because architects are paid only for what they build.

It is important to note that participation is *not* just a form of 'agora' that gathers people together to make a common decision. It must be a dialogue about differences, and about differences as production, even if this leads to confrontation. It must be a search for collaboration that can change representation to produce new differences and new dialogues. In contrast to what is always said about these processes, it is not about identity and rediscovering a common origin, but about creating and sharing a common space. Participative processes searching for a common identity tend to be quite conservative, and may be split by any event.

What is important is that representation, either political or spatial, is about something invisible, the abstract plan on which lines of desires cross, in which our lives are rooted. We have to build this plan, to make it more visible by participative processes, collective dialogues, sharing of knowledge. With new technologies such as the Internet, the processes of inclusion may be much larger than before, because they used to involve only the people who were physically there, but with new technologies you can now input people who are very far away. I take from Guattari the term '*plan de consistance*', a consistency of plan where things work together side by side; the word plateaux is an image of that. *Plan of consistency* is perhaps a little abstract but produces a collective setting within which it is possible to create together, without reference to specific fields of action.

Representing the invisible within society

New forms of representation for the invisible have to be found. The invisible used to be, perhaps, the revolutionary working class, which you met only on strikes and in demonstrations. Today in France the working class has become even more invisible. Social movements attract minorities with no common social capital, except the sharing of knowledge and intelligence. The new revolutionary subject seems to appear only in participatory processes, in gatherings, in digital exchanges.

In the former heavy industry there was a core of well-paid people: the managers, the researchers, etc., and they externalised things done by people who were invisible, people doing the washing, cleaning and repairing jobs. Then the only society with a right to speak was a society reduced to its core within the various sectors. No working class, no poor workers, no homeless, no students in the visible side of politics. How can architects make visible the invisible, create the new space to bring freedom? How can they begin to conceive this space?

This is a question about vision in architecture, and the vision within professionalism. It is not about competence, but about introducing into the profession some language that has not yet arisen there spontaneously. Inhabitants have their own building traditions, especially if they come from foreign countries. In France this has been overwhelmed by the desire to make a homogenous society. However, the memory is still there, despite the idea that it could be repressed and made invisible. These traces of history need to be captured by architects in both diverse and common settings.

The local now includes the global within it, and this can come out through collective development, not only through building, because building is limited to representing a certain moment in time. The language of space can nonetheless create more freedom than spoken language, so the subject of architecture and participation is very important.

City/democracy:
retrieving citizenship

> The forums of public life, like the city, are in a state of decay.
> Richard Sennett, *The Fall of Public Man*, 1986

In 'The urban question', an interview with *La Société Française* in 1989, Henri Lefebvre describes the transformation of Paris. He argues that whereas city centres used to be places of decision-making, the last thirty years have seen a transformation in European cities: 'only a few years ago Paris was virtually abandoned and then reoccupied in an elitist fashion'. He describes Paris city centre as 'museumified' and managerial, in a financial and not political sense, with the centre full of French and foreign tourists who come to look at the museums and recently built buildings. He states that the city appears to be lively but asks the question if it is 'lively in urbanistic terms'.[1] Lefebvre here is describing a very recent transformation to cities that has completely changed the meaning of the city and the citizen. For if the city centre is museumified, it implies that the city is fixed and will remain the same regardless of people's participation. The word citizen comes from the Latin, meaning 'member of a city'; to become a tourist when entering the centre of the city implies that one is not a member of the city, having the effect of placing citizenship somewhere else and therefore transforming one's political engagement with the city.

The theory of museumification in city centres can be applied to many Western cities, where the fashion for public buildings being design statements, with an emphasis on form, can be seen as part of a process where public buildings are becoming like museum exhibits. The Millennium Dome in London by Richard Rogers and the Jewish Museum in Berlin by Daniel Libeskind are two examples of new public buildings that all experienced the same problem after building – that of 'what to put inside them'. This raises a lot of questions to do with participation and the public realm, as these spaces are seemingly built with little idea of how the public will participate in them. While looking at Daniel Libeskind's Jewish Museum in Berlin, which centres around a series of voids, architectural theorist Anthony Vidler describes a sense of nostalgia; nostalgia for politics,

[1] H. Lefebvre, 'The urban question', in *H. Lefebvre: Writings on Cities*, trans. E. Kofman and E. Lebas, Oxford: Blackwell, 1996.

for the subject, for identity, for gender. He asks if the spatial world heralded by modernism is already lost, replaced by what he describes as the post-spatial void, 'a world that has little need for the human in the first place'.[2] In conversation with Libeskind, Jacques Derrida sees Libeskind's void as a space that excludes politics:

> The logic of the void space is the logic of a 'circumscribed emptiness' that excludes itself from the compromising realms of political and ontological visibility and discourse, whose exclusionary powers its exclusivity cuts off.[3]

Like the museum exhibit, Libeskind's void is sealed and non-negotiable, it attempts to remove the compromise that makes the future open and indeterminate, the very qualities that are central to democracy. It is not void of power relations as in the 'empty place' that becomes empty through multiple participation, enabling people to act freely and for political action.[4] On the contrary, Libeskind's void is filled with a dominant power that excludes them. On visiting Norman Foster's City Hall, the home of the new Greater London Authority, I was surprised to see that the building was largely made up of yet another void. Surely this is a building that should be about democracy – yet the void does have a role and that is to give the pretence of openness. Pretence because the meetings of the Assembly are not open meetings. The glass in which the building is clad gives an impression of democratic transparency – a pretence because it is not possible to stand outside and know what is happening in the Assembly room. The Greater London Authority itself cannot offer any spaces to the Forum: all space will have to be privately rented. We have discovered that London literally doesn't have official public space for political life.

At some point architecture and democracy have separated. In Ancient Greek and Roman societies the city and politics were the same: to the Greeks, the opposite of 'political' was 'private' or 'self-interested'. Unlike participatory politics today, political in ancient times referred to what was common and to what concerned everybody (with the exception of slaves and many women). The *polis* of the free and equal referred to citizens and to the parts of the city that were common. For Noelle McAfee, the Greeks were said not to think of the self as substance. The self was only as strong as the polity to which it belonged. She even goes as far as saying 'for the Greeks the city produced citizen-selves'. In contrast, the contemporary view of politics is based on the modern self being discrete, atomistic and autonomous. This view, she argues, puts us in a position of antagonism and clashing interests. Instead of seeing ourselves as overlap-

2
A. Vidler, *Warped Space: Art, architecture, and anxiety in modern culture*, Cambridge, MA: MIT Press, 2000.

3
M. Beechler, *On the Circumcisions of Architecture: Libeskind/Derrida*, paper given at the International Philosophy and Literature Conference, Rotterdam 2002, based on D. Libeskind, *Radix-Matrix: Architecture and writings*, New York: Prestel, 1997.

4
T. Hoskyns, 'The empty place of power', *Scroope, Cambridge Architecture Journal*, 2002.

5
N. McAfee, *Habermas, Kristeva, and Citizenship*, p.8, Ithaca, NY: Cornell University Press, 2000.

6
See M. Dillon and L. Garland, *Ancient Greece: Social and historical documents from archaic times to the death of Socrates (c.800-399 BC)*, London, New York: Routledge, 1994. Fragmented reports on the assemblies show the importance of public building within the city where, for example, much discussion was given to the building of the Parthenon and the infrastructure of Athens.

7
Some committees in Porto Alegre are delegatory but, unlike representative modern democracies, they will be from civil society organisations as well as from political parties.

8
T. Butcher, 'Direct participation in urban regeneration', paper given at the Contemporary Political Studies annual conference 1997. See also the Urban White Paper 2000 (*www.odpm.gov.uk*) and the Urban Summit 2002 (*www.urbansummit.gov.uk*) for UK government policy.

9
D. Trend, *Radical Democracy: Identity, citizenship, and the state*, p.9, New York, London: Routledge, 1996.

ping with the community and environment, and seeing that our communities are constructive of our being, we see ourselves as fixed and exclusive, with the community and others becoming sites of struggle.[5]

There was thus almost a shared meaning for public, political and city. The *polis* could be said to have been built by the citizens both politically and physically. Public buildings and spaces were places that citizens occupied and socialised, and where decisions including those about the city were made.[6] The citizens formed the public realm and, as it strengthened, the city flourished. A common argument against direct democracy in cities today is that cities have become so much bigger that direct democracy is impossible because there are too many people; however, as I will show later with the example of Porto Alegre, participatory democracy can work on all levels, from a neighbourhood to a global level, showing that a democratic city can be any size.[7]

It is accepted by all three major political parties in the UK that inner city problems such as urban decay, poor environment, unemployment, high crime rates and general social exclusion are important aspects of the late twentieth-century modern society; the government policies relating to community participation in urban regeneration are in fact an attempt to remedy these problems.[8] But it is difficult to see how what appears to be a symptom of a lack of political public participation in common decision-making, not helped by years of neo-liberal governments, can be remedied when the same political ideology remains in place. For many reasons neo-liberalism creates a theoretical and ideological clash or contradiction with the notion of real participation within the public realm: not only are we seeing a privileging of the private realm and a reduction in the public realm through privatisation, but also the transfer of power to increasingly elitist political structures and business.

The question of participation has been central to political philosophy since its beginnings. One way of looking at democracy within political philosophy can be to use a participatory continuum. At one end lies communitarian democracy, including the views of Aristotle, Rousseau and Hegel, where citizens participate in the common decisions for the common good. Towards the other end lies liberal or modern democracy, including theorists such as Locke and Rawls, and at its extreme the complete exclusion of people from common decision-making. The liberal argument against democracy in the communitarian sense is seen as a restraint on freedom and civil liberty; people are literally too busy pursuing individual interests to participate in politics and communal decisions may restrict the private market.[9] At the centre of the liberal democratic ethos is

10

E. Laclau and C. Mouffe, *Hegemony and Socialist Strategy: Towards a radical democratic politics*, p. 172, London: Verso, 1985.

11

Mario Pianta, 'Parallel summits of global civil society', in H. Anheier, M. Glasius, and M. Kaldor, *Global Civil Society 2001*, p.169, Oxford: Oxford University Press, 2001.

12

Ibid., p.170.

13

N. Klein, *Porto Alegre, Brazil: 'Bad Capitalist! No Martini'*, www.alternet.org, 2002.

14

In Florence 2002 and Paris 2003, and forthcoming in London 2004.

15

B. Cassen, *Tout a commencé à Porto Alegre: Mille Forums Sociaux*, Paris: 1001 Nuits, 2003.

the notion of the autonomous individual motivated by self-interest and free choice. Liberty and freedom refer to the freedom of the market, with a belief that the market can self-regulate from within the private realm, and any state intervention is an attack on individual liberty.[10] As a result of this, we see in modern democracies a constant reduction in the public realm and in political participation, an increasingly impoverished *polis*.

In practice, direct democracy has become a form of resistance to elitist, and often non-democratically elected, forms of governance. One of the factors of globalisation is a change in decision-making from a national level to supranational level, with intergovernmental organisations such as the European Union (EU) and the World Trade Organisation (WTO), and informal supranational organisations such as G7/G8.[11] As the influence of these supranational organisations has grown, parallel summits practising direct participatory democracy have been initiated by civil society organisations to confront the new power represented at summits of states and intergovernmental organisations. The first parallel summit, The Other Economic Summit (TOES), was held in 1984 to coincide with a G7 summit, but it was the parallel summit and street protests at the meeting of the WTO in Seattle 1999 that marked a turning point in the history of parallel summits. For the first time the participants had 'both the arguments and the strength to disrupt the official summit', while the movement also caught the attention of the media and the public.[12]

Since Seattle, the movement has grown enormously, giving rise to the World Social Forum (WSF) in Porto Alegre, Brazil, for three years (2001-2003) and in Mumbai, India, in January 2004, where the people of Mumbai used what is described as participatory planning for the city during the forum. The WSF was developed as an alternative to the annual gathering of the World Economic Forum, made up of the top 1,000 corporations, world leaders and opinion-makers who usually meet in Davos, Switzerland.[13] The social forums started on a global level and then moved to a continental level, the Asian Social Forum and The European Social Forum,[14] and then finally moved to the national and local level.[15] But if we look at Porto Alegre, the city where the WSF started, the story is actually urban and local.

The struggle for democracy in Brazil followed what is known as the 'authoritarian period'. Authoritarianism took its central locus of power at city level through a process of modernisation and urbanisation, resulting in enormous growth of Brazilian cities between 1950 and 1980. Decisions taken at the time led to the removal of the lower income population to the outskirts of the city, areas that

16
L. Avritzer, *Civil Society, Public Space, Local Power: A study of the participatory budget in Belo Horizonte and Porto Alegre*, Civil Society and Governance Programme, Institute of Development Studies, 2000 (*www.ids.ac.uk/ids/civsoc*).

07.01 – Arundhati Roy and Noam Chomsky at the World Social Forum, Porto Alegre, 2003.

received practically no investment in infrastructure. These outlying suburbs were like shanty towns, with large areas left unpaved and scarce sanitation, schools and health centres.[16] It is argued that the marginalisation of these city districts incited the emergence of an autonomous and democratic civil society organised around demands for urban facilities and public services, and from this movement completely new forms of urban government emerged, including the renowned participatory budget system at Porto Alegre.[17]

17
A. Latendresse, *The Porto Alegre Participatory Budget: An innovative experiment in urban govern-ance*, Alternatives 1999 quoting R. Abers, 'Learning democratic practice : distributing government resources through popular participation in Porto Alegre, Brazil' in M. Douglass and J. Friedmann, *Cities for Citizens: Planning and the rise of civil society in a global age*, pp.39-65, Chichester: John Wiley, 1998.

18
R. Abers, 'Daring democracy: Porto Alegre Brazil', *The New Internationalist*, December 2002.

The participatory budget for Porto Alegre started after the Workers Party (PT) was elected into municipal office in 1989. The administration found a city deeply in debt, demands from the community for investment and no money to spend. Faced with this situation, the new PT mayor decided that he would follow the party policy of participation; decisions involving the city budget would be participatory and transparent and the poor neighbourhoods would get priority.[18] The participatory budget is defined as a process designed to promote sound, transparent management by involving city residents in decision-making on budget allocations. Each neighbourhood decides on the priorities for that neighbourhood. Paving has been one of the big priorities for people in poor neighbourhoods because it is paving that defines a poor neighbourhood from a rich one; since the introduction of the participatory budget, the citizens have paved thousands of metres of streets. Rural communities directly control budgets for transport, social housing, education and rubbish disposal. Civil society councils, which govern together with elected government officials, control universal health care, reforestation, water reclamation, recycling, transport and

public safety programmes. The citizens of Porto Alegre have increased the proportion of the budget spent on the public parts of the
city from 2 per cent in 1989 to 30 per cent in 1999. They have completely transformed the quality of life in Porto Alegre, taking it from
slums to make it the most liveable city in Brazil and even Latin
America.[19]

Critics of 'participatory democracy' say that this form of decision-making is very time-consuming and inefficient, whereas with
'representative democracy' it is possible to make quick decisions;
they also say that it is practically impossible for all decisions made
by leaders to be popular and agreed by everybody and that a more
participatory democracy would consequently lead to what is known
as 'tyranny of the masses'. But as far as the city is concerned, participatory democracy creates a vibrant, cared-for and political public
realm.

From this urban movement the citizens of Porto Alegre have
participated in creating one of the greatest challenges to the world
political order through hosting the World Social Forum. The WSF,
described in its charter of principles as a 'public space', is open to all
individuals and organisations opposed to neo-liberalism and the
domination of the world by capital.[20] In 2003, 100,000 people participated in the five-day forum. The WSF took over every available
public space in the city by providing its own temporary infrastructure of meeting rooms, food courts, information points, Internet
cafés, press rooms and so on. The city was covered in civil society
stalls which meant it was possible to talk with participating organisations. The university, the docklands, and the sports stadiums
were all taken over for political meetings that ranged in size from
thousands of people in some of the big plenaries to workshops and
seminars of various sizes. Five warehouses in the docklands were
used as discussion spaces for each of the five continents, creating in
effect a temporary multipolar world parliament. The programme
for the Forum was the size of a tabloid newspaper, with the discussion based on five themes including 'civil society' and the 'public
realm'. Much of the discussion was on democracy; the former mayor
of Porto Alegre, Raul Pont, gave a talk on 'representative' and 'participatory' democracy. He argued that the roots of representative
political systems are found in the constitutional regimes of modern
states and that the individual subjects in the modern states only
'hold' rights but don't really exert them, and this far from qualifies
them as full citizens in the original sense of the word.

This debate expresses the distinct interests of classes and fractions of
classes in the passage of a society of small producers, artisans and

19
M. Strand Rangers, *Report on the World Social
Forum, Porto Alegre Brazil*, 2001. Contribution
to *http://lists.essential.org*

20
See WSF Charter of Principles,
www.forumsocialmundial.org.br

21
R. Pont, *Representative and Participatory Democracy, www.portoalegre2003.org*

farmers from the feudal yoke, to the consolidation of a new dominant elite typical of capitalism.[21]

One of the ongoing discussions of the WSF organised by HIC, Habitat International Coalition, and the National Forum of Urban Reform (FNRU) in Brazil, is about the realisation of a charter of principles on rights to the city, where the first principle is the full exercise of citizenship.

Recently I have returned to London's new City Hall, this time as a citizen, to an open meeting where we discussed the European Social Forum coming to London. One of the main problems of the ESF coming to London is the problem of space, with much of the public space in London, including the Dome and sports halls, having been privatised. The Greater London Authority cannot offer any spaces to the Forum. We have discovered that London literally does not have the recognised space for political public life. Participation in architectural design and planning, particularly in regeneration projects, can often be a smokescreen for privatisation. If architects and planners are thinking about real participation, they should be thinking both spatially and politically about developing the role of people as citizens, instead of as users, and about increasing, not decreasing, the public realm. The participatory budget in Porto Alegre means that citizens decide how the city budget is spent. This is very different from the types of community consultation in the early stages of regeneration projects seen in the UK, where participants have very little real power. Porto Alegre shows us that decisions on public spending made in participatory political structures are likely to favour spending on everyday improvements to living in the city over big design statements, and this may not favour the architect. Through taking control of our city's environments as citizens, however, we will be able to make the decisions that shape our future and quality of life for ourselves.

Another future is possible.

Histories of participation

Sixty-eight and after

1
His electioneering slogan of 1959, see E. J. Hobsbawm, *Age of Extremes: The short twentieth century 1914–1991*, London: Michael Joseph, 1994, p.257.

2
Ibid.

3
Ibid.

4
Notable examples were the satirical review *Beyond the Fringe* through which Peter Cook, Dudley Moore, Jonathan Miller and Alan Bennett became household names, the musical *Oh! What a Lovely War*, the television satire shows *That Was The Week That Was* and *Monty Python's Flying Circus* and Lindsay Anderson's film *If*, a savage attack on the public school ethos.

5
On the 1960s, see B. Miles, *In the Sixties*, London: Jonathan Cape, 2002, and S. Levy *Ready, Steady, Go: Swinging London and the invention of cool*, London: Fourth Estate, 2002. On the theory of structural reversal, see V. Turner, *The Ritual Process: Structure and anti-structure*, Chicago: University of Chicago Press, 1969.

6
For a cross-section of left-wing opinion at the time, see D.G. Cooper, *The Dialectics of Liberation*, Harmondsworth: Pelican Books, Penguin, 1968, papers from a conference held at the Round House, London, in the previous year.

7
For example, the special number of the *RIBA Journal* titled in red *Crisis in Architecture*, edited by Malcolm McEwen, 1969.

The Prague Spring and international student protest, especially May in Paris, marked out 1968 as a social and political watershed. It came at the peak of a golden age of economic prosperity, remembered in Britain with Harold Macmillan's famous phrase: 'You've never had it so good'.[1] It seemed all the brighter later, for with the depression of the early 1970s and the OPEC oil crisis of 1973, economic confidence collapsed and a more pessimistic spirit prevailed. The events of 1968 demonstrated the power of the new youth culture. Young people were more numerous in the universities than ever before, and also had greater disposable income, which was reflected in the arrival of youth fashion and the rise of the pop music industry.[2] Post-war prosperity had brought full employment, while the welfare state offered a reliable safety net, so anxieties about passing exams, getting a job and climbing the social ladder were relaxed.[3] At the same time, outworn conventions and hierarchies of the social establishment were mocked and undermined, and a generation gap opened up.[4] The atmosphere was generous, egalitarian, and optimistic, but driven by the anti-structure of a drunken new year's eve party, a Dionysian moment of chaos between the order of the old and the order of the new.[5] The injustice of the Vietnam War – the first in history to be televised – loomed large, and draft-dodgers from the US raised consciousness across the world. For many, the presumed innocence of the New World was irrevocably lost, while the dark shadows of a European colonial past loomed larger. As world communications increased, race-prejudice became more unsustainable, economic dependency more glaringly obvious: that the First World had responsibility for the Third could not be avoided.[6] The Vietnam War also showed the horrific effects of new technology, countering the technocratic optimism of the space race. With the energy crisis of the early 1970s, an awareness of the planet's limits and the arrival of books like E. F. Schumacher's *Small is Beautiful* (1973), faith in technical progress as an inevitable good gave way to a nagging doubt.

By the late 1960s architecture had reached its own crossroads.[7] The Gropius-inspired modernist orthodoxy that had swept the world became moribund and bankrupt. Although it had been at first a liberation and an inspiration, the call to Functionalism opened the way to the blandest economically-driven utilitarianism – to buildings dominated by the production and assembly process. This was typified in the tower and slab blocks that sprang up everywhere to solve the housing crisis. In Britain the technical and aesthetic shortcomings were underlined by the Ronan Point disaster of 1969,[8] but many architects believed that the new dwelling forms were appropriate and based on rational argument, that people would accept them once they got used to them. If these buildings failed to meet the promise of masterworks like Le Corbusier's Unité d'Habitation, it was argued, this was due not to misconception, but to

8
See V. Bignell, G. Peters and C. Pym, *Catastrophic Failures*, Milton Keynes: Open University Press, 1977.

08.01 – Typical page spread from Rolf Keller's *Bauen als Umweltzerstörung* (Building as environmental destruction) 1973: the repetition of the same banal housing blocks across the world.

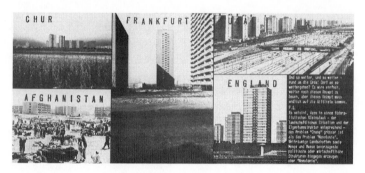

9
See, for example, Y. Friedman, *Toward a Scientific Architecture*, Cambridge, MA: MIT Press, 1972.

10
Tati's most ambitious film, involving the creation of huge and elaborate sets parodying Miesian architecture, shot between 1964 and 1967: see D. Bellos, *Jacques Tati*, London: The Harvill Press, 1999, pp.241–50.

11
CIAM meeting of 1933 led by Le Corbusier, discussed in De Carlo's essay.

12
Complexity and Contradiction in Architecture, New York: Museum of Modern Art, 1966, was the book by Robert Venturi that launched the postmodernist revolution.

compromise or restricted opportunities along the way. Aesthetic quality was somehow displaced onto a separate agenda, an almost irrelevant side issue, in favour of a supposed scientific stance.[9] The 'international style', as it had been called since 1932, was almost by definition placeless: the same thing repeated from city to city and for any and every purpose (Fig. 08.01). This tendency was powerfully satirised in Jacques Tati's films, especially *Playtime*.[10] The ubiquitous object-buildings also ignored the texture of the city, whose historic form, damaged by wartime bombs, was massacred all over again by road schemes and zoning policies handed down in the Charter of Athens.[11] The seemingly unmanageable complexity of the urban realm encouraged some architects to turn their back on the chaos, designing perfect islands of 'order in the desperate confusion of our time', to slightly misquote Mies. In reaction, calls for complexity and contradiction[12] and for a rediscovery of symbolism led in the 1970s to postmodernism and a fresh pillaging of history, but that took time and followed a more conservative attitude, as did the new attention to the city and new ideals of urban wholeness.

The mood of the late 1960s had been, by contrast, optimistic, utopian, egalitarian, and breathtakingly open. Anything could happen, and money did not seem to matter. As we arrived as students at the Architectural Association in 1966, Principal John Lloyd told us: 'I don't know what architecture is, it's up to you to find out', and we followed a very loose course, with far too much reinvention of the wheel. We were not taught by Cedric Price, but his spirit was ubiquitous. There did not have to be a building, we were taught: some kind of rethinking of the institution might do instead. You had to analyse the situation and make some brilliant leap of faith like

08.02 – Cedric Price: 'Think Grid' for Oakland, USA, as published in *Architectural Design*, June 1971, showing mobile 'information pods' and 'space mixer' in annotated drawings typical of Price.

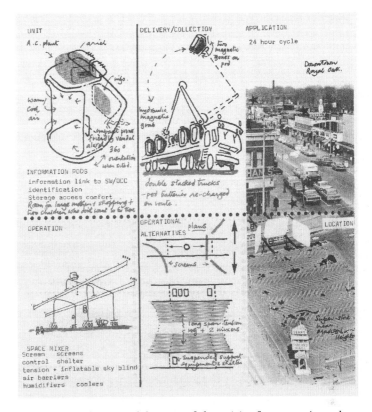

Price's Fun Palace, a celebration of the spirit of communitas, theatre as discovery; or his Potteries Thinkbelt, a travelling university on railway wagons (Fig.08.02). The Archigram group propagated the more image-driven 'Instant City', noticing pop festivals and borrowing the equipment of the travelling circus, while the Superstudio group in Italy posited the 'supersurface': a ubiquitous servicing grid to replace the entire built environment so that we could all become nomads. New technologies meant that old assumptions about communications, let alone about bricks and mortar, had to go. The main thing was the idea: captured by Price in those spidery sketches which show the promise without the drudgery, and which remain untainted utopia in an œuvre predominantly unbuilt.[13]

We did not draw nearly enough, as conceptual presentations were readily accepted, some of them almost entirely oral, and the AA was a far less visual place than it later became under Alvin

13
See S. Hardingham (ed.), *Cedric Price: Opera*, Chichester: Wiley, 2003.

14
The Architectural Association had its own
revolution in 1968, for after discussions
about a possible merger with Imperial
College broke down, Principal Lloyd
proposed running down and closing the
school. He was ousted and a new post of
Chairman created, to which Alvin Boyarsky
was appointed in 1969. Boyarsky created
international connections and launched a
series of world famous figures, but lost
English local authority funding.

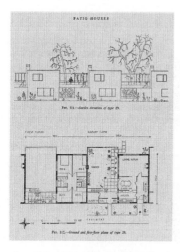

08.03 – W. Segal, 'Plan and Elevation of Terrace Houses'
published in *Home and Environment*, London: Leonard
Hill, 1948; 2nd edn 1955.

15
For biographical information on Segal, see
The Architects Journal, 4 May 1988, and for the
Segal method, *The Architects Journal*, 5
November 1988.

16
W. Segal, *Home and Environment*, London:
Leonard Hill, 1948; 2nd edn 1955.

Boyarsky, with his eye for the market and his smart exhibitions.[14] But towards 1968, an obsession with architecture's political implications made the consideration of measurable or buildable space for many trivial. The students' duty to right the wrongs of the world pushed them instead into a theoretical sphere, towards a calculation of new possibilities. A third aspect of Price's thinking, widely shared at the time, was his suspicion of institutions and the way they tend to consolidate their traditions in built form – Victorian buildings were scorned above all in the 1960s, overtly because of their borrowed styles, but perhaps more deeply because they represented so well the institutions of empire. History, largely cancelled by the Modernists, was now regarded as irrelevant. Price stressed the need for buildings to be flexible, to have age-limits and for inclusion at design stage of provision for demolition. He remained consistently outspoken in his opposition to the listing of historic buildings, seeing this as a damaging impediment to the natural growth of the city. As a member of the Labour Party (Old Labour – he was quick to remind us) and a committed socialist, Price relished the undermining of establishment hierarchies in favour of an egalitarianism whose new order should be allowed freely to express itself.

A contrasting figure also loosely connected with the AA and equally important for what follows was Walter Segal (1907-85).[15] Swiss-born and educated in Modernist Berlin in the 1920s, he had come to Britain as a refugee from Fascism in the 1930s, setting up a small practice and also starting to publish. First-hand experience of modernist housing experiments in Germany paid off when he threw himself into a long series of ingenious designs for every type of house, first serialised in *Architecture and Building News*, and later published as a book (Fig.08.03).[16] He must have hoped for substantial post-war commissions, but only small ones came, and he eked out his living from a one-man practice with teaching at the AA and a constant stream of publications. Taking at face value Modernist claims that the new architecture would arise out of new technological conditions, Segal was fastidious about solving issues of technical detailing, always on modestly priced projects. The switch in his career that brought him fame came in the mid-1960s, with the construction of a temporary house for his family's occupation while their own house in Highgate was being rebuilt. This little house, built for only £850 on a timber frame system almost without foundations, took its planning discipline from the sizes of materials available, using them uncut for later resale. Segal relished the challenge of the cheapest possible house, and his careful combination of mass-produced materials already on the market was a tacit critique of many stillborn systems invented by 'great architects'. Segal found himself with a more plausible 'temporary' house than he had anticipated: it stood until his death, and still exists. Seeing its potential as a self-build method, he started to offer it to clients in search of a low-budget house, and after small private projects had tested the system, it was adopted by the Borough of Lewisham for social housing (Fig. 08.04). The council provided site and materials, and volunteers on the local housing list built their own houses after an evening course of instruction from Segal. The method produced a strong sense of community even before construction was complete. For Segal, the participation of families brought social rewards that diverted his interest beyond the architecture, and he found satisfaction in the role of enabler exceeding that of a conventional practice increasingly beset with technical and bureaucratic hurdles.

08.04 – Walter Segal (left) talking to self-builders on a Lewisham site around 1978. (Photograph by Peter Blundell Jones.)

This attempt to recover a direct experience of people determining their own environment was a tiny and isolated experiment, yet in retrospect it is a symptom of its time. Segal's constant refrain was that one should 'free oneself' from this or that, and just as he tried to simplify the operations of the building site and reduce the number of drawings, so he also fought the tangle of red tape that restricts our activities and forces dependence on specialists before we take a step: bankers, lawyers, architects, builders. Against the top-down paternalist provision of housing under the modernist orthodoxy with everything predetermined, he offered a bottom-up self-realising pattern on its own scale and with its own logic, rediscovering a certain spontaneity. It promised not just a different landscape but a different way of life. The architectural historian Julius Posener – a fellow-student of Segal's in Berlin – made much of the

17
J. Posener, 'Memories of Segal', *The Architects Journal*, 4 May 1988, pp.38–41.

18
I follow the anthropologist Mary Douglas in the idea that dirt is matter out of place and thus as much a question of classification as of pathology: see M. Douglas, *Purity and Danger*, London: Routledge & Kegan Paul, 1966.

19
B. Zucchi, *Giancarlo De Carlo*, Oxford: Butterworth 1992, pp.26–38.

20
G. de Carlo, *Architecture's Public*

fact that one of the self-builders had imported a second-hand Victorian door against the architect's taste, but Segal calmly accepted it.[17] For many architects then and since, such violation of the integrity of a design is anathema, for they regard their imposition of aesthetic control as a right, a duty, and even a proof of competence. They fail to register the 'cultural and aesthetic class code' (to quote De Carlo) that such policing of style also undoubtedly is. Frequent claims by fellow professionals that Segal's work was 'not really architecture' reflected this violation of implicit codes of purity and professional good behaviour to indulge in what they could only regard as 'dirty architecture'.[18] Segal's work became an inspiration for several contributors in this book (i.e. Broome, Sulzer, Hübner).

Segal's anarchic, anti-authoritarian stance led to a slow revolution in his thinking which was approximately in gear with the events of 1968, if not exactly a part of them. Giancarlo De Carlo (b. 1919) also stood outside the established system, taking an independent and critical view, but he vigorously welcomed the events of 1968 as a sign of a major shift in attitude. Evidently he did not share the predominantly anti-historical stance of other 1968 revolutionaries: indeed it is precisely his ability to set the historical context that makes *Architecture's Public* (pp.3–22) still such a powerful and eloquent analysis. Born as a lecture in 1969 and published in 1970, this essay combines a critical but optimistic view of the 1968 student unrest with a swingeing critique of orthodox modernism. It is loaded with insider knowledge, reflecting De Carlo's role as one of the leaders of Team Ten, the breakaway group from the International Congresses of Modern Architecture that made the first coherent attempt to redefine the basis of the modernist project and to push it in new directions.[19] *Architecture's Public* has remained remarkably untarnished by the passage of a third of a century, and still offers an admirably concise and relevant statement about the political nature of architecture and the need for participation to re-empower the user:

> All barriers between builders and users must be abolished, so that building and using become two different parts of the same planning process. Therefore the intrinsic aggressiveness of architecture and the forced passivity of the user must dissolve in a condition of creative and decisional equivalence where each – with a different specific impact – is the architect, and every architectural event – regardless of who conceives it and carries it out – is considered architecture.[20]

De Carlo's critique undermined assumptions under which architects still operate today. Still deeply troubling, for example, is his revelation of the political nature of aesthetic decisions and questions of taste, which can no longer simply be innocently reserved to the architect or lightly be presumed to be universal. At around the same time that De Carlo was preparing his lecture, Philippe Boudon was writing *Lived-in Architecture*, about what happened to Le Corbusier's housing at Pessac (Fig.08.05).[21] The inhabitants had taken the master's provision of 1926 as a basis for further improvisation and *bricolage*, filling in spaces between pilotis, replacing *fenêtres en longuer* with narrow conventional ones, adding pitched roofs, murals, decoration and so on. The buildings proved wonderfully

21
P. Boudon, *Lived-in Architecture*, London; Lund Humphries, 1972.

22
See the essay, *Purism*, 1920, by Le Corbusier and Ozenfant, in R. L. Herbert (ed.), *Modern Artists on Art*, Englewood Cliffs, New Jersey: Prentice Hall, 1964.

23
P. Bourdieu, *Distinction: A social critique of the judgement of taste*, London: Routledge and Kegan Paul, 1984.

24
Note not only the departure from purity and Purism, but also the invasion of a chronological factor: the fact that settlements change and grow with their inhabitants. More of this below in relation to the work of Kroll.

08.05 – Housing at Pessac, Bordeaux, by Le Corbusier, 1926, with additions by the inhabitants, circa 1984. (Photograph by Peter Blundell Jones.)

convertible, but the changes completely undermined Le Corbusier's theory of Purism, his 'primary aesthetic' of universal good taste which was supposed to lie in pure geometric forms and primary colours.[22] The people of Pessac were not prepared to live under this image but remade it in their own way, according to their own values. It was not until later that Pierre Bourdieu demonstrated statistically the social basis of taste preferences,[23] but much of the groundwork had already been done. The importance of Boudon's book was that owners' alterations to the Pessac housing were taken seriously, and that the author dared to compare the people's expression with that of the master. Again it was dirty architecture, or rather dirtied architecture.[24]

De Carlo was always an architect as well as a theorist, and in his own work he attempted to put his ideas into action. Like his Team Ten colleague Aldo van Eyck, he stressed 'place' as opposed to 'space' and demanded respect for local context and region. His call for 'reading the territory' was exemplified in his own work through his sensitive re-planning of the city of Urbino, managing drastic changes of social usage while preserving – and even rediscovering – aspects of the historical context. De Carlo also made early and

08.06 – Housing on the island of Mazzorbo in the Venetian lagoon by Giancarlo De Carlo, 1986. Not only did De Carlo provide a harbour for the inhabitants' boats: the houses were modelled on local types and painted in bright colours following local tradition.

25
For Terni, see Zucchi, *de Carlo*; for Mazzorbo, see P. Blundell Jones, 'Lagoon grouping', *The Architectural Review*, July 1987, pp.21–7.

26
International Laboratory for Architecture and Urban Design, a summer school started by De Carlo and still running, set mostly in Urbino or Venice. It publishes a yearbook with Edizioni Quattro Venti, Urbino.

27
The best summary in English is Kroll's article 'The soft zone', published in *Architectural Association Quarterly*, vol. 7, no. 4, 1975, pp.48–59.

decisive explorations of user participation in housing, first with his steelworker's housing in Terni of 1968 which appears conventionally Modernist but allowed many user options within, and later in his more contextual housing at Mazzorbo in the Venetian Lagoon of 1986 (Fig.08.06).[25] In the latter project, De Carlo was already moving away from decision-making at an individual level and towards the definition of a local type involving the whole group – in other words to an exploration of the idea of a shared culture, which was intended to nurture the establishment of a community.

Lucien Kroll (b. 1927), a friend of De Carlo and participant at the summer school ILAUD,[26] made his reputation with a work that grew directly from the events of 1968: the Maison Médicale or Mémé at the University of Louvain on the outskirts of Brussels (Fig.08.07).[27] The university had already built a huge new hospital in the mechanistic and repetitive manner typical of that time, and were about to do the same with a hostel for the medical students when the students rebelled. Known locally for his interest in participation, Kroll was brought in by the students to lead a counter-project, and the intimidated authorities yielded the commission in a bid for peace. Kroll took the opportunity to experiment with a self-generating architecture, dividing the large programme among the staff in his office and developing its elements piecemeal, discussing everything with the future users. Rather than imposing a top-down masterplan, he used a physical model to document the developing design, with the rule that parties could only modify, never erase (Fig.08.08). The development became not only a reflection of the many needs and aspirations of the parties, but also a record of the evolving design process. Periodically, Kroll moved staff members from one

08.07 – Maison Médicale (Mémé) for the students of
the University of Louvain, outskirts of Brussels, 1971.
This anarchic-looking project managed by Lucien Kroll
marked a bold step in user participation and made his
reputation.

08.08 – The cumulative model through which Kroll and
his assistants allowed the Mémé to evolve. They were
only allowed to add and modify: 'You have to keep your
mistakes, nature does'. (L. Kroll)

group to another, so that they could not get too fond of a particular
element and assume authorship. The design process became a
voyage of discovery whose end remained unpredictable, and it
produced a building whose anarchic and anti-hierarchical image
flashed across the world. Contrast with the hospital next door
could scarcely have been starker: unified monotony versus creative
diversity.

Kroll also attempted to show how system building, then regarded as inevitable, could be used in a more humane way. He
developed a version of Habraken's modular grid to coordinate
assembly of mass-produced components,[28] showing how the system
could be played for maximum diversity instead of mindless repetition. This, and the early implications of computers in design and
production, were explained in Kroll's book *Composants* of 1985.[29] The
key to his work, however, is the recognition that the built world is a

28
Nicholas Habraken's system of 'supports'
and 'apports' was designed to allow flexibility: he has continued to develop his
theories about architecture as a series of
layers determined by different figures in a
hierarchy in his recent book *The Structure of
the Ordinary: Form and control in the built environment*, Cambridge, MA: MIT Press, 1998.

29
Published in English as L. Kroll, *The Architec-
ture of Complexity*, London: Batsford, 1986.
The German edition is called *CAD Architektur*.

landscape (*paysage*) that has always developed and changed, registering a diversity of interests. Lining people up in identical flats is like forcing them to wear uniform: it then takes an act of bravery even to paint the door a different colour.

Kroll has also been an outspoken critic of zoning. In several projects he advocated breaking an institution into its constituent parts, then linking them with a street or square which is given back to the public realm.[30] For example, the expanding School of Dance in Utrecht was intending to move to a new building in the suburbs, but Kroll recommended dividing the accommodation between two city centre buildings converted for the use.[31] Students would walk down the street from one to the other as they moved from class to class, part of the life of the city rather than being banished to the educational ghetto of an out-of-town campus. A further aspect of Kroll's work is his commitment to ecological issues, reflected among other things in an experimental ecological centre at Belfort and a school in France built to the toughest of environmental agendas.[32] But as readers will note from the text of his Sheffield lecture (see pp. 183-6), his whole œuvre resonates with the idea that architecture is always inevitably a political act, every new building a mediation of social relations. The architect's role is to read the local and social context, acting as intermediary and guide, while letting the process express itself.

Eilfried Huth (b. 1930) is a direct inheritor of Kroll's ideas and has pursued them sometimes to a more grass-roots level (see pp. 141–7). As partner in an internationally known office with Günther Domenig, he was one of the instigators of the New Graz Architecture, an architectural movement based in Austria's second city that became internationally famous in the 1980s and 1990s.[33] Domenig and Huth invited Kroll to Graz to lecture at city's school of architecture, along with his friend the Swiss architect Christian Hunziker, another pioneer of participation. This sowed the seed for a long series of participative projects within the Graz movement following the Modell Steiermark housing programme.[34] Huth became the local leader and spokesperson for participation and started his own most radical project, the Eschensiedlung at Deutschlandsberg, in 1972. He claims that it was the combination of the student revolt of 1968 and the oil crisis of 1973 that caused him to take this radical change of direction, breaking his partnership with Domenig in 1975. As is evident from his essay (see pp. 141-7), he is one of the few architects with the generosity genuinely to let things develop according to the ideas of the user, concentrating on the people and the process rather than the product, and allowing it to become what it will.

30
Both in an unrealised brewery project, with elements spread across the town, and at the Technical College in Belfort, where the open square which unites the departments is public: see 'Kroll's open school', *The Architectural Review*, March 1987, pp.63-8.

31
See 'Kroll drama', *The Architectural Review*, November 1989, pp.55-8.

32
See 'Green gauge', *The Architectural Review*, November 1996, pp.71-3 and 'Sustainable school', *The Architectural Review*, January 2002, pp.69-73.

33
P. Blundell Jones, *Dialogues in Time: New Graz architecture*, Graz: HdA, 1998.

34
Ibid. pp.86-8. They made a rule that any housing development comprising over 50 dwellings had to be put out to competition.

08.09 – Typical houses at the Eschensiedlung Deutschlandsberg, Styria (south of Graz) 1972 onward. Architect Eilfried Huth did his best to allow each family to develop their house according to their own needs and preferences, and no two have the same floor plan.

Peter Sulzer (b. 1932) and Peter Hübner (b. 1939) were both pioneers in the new technology of the 1960s: Sulzer as the designer of concrete components for Camus, Hübner for bathroom pods, kiosks and tropical building systems in plastics for Staudenmayer. Both had therefore experienced the advantages and the drawbacks of system building, particularly the problem mentioned by Sulzer that 'I never saw or spoke to a real user' (p.149). As a man of the left and a longstanding member of the Peace Movement, Sulzer claims he would never have gained his chair at the Technical University in Stuttgart in 1969 but for student support following the events of 1968. He was able to prepare the way for Peter Hübner, and by the late 1970s they were teaching courses together in building construction. Learning of Walter Segal's work through publications, they invited him to lecture at Stuttgart, and started to build experimental structures on campus using his system. Having produced some habitable rooms, the idea arose that they might build a whole student hostel, in which the students would become designers, then builders and finally inhabitants. With extraordinary energy and against countless obstacles the ironically named *Bauhäusle* (little

08.10 – 'Bauhäusle' on the Vaihingen campus of Stuttgart University, a student hostel designed and built by architectural students under the leadership of professors Sulzer and Hübner, as photographed by the author when nearing completion in 1983. It outlived its 15-year allotted lifespan and community spirit persists generations of students later, and across disciplines: in 2003 only one inhabitant was studying architecture.

Bauhaus) which started in 1980 was completed in 1983 (Fig.08.10), a cacophony of rooms in different styles and materials, mostly designed by first-year students.[35] The experience transformed everybody, for the students were able to test and enact their ideas at unprecedented scale, and to see how materials and details performed. But the building was much more than a materials laboratory and more than a temporarily usable hostel: it immediately gained a community atmosphere unrivalled by the best architect-imposed hostel, and this has carried on through generations of students over twenty years. For both Sulzer and Hübner it marked a turning point in their careers, as both became involved in further self-build projects, Sulzer in the substantial Youth-choir building in Landau (see pp.155-8), and Hübner on an endless string of youth clubs, hostels, primary schools, sports-halls and even larger complexes. This œuvre will soon have a monograph to itself,[36] but we include here one relatively recent project which shows developments in Hübner's methods (pp.161-79).

Hübner's early self-build projects were very hands-on and necessarily local, requiring great expenditure of time and energy by the architects. It first seemed unlikely that they could work at a national level because of the close supervision needed for such projects, and also because the German competition system seemed to preclude a participative process, demanding a *fait accompli* and precluding dialogue with the client. Hübner has won several competitions in the conventional way, but for the Gelsenkirchen school competition of 1993, part of the IBA Emscher Park development, he tried a different idea. It was supposed to be both an ecological school and a catalyst for reviving a socially deprived area, so rather than proposing an instant building, Hübner suggested a regenerative

35
See P. Blundell Jones, 'Student self-build in Stuttgart', *The Architects Journal*, 27 July 1983, pp.32-50.

36
P. Blundell Jones, *Peter Hübner – Building as a social process*, Stuttgart: Edition Axel Menges, 2004.

process. He sketched how it might work only in very general terms, but the drawings were accompanied by a fictional narrative. This was Kemal Özcül's speech on the occasion of receiving the European Environmental Prize in 2034 (reproduced on pp. 161-71). The son of poor Turkish immigrants, he had attended the school in Gelsenkirchen as a small child starting in 1994, and it had completely changed his life. The story charts the progress of designing and building the school, enacting its ecological policies, being inspired by a school-master nicknamed 'Eco', his family taking part in the development of self-build housing adjacent, and so on. As an adult, Kemal tells how he went on to do the ecological work for which he had won his European prize, so he owed everything to the school.

The competition jury missed Hübner's proposal in their initial selection, but when trying to penetrate beyond the parade of seductive images, were dissatisfied to find so little clue of how the designs would meet the ideals of the brief. Then one of the judges found Kemal's story on the reject pile and asked the others to read it. Was this not precisely what they were looking for? They ended up giving Hübner the prize and the school has been built. The open-endedness of the design left plenty of room for a real debate with the head, staff and pupils in preparation for the executed one. Stack-effect ventilation and ground cooling were incorporated, along with other energy measures which have become a regular part of Hübner's armoury, so it has ecological credentials. The money being readily available, much of the complex was built promptly with normal contractors, but Hübner injected diversity by assigning parts to various members of his office as Kroll had with the Mémé. The classroom blocks, however, are being designed by staff and pupils and added on a yearly basis, so the school grows and changes. Are there any Kemals there? Only time will tell.

Fragments of participation in architecture, 1963–2002: Graz and Berlin

Architecture is an instrument of mediation and of translation: it lies at the intersection between the collective and the individual, characterised by the relevant social and local environment. Architecture satisfies people's most elementary and most basic needs. Above all, however, architecture makes its presence felt; it is intrinsically and explicitly experimental. It is material, it offers itself to the senses in many ways: through smell, sounds, feelings, through its breadth or narrowness. It is about space, non-space, comfort and discomfort. The process of participation in self-help housing has almost become like a vocation. It is much more than a job.

My first experiment in self-help housing was the project 'Zellflex' of 1963-1965, to be built in Zeltweg with a prefabricated primary structure. This project was dropped before it could be realised.

Under the influence of Yona Friedman and later of the group Archigram, we started our own vision of a new town 'Stadt Ragnitz'

09.01 – Eilfried Huth and Günther Domenig, project for 'Stadt Ragnitz' 1965-9, a three-dimensional structural and servicing framework that could be inhabited in various ways.

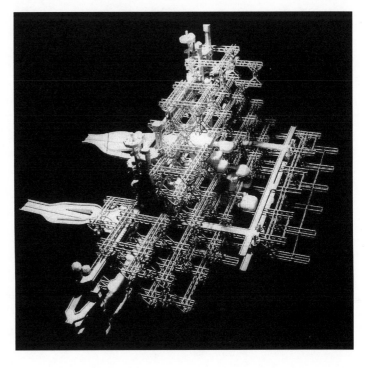

of 1965-69. In 1969 it won the Grand Prix International d'Urbanisme et Architecture in Cannes. Members of the jury included Louis Kahn, Henri Lefebvre, Makowsky, Jean Prouvé and Heikki Siren. Reyner Banham wrote in 1976:

> Not only did the Ragnitz scheme win the Grand Prix, but the very large model they (Huth/Domenig) built of it travelled to exhibitions in different parts of the world until it finally fell to pieces.[1]

1

R. Banham, *Megastructure: Urban futures of the recent past*, London: Thames & Hudson, 1976.

09.02 – Stadt Ragnitz: Close-up of model showing supporting structure and added 'pods'.

In fact, we had the model rebuilt in 2001 for the museum FRAC in Orleans. It consisted of a primary structure in steel or concrete and an added system of services and circulation. Within the frame were standard voids for occupation by dwellings, like artificial building plots. These artificial plots determined the volumes of the flats. For this we designed one special type – type X. Elements of the flat volumes (type X) are the KONZENT-POD (relaxation studio) and the HYGIOBILE (bathroom), here shown in a model and a construction sketch. Banham commented:

> Through the system were threaded vertical multiplex clusters of circulations (goods, passengers, services), horizontal ducts, roads and parking levels reached by expressways... In its complete form (which I never saw, alas) it was the richest, fullest, most complete academic mega model ever built, surpassing even Archigram's Control and Choice model.[2]

2

Ibid.

It was a dream, but we awoke to the reality. We saw on the one hand the devastation of the landscape through thousands of free standing houses – my home is our chaos – and on the other the desolation of high rise blocks of flats in the West and in the East.

We saw financial centres (like Frankfurt), headquarters of globalism, and at the same time native villages of the poor. We saw pictures of hunger and death. The darkness of globalism… millions of victims… The system of globalism is the 'new feudalism' of the multinationals, still dominated by male power today.

The effect of globalism is that a minority gets richer and richer, while the majority become poorer and poorer. One European citizen has the income of 300 inhabitants in most African countries. And so terrorism is often the result of rage and powerlessness. I think the future must lie with female power.

All ideas in housing had already been explored in the twenties of the last century. The one-family house is nearly everybody's dream (in Austria: 80 per cent), perhaps because it seems to offer individuality and identity, especially when built in the countryside. Individuality and identity in the city are by contrast an anonymous and independent feeling, so the city is often the compensation for the one-family house. But the dream to own a house remains a widespread ambition.

This dream is a mainspring of tourism.

Participation in housing has a wide range for different actions. The function of an element (inhabitant fE), the function of the sum of all elements (fEs) and the function of the system (fS) in relation to information (A), education (B) and consciousness (C) of the elements and the activities (partake, decide for, participating and suffering), brings more than 30 points of view.

09.04 – Eschensiedlung: site plan.

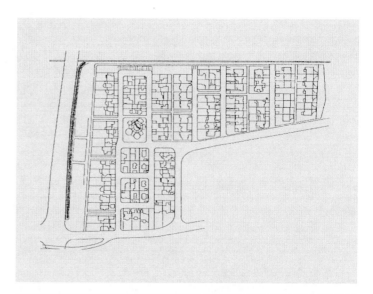

09.05 – Eschensiedlung: floor plans showing variations possible within the system.

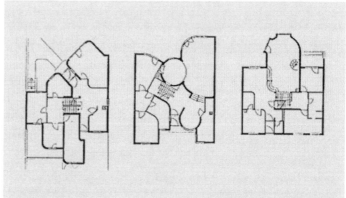

09.06 – Eschensiedlung: future inhabitants discuss a model of their future dwelling place.

09.07–09.09 (above) – Eschensiedlung: typical houses showing the freedom of expression allowed to the inhabitants.

Eschensiedlung

Our first and in some ways most radical participative scheme, the Eschensiedlung at Deutschlandsberg, dates from 1972-92. This was the pioneering example from which nearly all later participative housing in Graz took its cue. The innovation was as much political as architectural. The future inhabitants of 16-18 houses got together to form a building society, electing a building committee and chairman. There was participation in the design at every level, from deciding the overall plan in discussion with the local authority, to detailing the individual dwellings. Most of the houses were of a two-storey terrace-type with small gardens behind but some courtyard houses were also included in central locations. No two house plans are the same, and some are radically different from their neighbours.

The development was socially very mixed, from artisans to company directors, fortunately without visible hierarchical ranking. Although it was a bold and significant experiment, the great variety and specificity of the houses have helped to create a strong sense of place and a strong identification between the owners and their property.

With an architect's guidance the owners were able to make decisions about doors, windows and cladding materials, and finally also about the colours on the outsides of their houses.

09.10 & 09.11 – Housing in Graz-Puntigam, block model and finished houses.

Participative housing in Graz-Puntigam 1976-82

The next experiment in the same process as the Eschensiedlung

Because people joined in a group before it was built and experienced the process together, they got to know one another and created a real community long before it was finished. Some participated in the construction, other started to work on their gardens as soon as the main walls had been laid: they met on the site and had impromptu meals together.

09.12 – Discussion between clients and architect about Graz-Puntigam, with exploratory floor plans on the blackboard behind.

09.13 – Mimi Algersdorf, Graz, 1982-84. Participation of poor tenants in social housing process.

09.14 – Housing at Graz-Ragnitz, view of garden side, showing the varying use of the projected balcony.

Housing at Graz-Ragnitz
Participation of the owners (84 split-level flats)

The development at Ragnitz, a new suburb on virgin ground on the north-east outskirts of Graz, was completed by Huth's office in 1992. It was financed by a building society and the dwellings are being sold on to the owner-occupiers. The project began as a competition in 1986, the brief requesting a site layout and notional housing types, but no detailed design.

Participation is a matter of information, and especially of education. We must begin in the schools. We have carried out experiments of education in the aesthetics of housing in several different school-types: at an elementary school in Graz, at a high school in Graz and at the School of Arts in Berlin.

The experiments with school children ran through four stages:
1 Analysis of the general situation in housing today.
2 Ranking of the positive and negative effects.
3 Discussion within the group.
4 Envisaging a design for their own homes.

09.15 – Model building with pupils at the Hauptschule Deutschlandsberg, Graz during stage 4 of the eduction experiment.

And the programme with university students ran as follows:
1 Analysis of the general situation in housing today.
2 Design of a housing construction with different types of flats.
3 Every student designed a flat in a process of participation
    – once as an architect and once as a future user.
4 Discussion within the group and production of documentation.

Architecture provokes debate about the protection of human feelings and sensitivities, for planning involves organising such protection. If we are to support this human feeling – a matter of sense perception – our planning process must include some recognition of it: in other words it must involve the aesthetic. Mediation in planning therefore focuses on issues in the organisation of the aesthetic, such as the importance of the place, the proposed use, and the means of construction available, but with a necessary scepticism. In our teaching about the planning of buildings we aim, through the help of mediation, to achieve a spiritual matrix that permits us to work with the subjective organisation of the aesthetic.

Notes on participation [1]

1
This is the text of a lecture given at the
University of Sheffield, 16 April 2002.

In opening I should say that I do not regard participation in architectural design as the solution to world problems, and the projects
I am about to show you are but a small part of my life. Many of my
projects were standard architectural practice, that is to say with no
participation whatsoever. But in due course I shall present some
examples which stress the aspects of user participation and the
changing role of the professional, of the architect and the engineers. You will see that each project is different depending on the
conditions and the participants. In most cases I was the only architect, working alone doing all the drawings and specifications, and
always accepting responsibility both for the process and the result.

In the mid-1960s, I was head of a development group financed
by the building industry which had the task of developing a precast
concrete frame system, a simple affair. This frame was manufactured
in ten different factories belonging to two different companies. The
priorities at the time – as also in Great Britain – were speed and economy. As regards participation, what did we do? We tried to provide
flexible buildings, but I have no idea how well they worked: I never
saw or spoke to a real user. We built these so-called multi-purpose
buildings one hundred metres long, nine storeys high with stairs
and lifts. There was no specific space design, just the hope that
future users could arrange their offices. No participation at all!

A more recent project at Mutlangen could hardly be more
different. The Peace Movement was demonstrating in front of an
American base. The initial constructions were not my design: they
were just done by the people themselves, I don't know who. There
was always trouble with the police, so speed was of the essence – to
get the construction up overnight. When the police came, the building was already there: the user himself was 'architect'. Then the
Peace Movement managed to buy a construction site right opposite
the base. Together with two architect colleagues we planned a Peace
Centre. How can the Peace Movement participate in the design
process of a building like that? With ten thousand members it is
impossible. But it was vital that we discussed it with some members, if not all. The dominant considerations were speed, low cost

and self-build. People stayed overnight in sleeping bags, so this became part of the programme. We chose an octagonal plan, which has a special meaning in the peace movement, because it recalls the chapel at Frankfurt airport where there were battles between the Movement and the authorities. The project was delayed by legal struggles, and by the time we got the building permit in court the Pershing missiles had gone, so it lost its *raison d'être* and was never built.

The Segal method

10.01 – Peter Sulzer (right) with Walter Segal, late 1970s. (Photograph by Erika Sulzer-Kleinemeier.) For Segal method, see p.70 and for photographs of his Lewisham self-build houses, see p.72 and 131.

A strong influence on my work was Walter Segal, especially his self-build method used at Lewisham. Segal's innovation was to invent a building method using a modular grid of roughly 60cm. You buy standard plasterboard and cut it once down the middle, then it is joined with a sandwich detail. He gave this tartan grid to the user, but I do not believe the users really decided the plans, for Segal was a very strict architect (practically he was hopeless: he could not put a nail into a board!). But he got the users to adopt his method, and his plan was absolutely perfect. I invited him to teach at Stuttgart, and we built a prototype attempting to adapt his method to German conditions. It was not a building system: it was a method. We could not get the wood sections sold in Britain, but a student found that sections of 2 x 12 inches were used in scaffolding.

After experiments with Segal we moved on to produce our student housing project (See Figs. 10.02-10.03). I am always asked if it is a model for repetition elsewhere, but it is unique. When I became professor in Stuttgart in 1969, I saw that colleagues in the engineering department had experimental sites, so I asked for one. It was granted immediately by the University President. This was quite normal: I had a neighbour in the foundation business who had building machines on site. Once you have a site on campus, you get to know the people in the building department. A second generative condition for the project was that for many years we had asked first year students to design their own rooms. In 1982 some told me they could not find rooms in Stuttgart, so why couldn't they build what they drew? Their passionate commitment was a vital catalyst. We were also fortunate to have an enlightened University President, who not only let us do it, but even wrote supporting letters and came to lay the foundation.

We have a semester system, and between semesters students are on vacation. During this interval I and my colleague Peter Hübner – who was very important in this project – made a kind of master plan to link the student rooms with communal facilities. We tried several versions before coming up with the final arrangement.

10.02 – Bauhäusle student hostel, plan of the central communal building offering kitchens and bathrooms, along with a corridor: this was the core of the development, based on the Segal construction system.

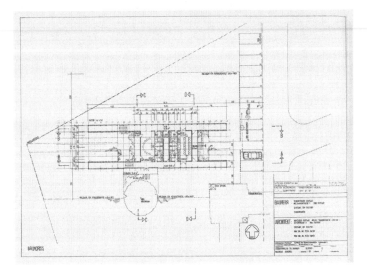

10.03 – Bauhäusle final plan, with groups of individual rooms added around the periphery and the tower-like structure by seniors to north-east. Photographs of the finished building can be found on p.138, 153 and 154.

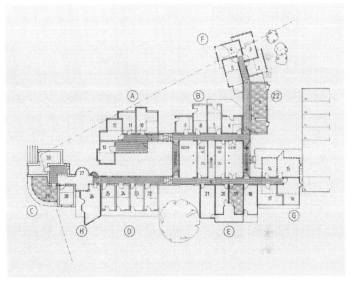

This is the macro structure for the project, with a central element that followed Walter Segal's method. The plan was based on two corridors, one each side of a communal block. We tried to minimise foundation work and service runs, so everything with water was put in the middle: two kitchens and four bathrooms. We kept the bedroom width to 2.84 metres on a modular system, so that a student going to the toilet at night had the shortest possible route; also the student association insisted that the corridors be enclosed. This restriction caused a revolution amongst the students, but as an architect you must insist on some things: to discuss everything would drive you crazy. We first intended to build twenty rooms, but in the end thirty were needed, all for first year students. The rooms were grouped in threes and fours to make 'houses' in between which were open gaps, so that they could be built independently. This also divided the responsibility, as the design development and execution of each house were controlled by one staff member. We begged materials off the building industry: one group got some roof tiles and another some asphalt felt. Each house therefore took on a different character. We built a mock-up in the entrance of the school for the students to study on their return. Participation changes the responsibility of the architect in many ways. Peter Hübner and I took on the role in this case, on top of the role of professor and total responsibility for the site. We had to discuss everything early with the administration before doing anything, but we found colleagues in the building administration open to the experiment. We made a building permit drawing outlining the general plan and the parts the students would build. Experimental buildings were limited to 4.5 metres, defined by a line. This was the condition set by the time the students returned.

10.04 – Models of the student dwellings exhibited in the university entrance hall.

The project ran parallel to my weekly lecture course, attended by 250 students in a big hall. The most difficult thing was to get the students to define precisely what they needed. What do you really need? You don't really need some spaces in a house: they are just used by spiders. We asked them to work on their rooms, to list their activities over a week and think about everyday habits. In lectures we discussed how to tackle the problem of student accommodation at a low cost. It is a question of integrating activities. A method we learned from the military is a scenario technique. So, for example, we ask what happens if your mother arrives at Sunday morning at eight o'clock. We also discussed questions of orientation: the most difficult rooms were the north ones without direct sunlight, so I took up this theme in a lecture, showing how by developing the section of the roof you could bounce some sunlight in. We asked the students to build scale models, which occupied the entrance hall of the school for several weeks (Fig. 10.04). We ourselves built a model of the communal area, which allowed much exploration of structure. We could see how the buildings would relate to each other, and the advantages of the timber frame. Whether dealing with students or real clients, you can make drawings and models, but they never really understand the building until they can step inside. With a wooden structure, once the roof is on people can enter. They can see how high it is and the direction of the sun. At that point you must interrupt the building process and return to the design. Now they understand what is going on. We experienced this in many projects.

Now the story of the macro and the micro. We were unsure whether these 200 first year students would really be able to build, and how many would be willing to do so during the holidays or during the lectures of colleagues. So we added a reserve group of fifth-year students to be sure of some decent results. They didn't work with the first years, but made an independent structure of their own. There were four, all men as it happened, and they wanted to build four rooms. For weeks they sketched and made models, and it was just a mess. So one day I sketched them a plan diagram (Fig.10.05) that provided a variable model for a room group attached to the main complex via the south. Each student (A, B, C and D) would get a square 3 x 3 metres. He can use the square for his room. But then A must discuss with B what happens in the shaded area between their spaces. If you want the sun, it would be reasonable for A to get the space below to let the sun in, but then C must be respectful. The same thing happens in section. We also suggested that there should be posts at each corner. Now each student can do as he wants to get what he needs inside, but he has to negotiate with the others. Suddenly they became architects!

In the end they decided on a rotational symmetry, which is not so reasonable if you get the north side rather than the south, but we respected the users' idea. The students were not content simply to follow Walter Segal's method respecting the right angle, but introduced the diagonal. It caused problems, because in Germany you cannot build a timber building without a controlling engineer, and we had to discuss all this with them: how many nails and what price and so forth. Again this is something for which the architect must be responsible, or he can't build the building. In the end the student with the diagonal gallery had the best room, and he was so glad! I had opposed it for not respecting the rules of the micro, but in the end it proved reasonable. They entered their house for an international student competition, but from the way they described

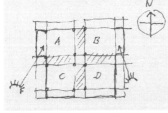

10.05 – Sketched plan diagram of the micro showing rooms A, B, C and D and the zones of negotiation between them.

10.06 – Plan of the micro, a tower-like group of four rooms built by senior students.

it, it seems that they never fully understood the design process. There was much detail work developed parallel to the design process. Some magazines have described this project as a complete improvisation on site, but that is quite untrue: the students did 1:10 construction drawings.

10.07 – Front of the Bauhäusle and path to the community building. Peter Sulzer is hekping out with a wheelbarrow of concrete.

10.08 – The 'micro', a tower of four rooms built by fifth year students.

In the beginning we intended one living room and one kitchen. But with thirty students the kitchen was going to be too small, so we decided on two kitchens and no living room. This was one of our best decisions: for a while one kitchen was for smokers and the other for non-smokers. Later it changed to people who washed up before dinner and people who washed up after. I went there recently with Yona Friedman, and one of the students who didn't know me – the original group having long ago moved on –

explained the story of the project. That I liked very much, and in the end when saying goodbye, I told them how in the beginning I had to do too much on the project. Now not a single architectural student lives there, but students of chemistry, engineering, etc. Even so, if there is a leak in the roof, they fix it, no problem at all. It was encouraging to see that the spirit of participation and self-build lives on for generations, we don't know how long. The building was never intended to be permanent: the initial permission was for fifteen years. When that time elapsed the students got every visitor to sign a petition, and so it continues for another fifteen years. They added another workshop, and when I asked who got the building permit, they told me it was one of the former students, now an architect. In 2002 the student housing association wanted to abandon the complex, but the inhabitants hired a lawyer and moved back in. The University President visited, and Peter Hübner, along with new students, has built a student café adjacent.

The Landau Cultural Centre

I started with self-build entirely as a method of teaching. But once your project appears in magazines and on television, people come and ask if you could do a self-build project for them. My first large client was a group related to the Peace Movement, about eighty people whose basic activity was singing. They met twice a week for practice, and they needed a kind of small concert hall. Everybody is very happy with the acoustics, without knowing that a colleague of mine who was an acoustician worked free for them. They wanted good acoustics, so as an architect I felt the need for the acoustician, who told me that the hall must be one metre higher. I wanted a simple roof, but I raised it and that is why it has a stepped section. This project was a complete self-build job. The hall has a totally free span. It began when the clients bought an old railway shed with the idea of transforming it. I advised them to tear it down, as it could never be a concert hall and didn't have any real foundations.

Now here you are, the architect, with about eighty people. How do you start? I gave them forms and told them to note down precisely what they wanted to do in the building. I got back a demand for a hall of 12 x 14 metres: already a precise size. It would have been better had they specified up to four hundred people, or something like that. They wanted to allow for theatre, singing and film. With the student housing project, the participation took a wilder, more hippy kind of direction, but these clients came from bourgeois families, so their taste was more conventional. This is another thing you must consider with participation.

As architect you have much work to do behind the scenes,

which you never show to the users. To find out what could be a good solution you also have to consult the town planning people. They said the new building should be at the top left corner of the site to allow extension of an adjacent park, but that has nothing to do with the participation of the users. I find it important to talk with these people at an early stage, and also with the fire chief. There were endless sketches, still without discussions with the users. How can you build a wooden structure without a contractor, and without a crane? All this must be decided by the architect and engineer. I arrived at a solution and asked them to build a model, which provided a basis for discussion. At that time the group had a conductor who was the intellectual leader, and seeing this model he said 'Columns inside? No!' So we had to omit the columns, creating a 12 x 12 metre free span, which is not easy in self-build. A worthy genius of a structural engineer joined in, working for, I think, 200 bottles of wine. He proposed the flat cupola octagon system including a tension ring. We made a new model adapted to the engineer's proposal.

Returning for a moment to what is essential, the architect has to invent a structure, not in the sense of engineering but in the sense of ordering. With this you can really start a discussion with the users. You can place the entrance here, and the toilets there. At first they did not include a housing element, but later they decided someone should live in the building for security reasons: it was a left-wing group, so they foresaw problems with right-wingers. It is also the architect's responsibility to deal with the energy question, even if it only emerges in the energy bill at the end of the year. So I did all that. There had to be working drawings understandable for self-builders, not for contractors. Second-hand windows complicated the issue: they had to be drawn, lots of details. The clients had a shed and collected used windows and everything. Self-builders make decisions, and if the architect's arguments are not strong enough, they decide instead.

10.09 – Landau cultural centre: site work in progress, Peter Sulzer in discussion with self-builders.

Now, you have to explain your drawings to them. And how do they understand it, and do you argue? The conductor was the type of man who always wanted to do it the other way. There was no carpenter on site, the choir members did everything. Someone was related to a local contractor and obtained scaffolding. They even started to make their own drawings, especially concerning the installation of services. They consulted I don't know whom, and arranged the heating and electricity themselves. As there was not much money, and as the old railway station had a felt roof, I wanted to make a felt roof. But as they came from petit-bourgeois families, they wanted red tiles. Red tiles were expensive, but they also pulled

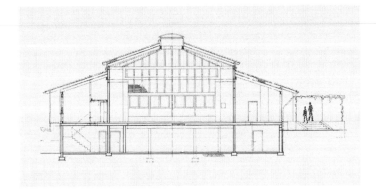

10.10 – Landau cultural centre, section through main hall and ancillary parts.

black tiles off the building next door: architects always ask me why there are two colours. A building merchant gave them for free the complete collection of sample wall tiles, and they cleaned the backs. Our students in Stuttgart threw their tiles on the floor, using the broken pieces to make beautiful mosaics in a hippy manner, but the choir members carefully sorted them, putting all those depicting trees in one room. All this is part of the participation experience.

10.11 – Landau cultural centre, a self-build project by the Landau youth choir designed by Peter Sulzer 1985-7. The hall for concerts and rehearsals is surrounded by offices and dwellings.

The moment the roof is on, you must interrupt the building process to celebrate. This happened about Christmas time, was very enjoyable, and relieved their exhaustion. Then discussions started again as they began to understand the building: the choir tried out the acoustics. I planned a gallery which remained unbuilt: 'Oh, we don't need that'. For the winter we clad the exterior wall with the kind of transparent sheeting normally used in roofing. We needed time to think. And also they had windows. I told the future users of the housing part to put in the windows where they were needed on the inside, just according to need and size. They did it but really they didn't believe me, for they made their own façade drawing which I found later. That's how it looks. And architects say to me,

Peter Sulzer | 157

that is beautiful, isn't it. I never designed it, and now the building has been in use for 20 years.

Cemetery Chapel in Gleisweiler

The village council asked three architects to make proposals. They expected drawings and perhaps a model. Instead I arrived at the council meeting with questionnaires. How should daylight enter the church? Together we drew on the blackboard. When I came up with my proposal there was much resistance to the wooden structure, but the projected costs were a third lower than the others. I did all the architectural work, including site supervision and ordering materials. The self-build activities had helped a lot: today the chapel is much appreciated by the village.

My own house

What about participation when the architect and his wife are the clients? In this project we had other problems: the house adjoined a historic monument, and permission was refused. We made a model, very much liked by my wife, then went to court with the appeal and won. Here was participation by users at a small scale: window in the bedroom, layout of the kitchen. More importantly, we had to get the approval of the neighbours; it had to fit in with the village.

Ecological houses in Edenkoben

The project was initiated by the owner of the land. We had the chance to start with the master plan, on which we had discussions with the first clients, all houses facing south. The idea: very large terrace houses, all rooms facing south, unheated space on the

north side. The architect developed a structure and a standard section, rooms on the upper floor with a gallery. The design process for each individual house was classic: discussion of the plan, size, cost. Each house is different, but standard details, tendering documents with options. An enormous responsibility for the architect; at cost of builder's houses, an acceptable group of houses.

Conclusion

The architect (along with the engineers) must develop an 'ordering structure': this we learned from Walter Segal. It cannot be done by the users. This structure must, however, remain open to the participation process. When the frame is erected and the roof added, there should be time for a second process of participation as the users start properly to understand the building: this involves allowance for changes!

The architect must be responsible for getting permissions, for a sound structure, and for architectural quality. You should not compromise on that! I tell the client: 'You should like the building – I would like to show it to my colleagues!'

Participation means more work for the architect, and every project is different, as I have tried to show you.

References

Blundell Jones, P. (1983) 'Student self-build in Stuttgart', *The Architects Journal*, 27 July, pp.32-50.

Sulzer, P. *et al.* (1983) *Lernen durch Selberbauen*, Karlsruhe: Verlag C. F. Müller.

Sulzer, P. (1987) 'Sulzer's Self-build: criticism of the Landau Protestant Youth Choir building', *The Architectural Review*, March, pp.73-6.

Kemal Özcül's acceptance speech [1]

[1]
Kemal Özcül received the European
Environmental Prize in 2034 for his services
in saving the forest of Lower Bavaria and
his efforts to re-establish a forest in the
Anatolian highlands. The following is an
excerpt from his speech at the prize giving
(decoded from a satellite photo script by
Peter Hübner).

In retrospect my schooldays in Gelsenkirchen were of the utmost importance, for I was lucky enough to experience the building of the new Evangelical School in the most literal sense. I arrived in the autumn of 1994 as a weedy lad of twelve with language problems. We were some 134 children in five classes, and we moved into a freshly repainted old building. As usual, the classrooms were too large, too bald, too bare. I was lucky enough to be assigned to class 5c, taught by a young and extraordinarily enthusiastic teacher nick-named Eco. His subjects were German, history and religious studies, but he was called Eco because he always talked about saving the world, about survival on a planet that had existed for thousands of years, but seemed on its way to extinction thanks to the unbridled overexploitation of nature. He claimed that only if every person took personal responsibility for his or her actions would it be possible to re-establish some kind of harmony between humanity and nature. Next to our school was a huge cornfield which in 1994 I saw being harvested for the last time, and I still remember that it was only my second day when the bulldozers arrived to turn this virgin ground into the place where I would spend a good part of my youth. Here over years and even decades, we would develop a place of learning that gave priority to the individual, fulfilling his/her physical and psychological needs while embedding them in a concept of nature which would be as relevant to later times as to our own.

We made hills and streams ending in large ponds, the so-called wet habitats of that time. It thrilled us, and started a process that has continued until today. As children we never understood why an area of land destined to be woodland, and planted with small trees of 30-50cm at half-metre intervals, had to be fenced off for the first two years, while another area was just left to run wild. But we soon saw that nature, left to herself, provides wonderful variety without seeds or fertilisers, and we saw the difference between wet and dry ground, meadows and marshes, each with its particular flora and fauna. I do not discount the importance of my later educators, but I feel, looking back, that my career in ecology was truly rooted here.

At the beginning of the school year architects, engineers, landscape architects and ecologists arrived at the school to present the whole remarkable project. We were told that we 134 boys and girls were going to build our own school, our own garden, our own world. We were full of the naive optimism of childhood, our teachers were young and open-minded, and the planners coaxed us on with their overwhelming enthusiasm, so that soon we thought of nothing but our new school. Eco was for us the driving figure, responsible for the concept that we, 5c, should develop in the making of our own classroom and its garden. Other teachers also became quickly engaged – memorably Mrs Kräutermayer of 5A – and classes competed to produce the best ideas. Dreams were indulged, the maddest notions were discussed, cloud-cuckoo lands, castles, caves and nests were lovingly drawn, and models were built as the ideas became more concrete.

Only four weeks from the start of the year we began a two-week project to build the workshop, which involved all five classes in shifts. The floor slab had been cast, and the architects had explained the building's circular form. At first it seemed complicated, but it proved easy enough as the repeated elements dropped into place, with the kind of simplicity we later rediscovered in our spiral stair. We were to assist the carpenter with the erection. A lorry load of wood arrived. The planks were only 5cm thick but planed smooth and with the delicious smell of Douglas fir. We helped unload the wood and to assemble the frames on a jig before they were craned into place. It was amazing that this workshop could arise from nothing in a mere 14 days! We had achieved 450 square metres of construction and felt we were real builders, grown-up carpenters, which certainly was not true, but we felt it. We had helped, we had identified ourselves with the building, and we took a pride in it. The rest of the construction was completed by trained craftsmen quickly enough for us to celebrate our Christmas feast in the new building. I still remember the first snowflakes falling on the glass roof, how they looked from below, and how single crystals combine to make a magic world.

In this workshop our models grew, made at the scale of one to ten and always including tables and chairs, stairs and galleries, greenhouse elements, etc. It was astounding how our wild ideas could be tamed into an orderly form with a frame of sticks 5 by 25mm, yet allowing the complexity of the spatial experience to remain. We had found a simple principle starting with a square, which could be extended with bays and projections to front, rear or above, into a real labyrinth with very differentiated elements. We had to keep within a strict budget, and the architects calculated each stage. For us this was when the computer entered the grown-up world. Computer firms provided free machines and programs for our study course to help with these calculations, and we learned in a few weeks how to use them and how to enter data for every part. We were excited to discover that we could not only print out plans and perspectives, but also move in and out of the house as if in a film. We made videos which helped us to understand and perfect our classroom design.

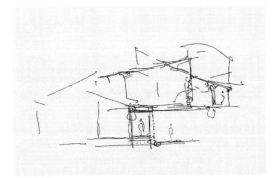 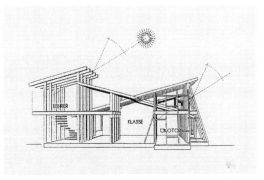

11.01 & 11.02 – School at Gelsenkirchen: preliminary sketch and developed computer drawn section through a possible classroom wing, showing solar exposure. Arrangements like this emerged out of discussions with pupils and teachers.

Locked into his muesli-eating habits, Eco was naturally against computers, only abandoning his doubts when he saw that he could fly through our unbuilt classrooms and on up to the staff room on the first floor, discovering a special greenhouse for his succulents perfectly placed on the roof of 5c. Maths Müller, who not only taught 5D but also information technology, was in contrast highly enthusiastic. His responsibility was costings. Each class had a set budget that was not to be exceeded: it covered both the paid craftsmen and the self-build component. So it proved advantageous that the computer carried the data for every option, so that we always knew where we were. Maths Müller's favourite task was in editing down: when a classroom became too expensive, he suggested reducing it by 10 per cent. I think this is how our classroom reached the cosy size that in the end suited us so well.

Our design was completed in February and March 1995. We had negotiated with 5B and 5D, our immediate neighbours, and were relieved to discover that 5A and 5E, at the ends of the row with free-space to east and west, had not managed so very much more – later we found too that their energy costs were greater. In any case, we middle-placed classes had made the most of our southern orientation. We decided to front our class with a two-storey greenhouse: behind this lay our nest and the gallery which for years was to remain my favourite spot.

At Easter, construction firms arrived to make the foundations and ground slabs for our classrooms. The architects had finalised all the details and engineering offices had calculated the stresses, so everything was swiftly documented, and we were asked which parts of our classroom we would like to build ourselves. Eco was delighted: already fancying himself a master carpenter after building the workshop, he insisted that we must ourselves construct the timber frame. The architects had accepted the responsibility of supervision, and two craft teachers were also there to help. As several classes were joining in, the Church provided funds to employ further specialist craftsmen, among them Mighty Max and Heinz, Master of the Art of Living, both of whom later taught in the school workshops. By building the workshop, we had established that the handling of the light 5cm thick timbers by us children was possible with careful supervision, and the erection of our classroom was great fun. The skeleton stood firm after only ten days, and the other classes competed with us. Seeing it going so well, Maths Müller had to revise his cost calculations and swallow his doubts, and it seemed that the architect had been right in his claims that our participation would bring commitment and identification.

Our teachers became increasingly creative in finding areas of instruction that could apply to the building site, and nearly all the pupils were so taken with the excitement of building that they stayed long after school, remaining until late in the evening if the weather was good. My uncle Mehmed, who had married the daughter of a Gelsenkirchen butcher, set up a kebab stall to cater for those whose parents had not sent them out with a picnic. The close friendships kindled on the building site in this first year of school lasted down the years, and soothed tensions that arose in those years when hatred of foreigners made headlines in Germany.

We were glad now that many parts of our classroom – especially the roofing with the waterproof skin, the windows and the glasshouse – were completed by building firms. We helped with the flooring, making fantastic mosaics and tile patterns. The placing of earth on the grass roof was accomplished by a human chain with a hundred buckets involving all the families and ending in a celebratory party. It was achieved in record time, and we were glad that the disruption to the ground caused by our building was now over. We were highly sceptical of the composting WCs that we had decided to include, but today it is almost beyond belief that such huge quantities of pure drinking water were then just flushed away, as is still the case in some old buildings.

Eco next got us going on the external works. All the fifth classes had decided to design and look after the entire garden area together, and they managed it for several years. In biology we had many tasks for individuals or small groups, and we found ourselves in charge of particular plots. I was responsible for the small rainwater pond filled by run-off from the roofs, and I had the same experience as Konrad Lorenz, who claimed that observation of small pools had made him a biologist. As we left for the long vacation, we saw that the unbelievable had happened: all the classes had developed so far that you could imagine moving in. Craftsmen helped to complete the rest of the work while we were away. Our return to our new home was celebrated with a great opening party involving half the neighbourhood. I still remember its enthusiastic reception by newspapers and TV, and the great pride of all participants. In the long vacation other things had also happened. The central 'street' though not yet glazed-in was paved, and rainwater was channelled through pipes and brought to various fountains, of which our favourite was the row of Wirbel basins in the main 'square' opposite the mosque. The mosque was actually a small prayer room, developed by a Turkish self-help initiative into a much more extravagant form. Diagonally opposite was an Evangelical chapel, also not foreseen in the first plans, so the 'square' had two tiny but distinct buildings alongside the large assembly hall and school library, and we called it 'the place of prayer'. Designed by different architects in different styles, the various buildings came together as with a natural process of growth.

In biology we learned about bark beetles, and Sven and Irina discovered that they used ordering grids like those we had seen in our school plans, with their main and side streets. The dining hall, the first of the 'public' buildings, was built to the plans of a foreign architect and soon became known as the 'Gasthaus'. Its sunny café terrace next to the 'Lake' became known as 'Big Bertha's', not merely because of Frau Kopletzki's girth, but because she was also our biggest friend, ever ready to listen and console us over our personal problems.

At the beginning of the new school year a new fifth class arrived and took over our old building, repeating the process we had been through, but this time spared the doubting know-alls who had plagued us at the start. The spores with which the architects had infected us had penetrated far and wide, and we had the impression that the whole world knew about our Gelsenkirchen experiment. Busloads of visitors arrived and hindered our work, so that eventually in the third and fourth year we had to limit the intrusion, but all the attention spurred Eco on towards a new initiative in which we helped: to spread the infection wider, to expose his model for changing the world to the largest possible audience.

In the second year, the building of the housing area began, at first with just a handful of houses. Our school, the houses and the landscape were planned as a whole, intended as an ecological renewal of the town of Gelsenkirchen for the millennium, part of the International Building Exhibition of Emscher Park. The fallow land stretched as far as the housing area, and left to itself, soon developed an amazingly varied ecology. This gave the first housing families some ideas. I remember a family of graphic designers who did absolutely nothing to their 'garden', to the extreme annoyance of their more bourgeois neighbours, until their wild garden slowly developed its own character with coltsfoot, nettles, mulleins, etc. Such wild-flower areas encouraged the cultivation of bees, and the hives of the Schwab family produced a local brand that fetched high prices.

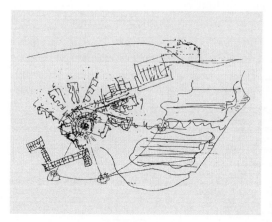 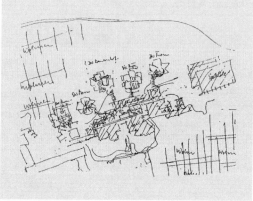

11.03 & 11.04 – School at Gelsenkirchen, competition proposal: sketches of possible site layouts. The previous school to be incorporated in the project is bottom left.

My father Suleiman, initially employed by the day, was fired in the restructuring and obliged to start his own second-hand car business. At last it began to make money, and we were able to buy a building plot to construct our own house, building as much as possible ourselves with the help of neighbours. We started with a core house designed by an architect, which was known as the sharp tooth because of its initially bald appearance and almost flat 3° roof. But a side wing was later added, and in the second year we put a south-facing greenhouse on the upper floor, which saved a lot of energy. We added a second glass house on the north side and used a transparent form of insulation on the side walls. This is now normal, but at first we suffered summer overheating, for the development of self-adjusting sunshades was then in its infancy. The solar cells which were donated by AEG, and which Eco had installed on the roof of the staff room, were replaced in the late 1990s by solar elements integrated in the window glass, which looked like very fine blinds but produced electricity through photovoltaic means. The now standard holographic elements were then in their development phase, and we used them as part of a pilot project in the year

2000 to make our own house energy self-sufficient, for at that time demand on the gigantic centralised power producers threatened to outstrip supply.

I have digressed enough, and must return to some important aspects of our school that served as impulses for society. Following the architectural competition we had long discussions about our school. We concluded that highest priority should be given to the pupils, followed by the staff, nature, and finally the buildings. The architects had wanted to build a tower in the 'marketplace' of the school as a memory of the winding towers belonging to the coal mines that had been the *raison d'être* of the area. The contrast between the disused towers and the wheat fields had left a lasting impression from their first visit. We decided to build this tower, and found in the process a fine form that developed from inside outwards, and certainly resembled a winding-tower, but not by direct imitation. It had to be wider at the top, for in our own picture of ourselves, the pupils must occupy the topmost layer, then the staff, then the architects, engineers and ecologists involved in planning the school. This tower became the heart of our school. From the terrace of the top floor, six stories up, we could follow year by year how the whole thing developed: how the housing dissolved into its natural surroundings, and how our school grew branches just as the bark beetle eats out fresh shafts. Luckily the patch of ground that we had stolen from nature soon returned in the form of green roofs on both school and housing: these supported a different kind of life, but an equally rich one.

Eco spoke of the need to clothe the earth with plants, and he used to quote the scurrilous Hundertwasser, who in the twentieth century upset architects with his pamphlets against the straight line. In his buildings he never got beyond the decorative colour effects which also animated his paintings, but this did not narrow his success: rather it encouraged it. Maths Müller used to say that art and commerce must walk hand in hand, or the economy does not work. From the balcony of the staff floor, Mrs Kräutermayer could look down on the roof of our canteen where she had planted a herb garden. This not only served our kitchens, but also provided some unusual herbs distributed locally from a market stall which we ran on Saturdays. In the fourth floor was the architects' office, with whom we had much contact. The experiences from teaching had to be integrated into classroom tracts yet to be built, and the Wednesday seminar, always at two, became an essential part of school life.

Energy problems grew ever more important, alternative solutions being presented and discussed. Our class built a large greenhouse at the beginning with passive solar energy in mind, and we included both a well-insulated heavy floor slab and massive mud walls at the rear. The heavy dividing walls between classes added to the thermal mass. The double glass wall had to be shaded to prevent overheating in summer. Later, we experimented with water-filled interstitial elements using old barrels and transparent polyester piping. These successfully combined shading with energy storage. When the plants had got going properly in our greenhouse, further shading turned out to be unnecessary, and we were the most celebrated class in the school, for our little 'survival ark' as Eco called it, won the top prize for Youth Research in 1999.

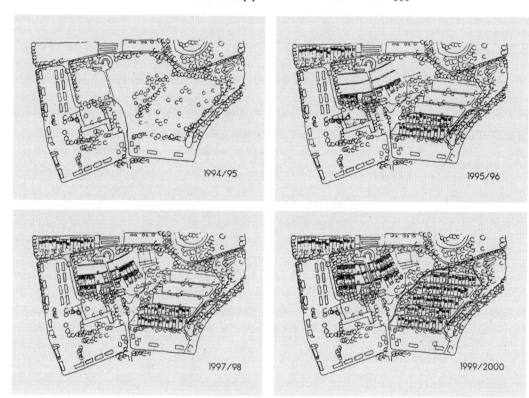

11.05–11.08 – School at Gelsenkirchen, competition proposal: dated site layouts of the proposed school and adjacent ecological housing, showing a plausible pattern of growth.

When we left the school in 2001, the central 'street' was completed along with all the wings of classrooms. The sports hall had been in use since 1998, and in the housing area three plots were still unbuilt, but almost everything else was done. Only the general structure remained the same from the beginning, for almost every element had changed in detail, but the plan proved strong enough to absorb all variations.

I returned to the old building in the second rank of the second level, and it was clear that this would never have worked without our being able to make some changes to the fabric. As 18-year-olds we were still unqualified, but the experience of self-build during our time at school had changed us through and through, and it was astonishing how easily we could create a living world out of those loveless rooms, while also reducing energy consumption. We had gained a sensibility: Eco's impulse drove us further, even though he was no longer our teacher.

I had been eight years in the school and had seen how from small saplings a great wood can grow. The first trees that rooted were already large enough for coppicing, and we could use them for many kinds of construction. Later I studied biology and ecology at university, and my interest in forestry never abated. At the end of my student time I wanted to become a teacher and was lucky enough to get a post as assistant in my old school. Having studied abroad, I had been out of contact, so I was very curious to see what remained of our experimental impulse. Eco and several other teachers were still there, though there were also many new faces. The timetable had stabilised, the school gave an impression of order and calm, but the individuality of the place had even increased.

Both the project teaching and the personal responsibility of pupils in taking on real-life tasks had proved themselves and been adopted into the accepted educational programme. The reform-curriculum seemed as modern and progressive as ever, and several delegations from the European Association of Education had visited the Gelsenkirchen School Conference, held twice yearly in the school's main hall. What I found most fascinating, though, was the way the pupils related to their own classrooms. Although these buildings had now passed to a fourth generation, they still seemed as personal as on the first day. The pupils claimed to have played important parts in their construction, which I knew to be untrue, since I had seen these classrooms erected. But even the small changes that they had been allowed to make had the same effect of creating an extra emotional link with their personal living space.

Essential aspects of personal responsibility were now taken for granted. Thus the whole energy issue and handling of waste were the responsibility of each class. In 1996 glass panels with a k-value of 1.3 were changed for the new gel-filled type with a value of only 0.3, a product of the building revolution. Each window became automatically a solar collector, and the energy absorbed was generally greater than the loss due to nocturnal radiation. Solar energy techniques had made astonishing strides, so that together with the reduced electricity requirement, each class also had its own photovoltaic array. The rubbish mountain at the turn of the century had raised such awareness that through careful separation the quantity of waste was minimised. Compostable plastic containers had been generally adopted, and were placed with other organic matter in garden composters. In the workshop area a small recycling hall had been built, where school projects in the separation and reuse of waste materials could be tested.

Eco had reached the age of 52 with undiminished energy, and was frequently asked to speak at international congresses. He had three similar projects going in Uganda, Honduras and Manchuria, which he had baptised and visited as adviser for two years. Now he had again a Fifth class, which I also taught. We had to cope with streams of refugees arriving in the Ruhr, and our pupils spoke eight different first languages. The integrative effect of working on small projects together was at first very demanding, but soon allowed the varied talents of the pupils to shine through, and before long our class had become an indivisible group. We reconstructed the gallery of our classroom and included a small kitchen corner. Eighty per cent of the pupils stayed at the school into the evening, and sometimes did not wish to go home, so we thought about the possibility of overnight accommodation as an extension of the guest wing.

I remained four years in the school and taught the last two in the newly founded Ecology Department in Humboldt House on our 'main street'. The open-ended planning of the buildings along this street, meant largely to be of two storeys, allowed extensions to be added relatively easy. We had planned our 'Institute' as we called it, as a three-storey structure linking earth and heaven. We had our own small weather station on the roof, and decided to make a fountain with our own hands in front of the terrace. Water had become the limiting factor in the entire region, and we began a project to purify waste water biologically and recycle it, drawing on our experience of the flow-clearing devices already tested in the school.

The whole two-storey layout of the school had proved most reliable, loved by the few wheelchair users. It engendered a general sense of solidarity, proved among other things by the fact that so many classes took place in the open air. The living growth of the school was helped by the fact that small changes could be made without the use of large machines, and that these changes did not disturb neighbouring parts, for each area was self-sufficient in its development. Life together was self-regulating, as in a town that has grown up by itself, letting the houses come together harmoniously with the minimum of rules.

The open discussion forum had proved itself, and the Wednesday meetings remained routine events, even if the content had changed. The old school building, still housing second-level pupils, had received numerous small extensions, so to the casual visitor it looked completely integrated into the complex. Both parts of the school had grown together into a single whole, offering itself as a social and cultural centre, not only for the adjacent housing but for the whole surrounding area.

I left our school with a heavy heart in 2014 to take up a post with the newly founded Forestry Institute in Ankara. I could hardly have dreamed that it would be possible to reclaim 14,000 hectares of desert in Anatolia by recultivation methods that we would pioneer, and you must allow me, in receiving this prize today, to share it with my mentor Eco, whom I see sitting in the first row among the honoured guests. We decided between us to spend the prize money on a very worthy project. We are giving the whole 2,000,000 Euros to the Fritz Sundermeier Foundation for our beloved old school, so that it can remain as young and lively as we saw it on our last visit three months ago. I've kept you too long from the refreshments: thank you for hearing me out.

K. Ö., Ankara, 29.09.2034.

Özcül postscript:
the Gelsenkirchen school as built

Architectural competitions, when well run, have many advantages. They encourage architects towards better solutions, generate debate about the building type, and provide alternative visions of the same institution that show the crucial role of buildings. Young practices are encouraged on their own way, old ones are stopped from becoming moribund. Yet competitions have one huge disadvantage: there can be little contact with the clients and users. All information about the social and political has been frozen in a brief, and it is neither practical nor fair on competitors to allow open discussion, so questions are highly restricted. The design thus tends to become a *fait accompli*, and knowing the power of the image, architects spend much time on a very finished presentation. The judges make their independent decision, and the users discover their new environment on the day they walk in, obliged from then on to make the best of it.

Peter Hübner has long been a socially-minded architect, relishing the opportunity to engage clients and users in discussion about what the building should be, and for him architecture has become a social process. Not only should users be consulted: they should be engaged in the process, working together with the designers and builders to create a world to a shared image. Invited to the competition for the school at Gelsenkirchen-Bismarck, Hübner was drawn to the social and educational ideals expressed by the organisers and also to their stated ecological concerns, but he felt that the provision of a static and finite design was all wrong: he had instead to put across the idea of an open-ended process. So he submitted not a complete design, but a series of sketches of what the school might become, accompanied by the narrative printed above. It nearly came to nothing, consigned to the rejects pile until a second round, but was rediscovered by one of the judges. On reconsideration, and with the enthusiastic intervention of Lucien Kroll, Hübner's project was adopted on the basis of the Özcül story, which is both construction manual and mythical narrative.

Özcül describes both the design and the process. The idea that a building completely changes a person's life may seem Utopian, and there was obviously a concern to include in the story all sorts of concerns that might appeal to the judges, from the happiness of wheelchair users to more general aspects – social, educational, technical and ecological. Nonetheless, many of the participative moments described are evidently based in detail on Hübner's own experience of having built several schools and youth clubs. They expose a methodology, and his knowledge and confidence shine through. Özcül's remarks about the fourth generation to occupy a classroom thinking they had built it was an echo of Hübner's own experience on visiting anonymously one of his youth clubs from the 1980s.[1] Remarks on the constructive process also cover examples he had already made, like the radial workshop which derives from the Stammheim primary school.[2] Aside from such details, the dominant impressions given by the text are first, architecture as a continuing process engaging the user; and second, narrative – preferably oral narrative – as a means of engaging the listener, the user, the co-builder, everyone in the process. Hübner's buildings always have biographies.

1
This happened more than once, particularly at the Youth Club in Stuttgart Wangen and the Bauhäusle student hostel.

2
See *The Architectural Review*, September 1990, pp. 49-53.

12.01 – Gelsenkirchen school from the front. The school cafeteria on the ground floor with classrooms above, and administration on the right; behind is the ventilation stack for the theatre.

The school and its background

Gelsenkirchen-Bismarck is a former industrial suburb in the Ruhr. It grew up in the late nineteenth century around a huge coal mine. Housing sprang up for the miners and their families, along with churches, schools and other modest social institutions, but it remained a grim place. The prosperity of the 1960s allowed expansion, and German families were replaced by immigrant workers mostly from Turkey. By the 1980s the mine became uneconomical and uncompetitive, its closure produced rampant unemployment, and Bismarck became a problem area. Illiterate in German, its Turkish children often had difficulty in escaping the vicious circle of poverty and depredation. The Protestant Church (Evangelische Kirche von Westfalen) sought to ease this problem with a new school. Fritz Sundermeier, an educationalist who had run schools in Tehran and Tokyo, conceived the idea of a multicultural ecological school as a catalyst for redevelopment. Not only was it to welcome people of many faiths – the Turks are Muslim – it was to be a cultural centre promoting ecological education. Sundermeier struggled for the support first of his synod, then of the city and regional authorities, and finally of the Education Ministry. The money was difficult,[3] but the financiers were convinced, and with the further backing of Internationale Bau-austellung Emscher Park an invited architectural competition was launched in 1993 for a school with ecological housing alongside.[4] The eight teams produced some attractive proposals, but only Hübner's shifted the emphasis radically towards process.

The new school has developed alongside an existing one built in the 1960s. It occupies a former meadow just behind the heart of the suburb, set between the old school and local sports facilities. Conceived as a 'village' (see plan, p.176), the group of buildings gathers around a central covered street with a kind of public square at the end where you enter it. Top lit and brightly coloured, this is an inspiring and exciting space. The precedents, and to some extent inspiration, are the street-like halls of Hans Scharoun's Marl and Lünen schools both built around 1960 and both to be found within a few miles. Those examples saw the school as a family of rooms rather than one monolithic lump, the central hall becoming street-like through accepting its irregular form from the more positively-shaped elements around it.[5] In Hübner's school the entrance is flanked to left by the cafeteria and to right by the library, with music rooms and chapel above. Beyond to the left is the theatre with its large side window and tree-like structure, while to the right administration occupies a relatively banal box. Then come chemist and cinema, workshop and laboratory, teaching spaces conceived as shops along the street, used by different groups at different times. The complex ends in a court adjoining the radial workshop. This whole 'public domain' is both for pupils and for local people, who can put on plays in the evening, or use the workshops and sports facilities. A large new sports hall has been built to the east of the complex next to existing open-air sports facilities. Though planned in close consultation with the teachers, all these buildings were contractor-built, only finishes being completed by the school. Hübner had wanted to hand out the separate buildings to independent architects, but the clients feared such complex patterns of

3
The church provided the initial few million, and the school had to borrow the rest of its money before reclaiming it from the state, which finally covered the bulk of the costs. After winning the competition, Hübner had to rework to a reduced budget, and a state guarantee was sought against excessive costs.

4
The housing component includes 28 self-build houses and a 72-house solar estate, the first in the Ruhr area. This part of the project is not covered here because the school is already so large and complex.

5
For the Scharoun schools, see P. Blundell Jones, *Hans Scharoun*, London: Phaidon 1995, pp.136–50.

responsibility, so in the end the parts were divided among members of his office to provoke the desired variations in style.

The classroom blocks were gradually added year by year as a series of side wings off this central spine. Their design and construction involved teachers and pupils directly, taking the form of free-standing pavilions like terraces of houses, added progressively as classes moved over. Initially only two groups of five were built,

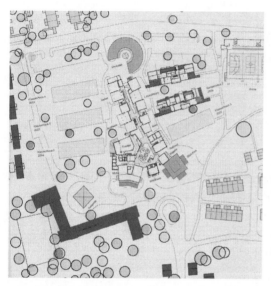

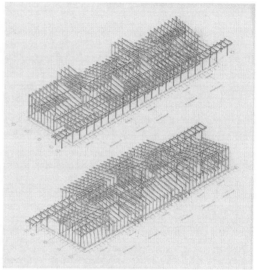

12.02 (above left) – General plan of the school in its context, north is top. The old school is the linear figure bottom right, while the new one is in the centre, its spinal street running upwards from the social 'market place' by the entrance to the round workshop. To either side project wings of classrooms, four of the six here shown only in outline. The two classroom wings drawn in detail are on the right.

12.03 (right) – Projection drawings showing the timber structures of two classroom wings. This construction system alllowed great flexibility in design, and each classroom was designed in collaboration with its pupils, encouraging them to consider it as a second home.

but two more groups were completed in 2000 and a further two in 2001. All were designed by their future inhabitants for, true to his word, Hübner involved the children in planning, modelling and construction. The process involved two pairs of project days when Hübner and his assistants visited the school to work with the pupils and their teachers. The children started by measuring themselves and making clay models at 1:10. Then they discussed the need for furniture and modelled their chairs and tables, setting out real chairs and tables in the playground to see the space needed. There were discussions about classroom and house: how many rooms are needed and of what kind? Should there be a garden too? Brainstorming sessions resulted in a brief for each class-house. Next came discussion of materials and structural principles, frame models being made with softwood. There was discussion of walling materials, of the relative advantages of flat and pitched roofs, of windows and their orientation, of need for light and avoidance of excess sun. Models of the emerging classrooms were assembled to see how they would fit together. Then the architects returned to their office to work up proposals based on the children's ideas. Six weeks later they returned for another two-day intensive session.

After discussion and adjustment of the design, the children built precise models based on the architects' drawings. At lunchtime on the second day these were assembled for a presentation to parents and the press. Further work by the architects then took the design through the bureaucratic hurdles and the basic structures were erected by contractors. Much of the subsequent fitting-out and finishing was done, however, by teachers, pupils and their parents.

12.04 – The spinal street and 'market place' looking back towards the main entrance.

Educational aims

Hübner enjoyed the enthusiastic cooperation of the school's director Rainer Winkel. The author of many books on educational theory and for years Professor of Education at the HdK in Berlin, he was glad of a chance to put his progressive ideas into practice. Interviewed in 2000, he summed up his approach under four headings. First it was a family school. Social problems being so severe, with poverty, broken homes, alcohol and drugs, many children lacked a stable background and this had to be remedied by the

12.05 – Pupils in the library sharing a computer.

12.06 – Pupils playing chess in their classroom.

school. Children were therefore assigned to classes occupying the same classroom-home for six years, and led by the same teacher-parents, a man and a woman to provide balanced role models. Hübner's method of letting them participate in the design and construction of their space helped to initiate this social unit. Second, though the school was based on Christian values, it was completely open to other faiths and concerned to accommodate them. With 30 per cent of children Muslim and 25 per cent Catholic, mutual understanding and tolerance are a high priority. Third, there was a concentration on learning by doing, extending the ideas of Dewey and Montessori, and introducing academic subjects through practical projects. The classroom design process is a gift to such an ethos. Fourth, it was a community school, part of the locality and usable by local people around the clock. The theatre was equipped for all kinds of productions, lectures, or film evenings, and there was space for a disco in its basement. The hope was that by coming there, the children could be kept away from other dangerous and drug-ridden venues. More than just an educational instrument, the school/village was conceived as a catalyst for the locality, giving people help as well as hope and inspiration.

Every country has its areas of poverty and depredation, with underfunded schools struggling against drugs, vandalism and disruptive pupils. In the UK the tactic, introduced by the right but since continued by the centre-left, has too often been a matter of measuring by exam results, then 'naming and shaming' so-called failing schools and even closing them down. Winkel has been highly critical. Interviewed in the year 2000, he feared that:

> Progressive education is threatened by a global impetus to bring all under control and make a ranking scale – but we are not horses, we try to help kids become human beings – you can't just reapply methods from other fields... We need to see the difference between a school and a factory... Education is a risk, an open structure. It has to do with faith and love and sympathy. We try to accompany children along the way. If you accept this you are shocked by the world-wide ideology that says bring all under control, give the money to those who reach our aims. You cannot measure everything! [6]

6
From an interview with the author taped in April 2000 at the school.

Examination results are surely too narrow a measure, for exam success is known to be linked with socio-economic advantage. Comparatively modest results in national league tables might conceal great success for a school in a deprived area, and be accompanied by longer-term social returns which remain unmeasured: less crime, less criminals in expensive prisons, less drug addicts in expensive hospitals, less dole paid out. But the church, of course, is concerned first with our respect for each other, with happier safer lives, more sharing of burdens and generosity towards the needy, more respect for the earth that we pass on to our children, Christianity by example.

12.07 – Pupils cleaning up outside their classroom in one of the side wings.

Energy saving and ecological values

Hübner's office has long followed a familiar formula: the usual site works in insulated concrete for foundations, then lightweight construction in timber frame, calculated and even cut to size by computer. Wood is a renewable resource, easily worked, and as frame and studwork flexible enough to absorb the varied shapes and sizes suggested by the participative design process. The roof can be flat or at low pitch, protected with a membrane, then covered in soil and allowed to grow plants. It replaces the ground, absorbs rain, encourages insects, and provides an extra insulation layer. The walls can be clad in a variety of ways, but usually in timber boarding, windows being inserted as necessary. The addition of thick insulation and judicious use of glazing renders the buildings thermally efficient, and classroom daylighting is usually a more pressing concern than heating, as a roomful of children produces kilowatts of energy. Natural ventilation is sufficient, provided that cross-draughts can be created.

It is the larger spaces that require more special treatment: the theatre and sports hall. Both have ambitious passive energy systems advancing concepts which Hübner and his consultants Transsolar have used before.[7] There are long underground inlet pipes through which air is drawn to be prewarmed in winter and precooled in summer. To create an airflow, both volumes also have thermal chimneys, two on the sports-hall roof and one in the wide end of the

7
See, for example, the sports hall at the Odenwald school (*The Architectural Review*, July 1998) and the school at Cologne (*The Architectural Review*, February 1999).

school's 'street' which can be opened to exhaust it or the theatre. Unheated, and allowed to fluctuate in temperature further than the permanently inhabited rooms, the whole indoor 'street' space is used as a climatic buffer, cold air arriving at the bottom and warm air escaping through vents at the top. The air movement helps ventilate rooms on either side, sucking in fresh air from the outside and exhausting into the central 'street'.

The ecological messages of 'learning by doing' applied not only to the building but also to the landscape. Landscape architect Christof Harms developed a concept involving the children and their teachers which was even more open-ended than the classroom design. It became part of their education to make gardens of vegetables, herbs or flowers, to develop small fruit orchards, to collect water from the roofs, to keep small animals, to encourage butterflies and bees. Like the buildings, the garden was conceived as an evolving entity, growing and responding with the efforts of the children. Harms decided the approximate layout, the hard landscape, the division of areas with fences and hedges, and the placing of large long-lived trees, but his landscape concept was otherwise open-ended, dynamic, interactive. It was the very opposite of the well-manicured unchanging park miraculously restored each day by unseen servants, which for many is the assumed gardening ideal. Children need to understand the landscape as a product of human endeavour, of our interaction and dialogue with nature. In seeing the results of their efforts to manipulate and control it, they discover their power to influence the world.

12.08 – Pupils gardening.

Practices of participation

Animal town planning and homeopathic architecture [1]

1
This text started a transcript of a lecture given at the University of Sheffield on 12 February 2002. It was subsequently revised for publication by Lucien Kroll.

Animal town planning and homeopathic architecture: these were the terms that I proposed in Vancouver once and they didn't understand at all. I'll give you an example. The donkey of Le Corbusier traces the lowest energy path into the hills. He is a holistic animal. By intuition he calculates, or rather he doesn't calculate like us but he knows before doing, his ancestors having discovered over millions of years what is the easiest way. Le Corbusier cites the intelligence of animals, but he decided to make all his roads straight on a grid anyway. It is stupid, but he didn't care.

A homeopathic architecture would mean that you don't have to decide everything as an architect. You don't have to decide the colour of the curtains, the kind of slippers to be worn by the lady client. When everything is designed, it too easily becomes a sort of concentration camp for the clients of the architect. The imposition is too much: we should instead try to organise a climate where a kind of friendly organisation is able to emerge spontaneously. We know that there are naughty architectures, and we should avoid them – I ignore for a moment the person of the architect. We should speak about and make gentle architectures. I think the definition of a good architecture is one where people are friendly because of the architecture. Perhaps this is fuzzy, but it means something. Just listen to inhabitants: they know perfectly...

We have to locate ourselves in the history of architecture according to the conditions of today. Yesterday was another day, and we live generally on outdated news; old news is not agreeable. For example, the economics of Adam Smith and the illusion of the free market. The free market is perhaps a good idea: we ought to try it some time in Europe! But Adam Smith was a moralist, not an economist, and he described a perfect system in a perfect world. In a way he was right, but he forgot the gangsters, who are as well-dressed today as ever. Friedrich Hayek is not an architect: hateable and fascinating as he is, he is nonetheless civilised. He says that the market originated in the Bronze Age. It was a technical period when they discovered something important: that by progress they could specialise, a sort of early Taylorism. People could specialise as farmers, as metalworkers, and they gained the opportunity of expanding their power and numbers: that's the Bronze Age system. Hayek says that as more people worked in more specialised ways, their production became ever more efficient, so they produced more goods than they could consume and so discovered the free market. They offered goods outside the village to anyone who could come and buy them. I was not there to see it, but I suppose it is plausible. There is, however, an alternative view. The philosopher Marcel Gauchet concentrates instead on the role of the individual, looking at it in a more psychological way.[2] Following him, I guess that before the first villager could take the goods and transform it into merchandise and propose it to others, something more essential occurred: the curiosity about 'the Other' with a big O. The curiosity was to realise that although he was not known, he was not necessarily an enemy. If he could be a friend, it was important to know him, and perhaps this need for knowing came before the invention of the market. So let us forget the market and remember the possibility of friendship with the unknown 'Other'.

These days globalisation seems unavoidable. I am against bad globalisation, but globalisation has arrived: we are global. I have flown a long way to get here, for instance, and it is important to do so, but I do so at the service of an old dream of humanity. This dream wishes to reconcile east and west, north and south, and to exchange not merchandise but philosophical or religious thoughts, art, ideas. Money inevitably gets involved in these exchanges, but it is the last rather than the first thing. Our big mistake is that money has become the obsession, it has eaten the whole inventory.

What kind of architecture or town planning can coexist with this evolving situation? For years we have been trying to find the answer, aiming at a landscape which is pluralist, and perhaps more easily defined by what it is not, than by what it is. It is not enough to describe the negative aspects, but it is easier to begin with them. It would be a landscape that doesn't obey a central form, an authority, any kind of unifying system that is obligatory. If you remove such centralised authority, you generate an area of creative freedom; and believe me, if you leave people free to design something, or to propose an idea, twelve people will produce at least twelve different ideas. They will certainly not rediscover the military uniform that defines social housing in all our countries. So our aim must be to define a place of freedom, to determine the circumstances for self-affirmation and low energy.

If we are independent individuals we do not find it necessary to stand together against an enemy, so we can be ourselves, each dressed differently, without uniform. The tragic question is, are we

2

Gauchet published numerous works. See M. Gauchet, *La Religion dans la démocratie: parcours de la laïcité*, Paris: Gallimard, 1998; *La Révolution des droits de l'homme*, Paris: Gallimard, 1989; *L'Inconscient cérébral*, Paris: Seuil xxe, 1994; *Démocratie contre elle-même*, Paris: Gallimard, 2002; *La Révolution des pouvoirs*, Paris: Gallimard, 1989; *Le Désenchantement du monde*, Paris: Gallimard, 1997; *Réligion dans la Démocratie*, Paris: Débat/Gallimard, 1998.

obliged, forbidden or allowed to design identical houses for different families? It is a 'functionalist' question, but the functionalists have answered to the contrary: they say 'yes, we have to rationalise'. Rationality is common sense reduced to the level of stupidity. It means concentrating on a half dozen calculable arguments in making a decision, and ignoring the millions of low-energy arguments, which are so much stronger and more important. The latter are not taken into account. With such limited rationalities we design so-called rational architecture. We are in a building [3] where we were late because of the elevators: doubtless they were calculated by good architects and engineers in the usual way. But... badly!

I have prepared another more adventurous line of thinking: but I hesitate, for it is difficult to define ourselves not in terms of what are we doing but why are we doing it. I wouldn't call it a philosophy but a direction, and the recent death of the French philosopher Pierre Bourdieu – I don't know if you know him well – is a good occasion for that. Pierre Bourdieu was against almost everything that was part of the French establishment: official university or administration or politicians or media or journalists and all the ways of talking to the masses. He studied the way that people live, first in Algeria and then in France. It was not so much a question of square metres as of what kind of symbolic space they live in. The German sociologist Axel Honneth remarked that in Germany you had two schools of sociology before the war, the first was Georg Simmel and the other was Max Weber, the founder of sociology. Simmel, with Siegfried Kracauer, studied the culture of everyday reactions and the way of life of employees in the inter-war years from a social and political point of view. They claimed that in every symbolic culture objects are a sort of self-defence, tools for dominating the others. We now call this institutional analysis, but the term came later. Walter Benjamin, who died at the beginning of the war in the Pyrenees in fear of being taken by the Nazis, had studied the furniture of the petit bourgeois houses in Berlin before the war in exactly the same way. It was not merely an affirmation of class opinion or a class's attempt to dominate other classes: it was both. The second sociologist, Max Weber, initiated the theory of actions. It was not a contemplation so much of how people live but of what they do, and he spoke about the domination of a social group through the accumulation of symbolic goods, constructing knowledge, culture and relations. All these things are fortifications to make sure that they remain in a dominant position, with authority over the rest, like tribes. They say that these two schools of sociology had no opportunity to combine contemplation with action because of the Nazis and the war. Suddenly they were chased out of

3
The School of Architecture in Sheffield, a listed tower block by Gollins Melvin and Ward built in the Miesian style with 19 floors. The lecture took place on the 15th floor.

Germany, being sociologists, and institutional analysts became dangerous. So after the war it was half-forgotten, until Pierre Bourdieu came and analysed the system of domination in Algeria and France in the same kind of way. That is to say he looked at domination through the tools of cultural objects, but at the same time he was so active and reactive that he was against many things and always making demonstrations against the authorities or against oppressive force (the press and television, for instance). So he combined his contemplation with action.

Why have I been talking about sociology? I find myself a follower of Pierre Bourdieu because we do exactly the same but as architects. I mean that the vocabulary of modernity, in furniture, colours, forms, outside, inside, etc. is a tool of domination. Inevitably this is not a discovery. What do we do when faced by these questions?

Should we choose a form of domination, say those of Walter Gropius or Prince Charles?

There is really no choice, for both are outside the question. What we need instead is an area of freedom to help creativity. What we have been doing for years in our office is to go to the place and ask the people to help us in organising their landscape. We are the architects, and I don't want to escape from the responsibility of being or deciding etc., but I do not want to decide alone. What I say is half-theoretical, because when we have the opportunity of doing it, we know how, and how to be helped by sociologists and by the inhabitants. When there is no chance of such collaboration we do without, but we act in the name of the inhabitants, and if this is a hypocritical attitude it is nonetheless probably more authentic than authenticity. This is because you escape from the duty of being authoritarian even in trying to guess what a group of inhabitants would design in those circumstances. The first thing is diversity, and I simply hate repetition: the deaf repetition of identical objects for any kind of reason or motive, all are false (contrary to Adolf Loos, crime lies in repetition, not in decoration). Up to now, prefabrication has never been cheaper than the hand-made, even if tomorrow that could change. It is a matter of principle, deep principle, not a matter of objects. I have nothing against industry or against intelligence, but if you need to use industry and industrialised components, you can at least use different components and mix them so that it makes a difference. The material is not important as such, naturally we could dream with nostalgia about hand-made materials, hand-made architecture etc. It is probably not the time, at least not yet the time, but certainly it will come back.

What if?.. A narrative process for re-imagining the city [1]

[1]
Title borrowed from A. Carpenter,
R. Nicolson and D. Robinson (eds), 'What if':
Fifteen visions of change for Britain's inner cities,
Community Links, London: The Short Book
Company, 2000.

Participation: What for?

What do we think we can achieve with community engagement and participation? Why do we believe in 'creative' consultancy? It is a process where success hinges totally on those people you can reach and that you can entice along to events. How can it be democratic when there are large swathes of people who cannot, or will not participate, who think their voice cannot be heard? When the project concerns large numbers of people or whole communities, we tend to hide ourselves in layer upon layer of consultation, a plethora of community events until we feel something has happened. The process can be good; it can often be chaotic; but I believe we need to engage boldly and creatively with the ideas it can inspire.

This chapter suggests narrative as a form of inspirational engagement during a long and often frustrating process – a device to help us develop a set of background ideas, an identity for a place – a 'there' for somewhere that was not there before. This chapter describes an ongoing project for the regeneration of North Sheffield in South Yorkshire, an area with 50,000 inhabitants, a tenth of the population of Sheffield.

Southey and Owlerton comprises six neighbourhoods but is largely one enormous housing estate, with run-down local centres. Laid out in the 1950s it has a curious semi-rural/urban feel; effectively garden city planning. The communities are well established with large extended families who have been on the estate since it was built. Recently a new set of residents, young families with single parents and no employment prospects, have been placed there. Although a familiar scenario, the problem is exacerbated due to the area's remoteness from the city centre. Transport links are poor and the hills do not help.

Most of the neighbourhoods have been neglected over the last 20 years during the period of falling unemployment due to the contraction of the steel mining industries. It is an area of multiple deprivation. The physical condition of the houses and the green spaces has declined. They are also remote physically and psychologically from the city centre. Many, however, are in beautiful natural settings, surrounded by ancient woodland or with long views to

14.01 – Relief map showing the dramatic topography of
Sheffield with the SOAR development area and Parkwood
Springs highlighted, and illustrating the housing landscape
of the area. (Drawn by Howard Evans.)

adjacent hills or towards the city centre. Community networks and tenants organisations are very well developed in Southey and Owlerton. There are approximately 200 different groups, and some of them are highly politicised.

Faced with the task of this urban transformation the Southey and Owlerton Area Regeneration Board (SOAR),[2] commissioned consultants to prepare a physical development framework plan for the area. This top-down and relatively unimaginative report suggested mass housing demolition and the development of pockets of private developer housing. The report had some sensible suggestions but was very contentious. After vociferous objection local residents and SOAR unceremoniously rejected it.

The regeneration board recognised a number of difficulties with the first plan. First, because of the size of the area the proposals were extremely diagrammatic, there was no detail at neighbourhood level, the plan had no visual information other than diagrams and this limited its potential to communicate ideas. It was formal and rational, like the analytical, engineering-based infrastructural planning of the nineteenth and twentieth centuries; an archaic process that continues to interpret social problems in quantifiable and physical terms. Finally, local people had not led the process.

The regeneration team had a major rethink and embarked on an experimental process, developing six individual neighbourhood strategies with full engagement with the communities and tenants' associations, that would lead ultimately to the framework document for North Sheffield. The process was experimental in the way they used consultants to fill gaps in expertise in the neighbourhood and council team rather than handing it over to consultants.[3] These gaps centred on new methods of engagement with local people and developing and communicating the ideas of the different communities. Miranda Plowden describes the role of planning in the framework document:

Today there is a recognition that cities need to embrace social, environmental and economic issues and to cope with periods of dramatic change. To do this they will need new tools that make connections between problems, rather than separating them into boxes, that open up new ways of looking at issues and that respond to the personal, the local and the everyday, as well as the strategic and the visionary.[4]

Multilayered narratives ranging from an image of the whole city right down to personal stories of residents in the communities underpinned the whole process. Some narratives were developed by

2
Southey and Owlerton Area Regeneration Board, the regeneration body representing North Sheffield.

3
The team comprised Sheffield City Council officers, a community enabler, arts regeneration specialists, a landscape architect and myself an architect, with the Sheffield School of Architecture diploma students participating during a six-week 'live' project.

4
Extract from the framework document written by Miranda Plowden, the Regeneration Officer for North Sheffield working for the Inclusion Unit in the Chief Executive's Department of Sheffield City Council, who led the whole project with clear thinking and insight.

the team after consultation and then presented back in 'loose' form to the community for their input again; some were generated directly by the community. All were treated as part of a story about the area that would resonate with the largest number of people, from the policy-makers at national level to the community 'stakeholders' and residents at local level.

Narrative

Narrative in the context of the SOAR project is both active and forward-looking – involving the construction of narratives of the future through storytelling and scenario playing, but also more passive and descriptive – the uncovering or representation of personal and social lives within the city.

A narrative can be constructed or understood in many ways. James Holston talks of city surfaces telling stories – cities are full of stones in time: 'their narratives are epic and everyday... they tell of migration and production, law and laughter, revolution and art'.[5] City narratives as a result are 'both evident and enigmatic, knowing them is always experimental'.

Dolores Hayden reminds us that narratives 'locate us as part of something bigger than our individual existences, make us feel less insignificant, sometimes give us at least partial answers to questions like who am I? Why am I like I am?' Memory locates us as part of a family history, community as part of city building and nation making. Specifically storytelling with the *'shapes of time'* uses the forms of the city, 'from the curve of an abandoned canal to the sweep of a field of carnations',[6] to connect residents with urban landscape history and foster a stronger sense of belonging.

David Harvey, the cultural geographer, warns us that the popular approach to regeneration in New Urbanism,[7] with its concepts of neighbourhood and community and urban village, is woefully inadequate to deal with unemployment and deprivation because it often lacks the narratives of history, collective memory and identity that make a place. It 'builds an image (only) of community and a rhetoric of place-based civic pride and consciousness for those who do not need it, whilst abandoning those that do to their underclass fate'.[8]

Architects' narratives tend to be positive: we tend to put a gloss on social issues and want the world to be a better place with our help. To find alternative narratives of the city, one has to look to the Situationists in the 1950s, or today's psycho-geographers such as Iain Sinclair who challenge the idea of the perfected and confident city and introduce readings that engage the views of the community.[9] What the methods and techniques of psycho-geographers

5
J. Holston (ed.), *Cities and Citizenship*, Durham, NC: Duke University Press, 1999.

6
In the highly influential D. Hayden, *The Power of Place: Urban landscapes as public history*, Cambridge, MA: MIT Press, 1997, p.227.

7
David Harvey in 'the New Urbanism' – discusses new urbanism as proposed by Peter Katz, Leon Krier, Prince Charles, Urban Villages Forum and others. D. Harvey, 'The New Urbanism and the communitarian trap', *Harvard Design Magazine*, vol.1, 1997, pp.68-9.

8
Ibid.

9
Eammon Canniffe in *Urban Ethic: Contexts and constructs in the design of the contemporary city*, London: Spon Press, forthcoming 2005.

give us are multiple narratives of the city that intersect and overlap, connecting people to places and to each other. These are not likely to generate the creation of space, but instead help us see the city anew and take on board the stories of those we do not understand. We need to understand and be exposed to the existing narratives for a city or a community to allow us to make new narratives and to raise those issues that remain covered.

What most agree is that any narrative of the city is a shared process. It demands a willingness to listen and learn, to focus on a 'shared authority' and to be at the core of the engagement with community. It takes a great deal of research, community involvement and inventive mapping to find those narratives.

Charles Landry in *The Creative City* talks of narrative communication. 'Narrative communication is concerned with creating arguments; it takes time and promotes reflection. Its "bandwidth is as wide" as its scope is exploratory and linked to critical thinking.'[10] He distinguishes this from iconic communication, which triggers a response and has a highly focused purpose. An example he uses is that of Common Ground's [11] river-based songs for London's riverside communities. They used a participatory event about the songs as a springboard to enable people to meet and link with cultural and political regeneration and prepare the ground for other issues once commitment and motivation have been enhanced. Landry stresses: 'The challenge of creative urban initiatives is to embed narrative qualities and deeper principled understandings within projects which have iconic power.'[12] In Sheffield the two are completely interlinked; the iconic event is a constituent part of a consolidated story for re-imagining; narratives are worked and developed and retold to become the process.

What we learn from the narrative process more than anything is that it breaks through professional codes, it appeals to the majority – to lay people uninitiated in the private world of conventional architectural or regeneration 'language'. Narratives are easily remembered and are bound up with memories. Almost everyone can place themselves somewhere within them '... opening a way for the imagination into the wilderness of a kingdom as yet unmade'.[13]

Narrative as a utopian process

We used our storytelling further in North Sheffield to create a 'utopian' process, an overarching narrative developed with the community that was as much to do with social and economic as physical development. It was based on the political, historical and local knowledge the community had communicated to us, combined with an ambitious visionary statement for the future – a soft

10
C. Landry, *The Creative City: A toolkit for urban innovators*, London: Earthscan Publications and Comedia, 2000, p.64.

11
Common Ground are a participatory landscape group, based in London.

12
Landry, *The Creative City*, p.65.

13
Rodney Hall in his novel *The Island in the Mind*, set in the eighteenth century, talks of a composer writing an opera that describes the whole vision for an empire.

utopia. However, we were wary of being considered too utopian. Throughout history utopias have sought to address problems experienced at a particular time. But they are not just part of deep history, they have persisted in various forms throughout the twentieth century. However, history both far and near teaches us that the days of empire building and grand narratives for cultures and countries are at best deeply problematic and even dangerous. Such visions have been riddled with contradictions and have failed society too many times to be taken seriously. They remain as a critique of society and a mirror with which to look at ourselves.

According to Dieter Hassenpflug, postmodernity let go of the idea of utopia and its attempt to configure society. We are now more interested in spectacle, a-topia.[14] He describes a-topias as real and at the same time without site, potentially everywhere and at the same time nowhere, whereas utopias create an image of a better life in the space and time of a nowhere we can recognise now.

The City of Sheffield has had its share of utopian visions,[15] utopian housing schemes, city centre planning utopias, and lastly smaller highly politicised and anarchic utopias. Edward Carpenter,[16] for example, the writer and 'explorer of ways of simplifying life' started an openly homosexual utopian community in the repressed climate of the turn of the century. It began as an eight-acre smallholding on the outskirts of North Sheffield at Millthorpe. It continued for fourteen years and inspired Ruskin's later experimental project for a utopian community farm nearby. It responded to the 'idea' of Sheffield as a craft-based and productive city surrounded by a productive landscape. This idea of Sheffield still exists and is relevant to the way the communities perceive themselves on the edge of Sheffield and to the notion of Sheffield as a place of production. This notion was also captured in the SOAR project and in the resultant Framework document.

Image, identity and a city-wide narrative
So can we re-imagine a city or part of a city through narrative, propose a structure and a process – a soft utopia, a re-visioning for the new century? Does a creative 'meta-polemic' have any validity at all? Have we lost the possibility to think, to be imaginative, on a city-wide scale? Not just in strategies that operate at city level, but in a consistent and creative narrative that is appropriate for planning a future for a particular place and particular people.

The closest thing to a 'vision for a city' is usually its marketing strategy, how the city is packaged to attract investment. Hans Mommaas, in his essay 'City branding', talks of branding as a strategy to provide cities with an image, a cultural significance that will

14
D. Hassenpflug, 'From Utopia to A-topia', in *Social Utopias of the Twenties*, Berlin: Bauhaus Dessau, 1987, as discussed in A. Graafland and D. Hauptmann, *Cities in Transition*, Rotterdam: 010 Publishers, 2001.

15
Park Hill, perhaps the best known, was preceded by Abercrombie's radical plan for the city centre in 1924 and an eighteenth-century 'new town', the brainchild of the Duke of Derbyshire, of which only one house was built.

16
See D. Hardy, *Utopian England: Community experiments 1900–1945*, London: E & F Spon, 2000.

give added symbolic and economic value and exclusivity. A city's brand can also serve to raise its status as a tourist destination or as a residential or business location. 'City branding is associated primarily with the economically-inspired desire to position cities more positively in the midst of a scaled up, more mobile and flooded market of locations and destinations.'[17]

17
H. Mommaas, 'City branding: The necessity for sociocultural goals', in V. Patteeuw (ed.), *City Branding: Image building and building images*, Rotterdam: NAi, 2002.

Branding a city or giving it an image or icon is usually an empty gesture in terms of the physical environment: it says little about the identity of a place. It can be useful for the external view but it is not relevant or recognisable to many. A city's 'image' has always been important, but it needs constant attention to remain relevant. It has to be broad enough to encompass different interests and cultures. Also, it needs to look to unimagined futures and other possibilities.

Sheffield One, the development company charged with the regeneration of the city centre, wishes to create a 'new' vibrant city achieved through a knowledge-based development. This is a popular European objective. Their aim, and the city council's, is to attract high technology and e-technology companies to Sheffield, in addition to retaining the talent emerging from the two large universities. This aim is not ambitious or specific enough to Sheffield; it is the same aspiration as most other cities and it does not prioritise quality and innovation. However, if this expectation of a high technology city is placed against another trend for a healthier, more natural mode of living and a more responsible attitude to the planet, we have an interesting, almost unique set of relationships. This could be a powerful selling point for the city. This relationship between technology and nature became a constant linking thematic behind the narratives developed during the participatory process in North Sheffield. At both city scale and building scale there seemed a resonance in the relationship.

In terms of branding Sheffield is probably in the second league of World Cities. These cities are often post-industrial cities or have lost their focus. They are more approachable than the capital city or the region in that they are smaller, more understandable and have more coherent possibilities. However, they do not have the draw or the intellectual pull of capital cities. Often cities of around 1.5 to 2 million people, they include Malmö in Sweden and Portland, Oregon, in the USA. Interestingly, they seem to follow similar themes that are important in their marketing and their image. Malmö is successfully developing a sustainable and ecological image that is making it notable at a European level, particularly with new housing and the community recycling schemes. Portland is becoming known as a 'liveable city' and is marketing itself as the 'greenest city in the USA' due to the linear network of urban parks and transport routes and in particular the forest park coming right in to the centre. Despite massive competition from other American cities, to the European eye it is impressive and ambitious. A local lobbying group managed to move a motorway to reveal the hidden riverside of the Willamette River. The impetus for change is coming from ambitious community groups.

Portland is a useful comparison to Sheffield – they are both surrounded by hills and have an industrial past – though Portland is also a port. In Portland grizzly bears come into the city centre; in Sheffield roe deer and foxes make their way to the centre, by way of the linear parks and routes from country to city centre. Where Portland and Malmö differ from Sheffield is in their ambition. Portland, perhaps because it is an American city, has managed to change its image and carry out ambitious projects we in Britain can only dream about; our top-down planning processes and limited ambitions restrict the development of visions that can be developed through both institutional and community-based processes.

Mention Sheffield to someone who lives in London or Paris and the image, from films such as the *Full Monty*, will most probably be one of a rather sad, grimy, industrial, or rather post-industrial, city. It is seen as poor, somewhere in the middle of England and surrounded by a nondescript landscape. Of course in some ways these views are accurate – what is most inaccurate about this mass of externalised images of Sheffield is the varied topography and the dramatic landscape of the city.

The relationship between *nature* (landscape) and *technology* (innovative industry) is particularly apposite to Sheffield, whose great strength and *raison d'être* historically are based on its topography. Sheffield has seen extraordinary change over the past 1000 years due to the relationship between technology and the land form. It was at the centre of the first wave of advanced technology in the Industrial Revolution. The rivers and the valleys harnessed power and drove the bigger and bigger production base for steel.

It is this relationship between nature and technology that we used to provide a theme for a narrative strategy in order to give the whole of Sheffield a new image. To find a base to explore such a vision the starting point has to come from a wide range of disciplines describing processes apposite to twenty-first-century society; processes that allow an over-arching vision on one hand and an interest and involvement in the most minute detail of personal experience and community needs on the other. These processes include exploring the dialectic of nature and technology, looking at the city as landscape – the topography and topology – understanding

14.02 – Vulcan on the Town Hall

the ecology and developing sustainability. Also, it demands encouraging a more feminised city, one where the needs and voices of women are visible, exploring new forms of practice and using and understanding the political processes. Sheffield needs to capitalise on the factors that make it a unique location to dwell in, exploring a sense of a distinct geographical place as well as other local, cultural, historical and social differences. This also involves engagement with topographical, meteorological, seasonal and diurnal cycles.

Sheffield's success depends on developing this high technology future as a distinct 'valley' or cluster or region, a 'silicon valley' in the north of England. These highly successful concentrations of expertise encourage a new type of regionalism and distinctiveness. Peter Hall, in an interview discussing the Ruhr valley, supports this view:

> I don't believe the world is simply becoming one world, local interactions between people, talking to each other, people sharing each other's thoughts, people working on problems together is likely to be far more effective. It is still far more likely that you get effective results if people are able to communicate on a day-to-day basis – people are far more likely to interact creatively over short distances.[18]

18
Interview with Peter Hall, May 2002 in MVRDV and H. Cantz, *The Regionmaker – Rhein Ruhr City: The hidden metropolis*, p.54, Düsseldorf: NRW-Forum Kultur und Wirtschaft, 2002.

A key issue in the success of a city is its ability to build and maintain successful existing neighbourhoods in the suburbs of the city. So North Sheffield, or Southey and Owlerton as the area is known, is instrumental to the success of the whole city of Sheffield. The population here forms a large part of the population of the city and the economy of the city is therefore dependent on the success of Southey and Owlerton. The SOAR team explored this broad thematic idea to describe an ecological city landscape, one that builds on all its assets to build a sustainable future through its history, its people, its politics and its economy and through the physical environment.

The overarching themes

History and politics
Sheffield's past is a political one, and it is still suffering from political acts in its recent past. Potent symbols of Sheffield are evident in the physical form of the city. It was heavily bombed because of its industry in the war and it was marginalised in the 1980s and 1990s because of its politics. It became a poor northern city, like many others in the same post-industrial predicament. But Vulcan still stands on top of the town hall and high quality stainless steel is still manufactured in the city. The decline of wealth in the north of

Sheffield, an area of steel workers' housing built in the 1950s, is entirely due to the decline in the size of the workforce for the steel industry.

The topography

'You can see the rain coming round the corner from Bakewell'
Resident from a Norfolk Park high-rise housing block in Shefield.

At city level it is the topography – the hills and valleys, the rivers, the trees, linear urban parks and the clustering of the built form – that gives Sheffield a distinctive image.

14.03 – Sketch of an altered topography.

The city centre sits on a raised acropolis in the central valley surrounded by seven hills. In order to strengthen this image the city centre could be higher and denser, more city-like. Second, the hills need to be more identifiable from the city centre, something that gives them a specific image.

The assets and attributes of Sheffield became a catalyst in the relationship between *nature* and *technology* – this became for us an appropriate citywide strategy for Sheffield that North Sheffield could be a part of.

Landscape as a tool to reimagine an area is a popular theme today. The Dutch architects MVRDV,[19] in their polemic scenario, use 'park city' as one of four proposals in their regional plan for Rhein-Ruhr City. When the inhabitants of Essen were asked what they thought was beautiful about their city in the Ruhr they mentioned only the landscape and the amenities. In 2003 Will Alsop in his commission to look at Bradford uses the idea of the city as a park to rethink public buildings. In the North Sheffield Regeneration plan produced in 2001, the idea of park city becomes one part of a narrative for the area. These ideas were taken further with the intimate

19
MVRDV, the Dutch architects, described in MVRDV and H. Cantz 2002.

20

The 'Little Mester' is an eighteenth-century regional term used to describe Sheffield's self-employed cutlers. They rented space in factories and their finished goods were sold by the factory owner. They were the backbone of the Sheffield cutlery industry and were instrumental in helping Sheffield achieve a worldwide reputation for craftsmanship. The term is also more widely used to describe almost any self-employed craftsmen working in metal or steel.

21

Joseph Hunter from: *A Brief Memoir of the Late Joseph Hunter, with a Descriptive Catalogue*, London: J. E. Taylor, 1861.

22

D. Matless, *Landscape and Englishness, Picturing history*, London: Reaktion Books, 1998. The subject is problematic due to the overwhelmingly white middle-class use of the countryside in Britain.

local knowledge of the use of the green spaces and the relationship and identity of them now. Early community engagement brought out the themes of industrial past and of landscape – mainly through the importance nearly everyone placed on views. Like Carpenter's experiment and the smallholdings of the little mesters,[20] like the ring of allotments today around Sheffield, the landscape is ever present here. Even in the nineteenth-century days of industrial grime and deprivation, Joseph Hunter, a historian and writer, describes Sheffield as '... so beautifully clothed with a forest verdure, the ground declining to the river Don'.[21]

This 'world as landscape' sensibility is not exclusively an English notion, but it is particular to the English ideas of the picturesque and the sublime, the key themes within the eigteenth-century landscape obsession. Lately this has been both a problematic and nostalgic image but David Matless[22] reminds us that the idea of landscape has not always been nostalgic. From the interwar period through wartime and reconstruction, landscape became central to a vision of England, modern and traditional, urban and rural, progressive and preservationist. Having identified a potential vision for the city and processes through which this vision might be negotiated, the team then developed specific aspects of the vision. These were then used as the starting point for informing and constructing the narratives in the participative stage of the visioning exercise for North Sheffield.

Specific aspects of a vision for Sheffield

A different attitude to the rivers and the water
Redefining the role of water, not only as an amenity for leisure pursuits but also as something more fundamental to the urban landscape, as a workplace or part of the living (home) environment. A different set of values could be developed based on an ecological viewpoint and this in turn could be incorporated into the design of the urban landscape. Power could be used in a different way, harnessing the rivers again.

The linear parks – park city
Sheffield's greatest asset and a relic of its industrial success. The linear parks are an ecological and pleasurable way to reach the countryside as well as providing green corridors coming right into the centre of the city. If all the linear corridors were improved and connected, Sheffield could become a truly 'green' city. Still polluted parts of the Upper Don Valley and other post-industrial sites can use new landscape practices to restore them and connect them to other

linear routes. Through the process of pollutant removal people are made aware of their industrial heritage. The whole area is archaeology and provides multiple readings for people's memories. The walk as narrative...

14.04 – Timber industry along the rivers, an image illustrating a possible timber mill as part of a collaborative new type of industry. An example of the type of images used in the participatory visioning stage. (Image by Alex Mingozzi.)

Using the trees

Sheffield is one of the most wooded cities in the country. From an elevated position from most parts of Sheffield you can barely see urban form in amongst the trees. Productive industries using timber thinnings could be a viable industry in Sheffield and have been part of Sheffield's history. Using the trees can help transform the post-industrial image of Sheffield and heavy industry to a more natural ecological image.

Recycling as a productive high technology industry

Recycling is important to the city, with the city-wide 'Sheffield Heat and Power' already established and other recycling ventures, including the traditional scrap metal and tyre recycling that defines the area near the Wicker Arches. There is a strong base to make this part of the high technology revolution in the city. Sheffield could pioneer new disassembly plants for recycling cars and other by-products of our consumer society.

14.05 – An image used in the participatory visioning sessions to illustrate future work practices for a knowledge-based, high technology future; the office of the future, set in an existing wood in Shirecliffe, North Sheffield. (Image by Alex Coppock.)

A knowledge-based, high technology future

The city's aim to attract high technology and e-technology companies to Sheffield raises two key issues. One must be to radically increase the small moneyed professional and skilled population in order to provide a better economic base for the city. This asks the question – what would it take to attract those new citizens? Make it *the* city to move to and be in; encourage the large numbers of students at the two universities to stay.

Developing the neighbourhood strategies leading to the regeneration framework

The regeneration board SOAR and the professionals worked together with the community and 'stakeholders' to see whether a physical 'identity' and image from the city-wide narrative agenda were appropriate to help develop the social, environmental and economic regeneration plans for Southey and Owlerton. Our working process incorporated new ways of working, talking and mapping all informing specific narratives for the neighbourhood strategies and the regeneration framework for the whole area. The new ways of working meant putting local people at the centre of a partnership with the council, other agencies, professionals and city-wide institutions. The council team included officers from each directorate so that important links could be made between issues. For example, the housing department for the first time worked with the parks department to look at the relationship between the problems in the park and the housing backing on to it, rather than fronting on to it. New ways of talking involved using artists and facilitators to open up the dialogue between local people and professionals. Participatory games and structured events surrounding personal experiences and memories used new types of visual information to test out ideas and help build the narrative from the repertoire of stories. New ways of mapping took as a starting point what local people told us about their neighbourhood from their stories. The information was recorded and mapped and used to further investigate and draw out themes missed out by conventional maps and reports. Favourite walks and special journeys, and the particular views that had important family events attached were recorded.

14.06 (above) – Topiary sculptures, part of a narrative for rethinking the gardens and green spaces.

14.07 (right) – Mapping the popular places and walks in Parson Cross.

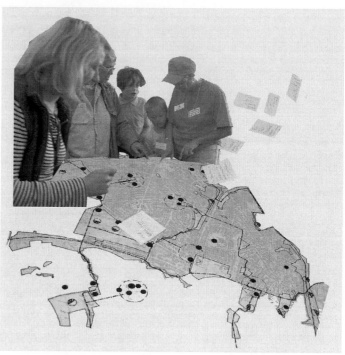

23
Neighbourhoods making up the SOAR area of North Sheffield are Southey Green, Hillsborough, Foxhill, Owlerton, Shirecliffe, Longley and Parsons Cross.

Each neighbourhood[23] chose to consult and develop its strategy in its own particular way, but there were many common features that allow a generic narrative process to be recorded.

All the neighbourhoods used neighbourhood and guided walks, creative workshops, storytelling, visits and feedback sessions in the development of their own strategies. These events relied on the need for regular communication, careful judgement of how and when professionals should present their ideas and observations, and continual reassessment of the tools and techniques used. The process started with no preconceptions about what could come out of it in term of ideas and stories. There were some themes that were important to all of the neighbourhoods and there were some that were specific. Issues like the views, the problems with transport to other parts of the city, lack of community facilities, security, lack of child care, lack of health provision and healthy food available were common to most neighbourhoods.

Often the overarching themes could be related to the whole city. Ideas moved from neighbourhood level to area to city-wide level and back again, and a dynamic top-down bottom-up narrative began to appear. A particular game we played at a Parson Cross festival applied ideas to issues that had come out of the mapping and walks. We asked residents to make comments on a series of images that developed a narrative for a more sustainable future, with new forms of energy, refurbishment of their homes and other ideas to improve their environment. All the ideas were collaged on to the streets and parks of Parson Cross. They were loose, sometimes controversial and open to interpretation; they were not designs.

14.08 – Image board suggesting street side improvements. (Image by Louise Ciotti.)

Work was brought together from the consultation on the wider ecology and nature of the area, what the opportunities for the residents were and how to create further opportunity. From this, taking a 'step back', some overarching ideas emerged, reflecting each neighbourhood in the wider area. These ideas, put together as a storyboard, would help change people's perception of the area. It would highlight and celebrate the character of the place and hopefully encourage others to visit and make the whole area more visible in the city. This is summarised below:

A dynamic narrative for North Sheffield – five big ideas
Although the ideas look primarily concerned with landscape, in each case our concern was to make a connection between the natural and built environments and between the communities: joining the green spaces and key routes to centres of community activity,

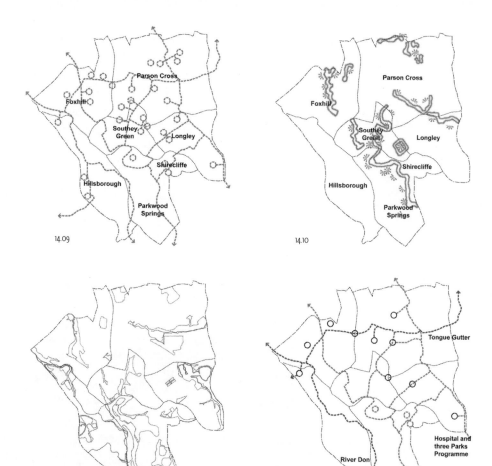

14.09

14.10

14.11

14.12

Tongue Gutter

Hospital and
three Parks
Programme

River Don

Edges

14.09 – *Park City* – all the open spaces could be linked
to form a green web.

14.10 – *See and be seen* – the topography makes
particular ridges and areas very visible. These need to be
marked to make them visible throughout the city and to
each other.

14.11 – *Identity from landform* – the vegetation patterns
are distinctive and linked to the topography. Grassy
tops, wooded slopes and river valleys can give clues to
the types of physical development.

14.12 – *From city to country and back again* – by joining up
footpaths and trails distinctive routes emerge into the
city centre and out to the countryside.

14.13 – *Green arteries* – these link the key open spaces
with community facilities, emphasising the green
parkland character of the city.

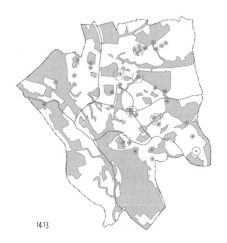

14.13

using built form to make the area visible to the rest of the city, reflecting the identity of each particular neighbourhood, and using the green web to support local facilities and enterprises (See Figs. 14.09 – 14.13).

Parkwood Springs: The next stage in the development framework for North Sheffield.

Shortly after the completion of the framework document for Southey and Owlerton we were commissioned to develop a detailed community vision for Parkwood Springs, a largely landscape area partly inside and partly outside Southey and Owlerton. This provided us with the opportunity to build on the techniques we used in the preparation of the framework document and to try out the 'five big ideas' narrative that emerged from the process. Would it work at a smaller scale? Would the communities around Parkwood Springs find the narrative and the approach relevant? (Why should they be different from SOAR?)

Parkwood Springs is a vast scarred landscape, a largely redundant area of the city with many challenges.[24] It also has moments of great beauty and importance; an historic graveyard, a beautiful river landscape, some successful businesses and small industry and a very popular dry ski slope, one of the biggest in Europe. The communities and stakeholders involved were diverse, ranging from the utilities providers such as British Gas (whose above-ground pipes cover the lower reaches of the site), to displaced communities (who still meet up after 50 years), to the friends of the historic graveyard. Two of the biggest owners of the site are the ski slope and the most controversial – the vast landfill site. The whole population of Hillsborough look on to Parkwood Springs and the site is ringed with housing.

The complexity of ownership, involved communities, stakeholders and issues indicated that the most important task of a participative approach was to break down conflicting interests and develop a consensus that everyone could work with. We now had an initial narrative for the city and the more specific physical narrative of North Sheffield to use as the basis for starting the process. The strength of the narrative themes worked well to encourage all the interested parties to work together. We developed a series of workshop events to encourage a variety of stakeholders to come and give their views on the long-term development of the site. Perhaps the most successful, however, was the launch of the visioning process at the Hillsborough Winter Fair – it imagined the first vintage of wine produced on Parkwood Springs and asked local residents to give their views and try the mulled wine.

14.14 & 14.15 – Local press about Parkwood Springs.

24
This project became one of the first commissions for the BDR (the University of Sheffield Bureau of Design Research) when we won the commission to develop the community vision for the Parkwood Springs Steering Group, after 'live' project by School of Architecture diploma students re-imagined the site for the Department of Environment and Leisure (DEL) of Sheffield City Council in 2001.

25

Sheffield School of Architecture diploma
students produced the images used in the
storyboards, again during a 'live project'.

This opened the discussion to the storyboards [25] that suggested all the things that could happen on the site based on early consultation with the council, the stakeholders and community groups for what was needed. It also suggested a bold framework the ideas could become part of based on the five big ideas narrative for Southey and Owlerton. It created swathes of different landscapes

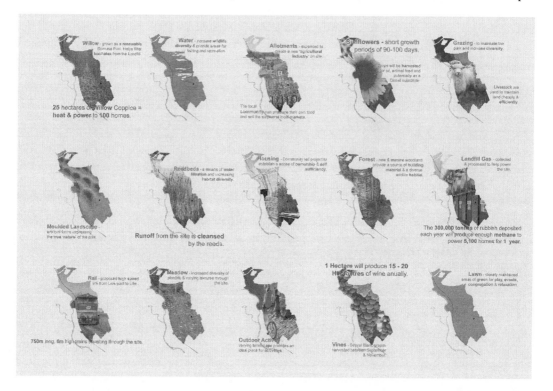

14.16 (above) – Building a narrative for a sustainable
future for Parkwood Springs.

14.17 (opposite page) – The plan 'jigsaw' used at a
collaborative workshop allowing participants to move
pieces around and remove and add elements and
facilities agreed on.

with leisure and sporting facilities dispersed around the landscape. It made connections to the green arteries and connected the site to the city centre and to the countryside. It became part of the green web. Some of the visitors to the Winter Fair recognised the narrative ideas and appreciated seeing them visualised in the vision for Parkwood Springs. Comments were diverse. What was surprising is how many of the ideas suggested had already been tried on the site. Many of the allotment holders who had been on Parkwood Springs for generations had tried growing grapes, for example. They did well if they were protected, but the wind was too strong.

The vibrancy of the event and the enthusiasm and knowledge that residents had of both Parkwood Springs and the wider area ensured many comments from all age groups. This gave us the questions for the more in-depth participatory events where a specific plan emerged. The process here, we are convinced, went more smoothly because we had a relevant framework, a story to underpin

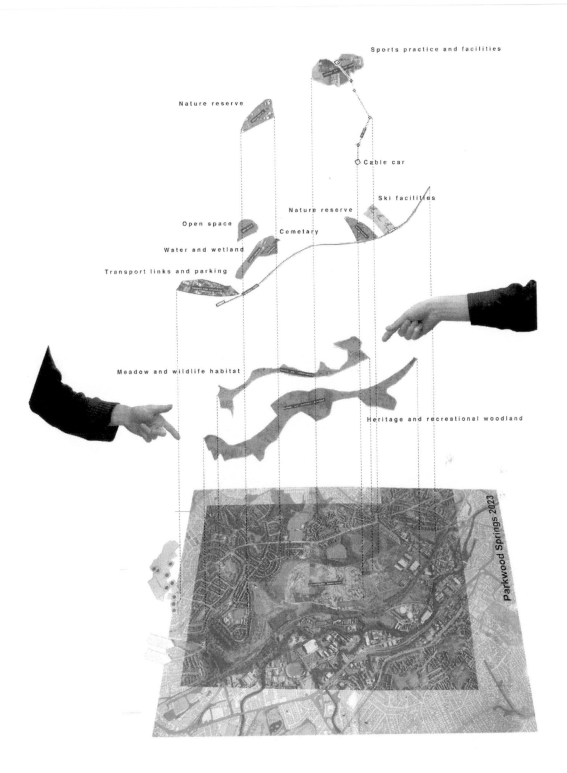

Sports practice and facilities

Nature reserve

Cable car

Ski facilities

Open space

Nature reserve

Cemetary

Water and wetland

Transport links and parking

Meadow and wildlife habitat

Heritage and recreational woodland

Parkwood Springs 2023

the development ideas for Parkwood Springs that everyone felt had relevance and resonance to Sheffield.

What if?

26
L. Sandercock, *Towards Cosmopolis: Planning for multicultural cities*, Chichester: John Wiley, 1998.

Planners and planning are changing. Leonie Sandercock,[26] a Canadian planning academic, discusses new planning epistemologies leading to bottom-up – insurgent or radical – broader processes that now should take the place of top-down – narrower and more politicised thinking. The problem is still that the planning processes are multilayered, with community-led action still at the bottom – there is a perception that it will not be visionary. What if policies developed ensured that there was effective corporate working at both strategic and project level and that the community-led projects were supported at regional, national and local level? That would be another story.

The SOAR team have had their framework document endorsed at local and city level. It represents where we are now; things might change and develop. We hope they will, for that is part of the process. The strategies developed comprise an ambitious programme of improvement and change for the whole area over a ten-year period. Now the ideas have been developed, they need to be implemented. The neighbourhood groups in each area, responsible for their own strategy have now been given executive responsibility to allow them to continue in crucial roles for the implementation of development projects in partnership with a corporate team of council officers and other agencies. A step change in design quality is being achieved by developing project criteria that ensures all projects (whether capital or revenue) involve participation, combine social, environmental and economic benefits and reflect the nature-technology identity. All physical projects will be tested against the five big ideas narrative and showcase new ways of bringing nature and technology together. SOAR have ensured that all projects would need to show how they help bring opportunities for training and jobs in new technologies, such as digital, cultural and environmental industries, and this will be incorporated into the scoring criteria for all bids to SOAR. This represents a large step towards a truly top-down/bottom-up regeneration process and hopefully a new story.

Chapter 15

Marion von Osten

Politics beyond the white cube

1

C. Kravagna, *Agenda: Perspektiven kritischer Kunst*, Vienna: Sachbuch, Folio Verlag, 2000.

In 1999, the artist Julie Ault, a member of the artists' collective Group Material, pointed out in the publication *Agenda: Perspektiven kritischer Kunst*[1] that the practice of viewing an exhibition usually put the viewer in a specific silenced and disciplined position. Referring to exhibition projects like 'Alt Youth Media' in the New Museum, New York, in 1996, Ault argued that in contrast with most art galleries, this show gave the public much more space for everyday life practices in the exhibitions hall, such as magazine reading, video viewing, copying fanzines, doing research, meeting with friends, music listening, etc. Her statement referred to exhibition practices in the 1990s that not only involved the audience in transdisciplinary and participatory ways, but also were strongly issue-oriented, addressing politically and socially relevant questions. Project exhibitions of this kind have been developed as collective artistic practices or by artists who started to curate shows in collaboration with actors from other fields for specific purposes. For example, the exhibition 'If you lived here' at the Dia Arts Foundation in 1989,[2] organised and initiated by the artist Martha Rosler, focused on gentrification processes and homelessness, not just because this was a relevant issue, but because the gallery itself was located in a specific gentrification area and because of this, it had been involved in the transformation process. The exhibition addressed the bohemian surroundings of the new gallery location, which constituted both the potential audience of the gallery and the important actors of the gentrification process. This example shows how the art audience can be addressed in terms of actors related to the issue of the exhibition, and also how in such a case audiences other than the conventional art public have entered in the gallery space and participated in the project (i.e. political activists involved in housing projects, homeless people, urban planners and social workers).

2

M. Rosler, *Discussions in Contemporary Culture #6: If You Lived Here..*, New York: Dia Art Foundation, 1991.

The potential of the cultural space to establish a specific public includes also the potential of its alternative use: to address and involve in the project, different audiences who are usually separated by their disciplines or their social and class order. In that sense, the project exhibition used the 'white cube' (the gallery space) as a communicative platform, a place for public encounter, a stage exhibiting not just knowledge but ideas about collaborative practices, and where new spaces of discourse have also been established.

Traditional exhibiting is, in Tony Bennett's sense, 'a set of cultural technologies concerned to organise a voluntarily self-regulating citizenry'. The exhibitionary complex, a technology to exhibit knowledge and artefacts to a broader public, that began in Europe in the late eighteenth century, was in Bennett's opinion already a response to the problem of order, but one that was seeking to transform that problem into a problem of culture. The historical emergence of the art exhibition was closely related to that of a wider range of institutions: history museums, natural science museums, dioramas and panoramas, national and, later, international exhibitions, arcades and department stores. All these served as linked sites for the development and circulation of new disciplines (history, biology, art history, anthropology) and their discursive formations (the 'past', 'evolution', 'aesthetics', 'Man') as well as for the development of new technologies of vision.[3] For example, the first large exhibitions in London showed artefacts and crafts from abroad, in particular from the British Empire and its colonies. Since the beginning of eighteenth century and later, in the nineteenth century, the relation of the 'exhibitionary complex' to European colonialism was crucial. Because of this colonialising structure behind this practice of 'showing in public', a dichotomising system had been institutionalised and, with it, a great number of current paradigmatic oppositions were constituted: traditional versus modern, oral versus written and printed, agrarian and customary communities versus urban and industrialised civilisation, and subsistence economies versus highly productive economies.[4] Beside other educational forms, the emerging western civilian has been governed through a variety of forms of displaying and staging knowledge within this emerging exhibition complex. The project of 'showing' was grounded on eurocentric, dichotomising systems, established national tastes and fashions and the self-consciousness of a 'civilised world'.

It is crucial for the understanding of new participatory and political practices in the art world that the art gallery stood from its beginning in the context of other bourgeois institutions, which had not only the power of privileging knowledge and creating specific normative narrations, but also the educational aim of creating a bourgeois, distinct, well-behaving public. Before the 1960s and the transgressive practices of artists at that time (conceptual art, happenings, performances) the art public were never addressed as a participatory public, or as I would like to emphasise, as potential pro-

3
Tony Bennett, 'The exhibitionary complex', *New Formations*, 4, 1988, pp.73-102.

4
See Valentine Mudimbe, *The Idea of Africa*, Bloomington, IN: Indiana University Press, 1994.

5
See B. O'Doherty, 'Inside the white cube:
Notes on the gallery space (Parts I-II-III)',
Artforum, March/April/November, 1976.

ducers, but only as spectators viewing and reflecting on an artefact. The body politics of the exhibition space in general corresponds to the assumption that the spectator's eye is the privileged sense. It is not only the art gallery, the white cube,[5] that has been constructed around this assumption, but the total displays of modernist orientated exhibitions (such as those designed by Herbert Bayer) as well. The privileging of the spectator's eye has constructed an audience of passive subjectivities, neutral, objective arrangements of space and product-oriented visual cultures.

It is not surprising to see photographs of art exhibitions where the spectator is left out, or if visible, is always shown from behind, and is usually male. This passive gendered role has to be understood within the background of the strict division of labour in the art world. Nobody questioned the divided roles of the artist as autonomous producer, of the curator and the gallerist as autonomous distributors, and of the audience as a passive consumer, before the artists belonging to the institutional critique movement in the 1960s and 1970s, and related practices in the early 1990s.

But the history of the exhibition space as a social space is still unwritten. If we look more closely we will always find a more marginal tactical use of the institutionalised spaces by the so-called consumers, by groups of artists or small collectives. These tactics are active in the shadow of the strategies of control, as mentioned above, and they show other kinds of attempt to master the unmasterable. The extensive counter-cultural use of the art space, observable since the early days of modernism, has been intensified in the 1970s and again in the late 1980s and early 1990s.

The intention in my work as an artist and curator relates to these concerns, and tries therefore to change the perspective on 'the gallery' as a stable and neutral setting. The exhibition project *Sex & Space* (Shedhalle Zurich 1996), for example, was related to questions of gender and marginality, focusing on the need to connect gender debates with their context in various hegemonic settings in architecture and urban planning. In the public workshops geographers, architects, media activists and city planners were confronted with artists, critics and political activists; and the same process occurred the other way round in specifically organised panel discussions in a TV studio setting used to record the events. This included the fact that the exhibition space was misused for personal activities.

In terms of a feminine practice that analyses power structures, but also produces specific relations, solidarity and forms of collectivity that go beyond reduced identity articulations, the field of everyday life and the living conditions as well as the symbolic space of representation have the same importance; and as such, they are shown as being relevant for the production of (art) 'works'. In highlighting this usage aspect, the project went beyond linear speaking structures (i.e. one-way communication from institution to its audiences). The institutional framework (the exhibition) was transformed into a communicative space, and the audience/public integrated into it as part of the project's central questions.[6]

MoneyNations, another project at Shedhalle Zurich in 1998, was an exhibition, a radio workshop, an international congress, a web site and a video programme; but, much more importantly, it was also a network of producers, an initiative of a supranational community, between west-, middle-, east- and south European cultural producers from different disciplines, who developed projects from a cultural perspective over the Schengen (visa) border by making the border itself into an issue. In *MoneyNations*, the exhibition space was transformed into a space for political theory and interdisciplinary collaborations rather than a space for visual and textual representation and artistic works only. The institution was used as a producer of content and connectivity, as a social and participatory space and as a space for critical issues, theory and anti-racist politics.[7]

In the most recent project, *Be Creative. The Creative Imperative!* that I produced in collaboration with artists, ex-students and theorists for the Museum of Design Zurich in 2002, the central concern was the current educational, spatial, economical and social concepts, and practices that involve a shifting emancipatory vocabulary within neo-liberal politics.[8]

With this background, I would like to finish with the remark that since the democratisation movement of the 1970s and its claims for political co-determination, the participative approach has also been used as a strategy for optimising take-up. Working for a maximal inclusion of all those involved in the decision-making process wherever possible, the participative approach involves a bundle of basic anthropological, psychological and sociological measures, and also a repertoire of strategies and tactics for making the participation imperative operational. Concepts like 'empowerment', 'civic commitment' or 'action research', procedures like round tables, open space, future workshops or mediation are used in a whole variety of social settings today. They support the formal democratic decision-making processes, but also compete and conflict with them.

The exhibition projects that work today with participatory elements need to reflect on these new paradigms of cultural technologies 'concerned to organise a voluntarily self-regulating citizenry'.

6
See *www.k3000.ch/sex&space*

7
See *www.moneynations.ch*

8
M. von Osten, 'Be creative. The creative imperative!' in *Norm der Abweichung*, Vienna: Edition Voldemeer Zürich and Springer, 2003.

Chapter 16

Muf (Liza Fior, Sophie Handler, Katherine Clarke and Kath Shonfield)

Rights of common:
ownership, participation, risk

1

Liza Fior gave a lecture at the University of Sheffield, in the Forum series 2002. The text of this article is credited as Liza Fior, Sophie Handler, Katherine Clarke and Kath Shonfield.

When I went to lecture in Sheffield I spoke without notes and the lecture was videoed.[1] Some time afterwards, we were asked to be part of the book which developed from the lecture series and video transcripts. But the transcriber lost our tape. So in the spirit of 'The cat ate our homework' we present some current work. Architecture is slow, so they are the same projects as described in the lecture but in a different guise: drawings are now site photographs, what was a strategy is now being implemented, and lastly, the way theory participates in our practice is now our sole responsibility.

The collection is called *Architecture and Participation*; the theme is collaboration. Since the lecture was given, Kath Shonfield[2] – the long-term Muf collaborator – has died. The obvious theme for this essay is therefore Kath's contribution to our practice, the way that she gave shape to our thinking for external consumption, and for us too. And yet it is too soon, and too sad to do her contribution justice. In part because she is still around, she made generous claims for our work which we are still attempting to make good on.

2

Kath Shonfield was later to change her name to Kath Vaughan Williams. Her contribution to this book, the following chapter, is credited as Vaughan Williams.

The *Muf* formula is detail/strategy = DETAIL: the utopian projections of strategy are simultaneously understood through the transformation of a tiny bit of the here and now. So strategy derives from the up close and personal, and DETAIL from an up close look at a strategic 'What if?'[3]

3
From Kath Shonfield's introduction in:
K. Shonfield and Muf, *This Is What We Do: A Muf Manual*, London: Ellipsis, 2001.16a

This wild generosity of thought, this largesse, is perhaps a prerequisite for participation to become a reality. We present two pieces of work: one a body of work in Tilbury and the second a reprint of Kath's last piece of writing about a Muf project.

Assertions and wild claims:
1 'The design for the community garden makes a public contested space genuinely public.' Liza Fior, Sheffield
2 What is a horse without a field? What is a field without a horse? Posters in bus shelters, Tilbury. *The Horse's Tail.*
3 'I'll be your Reyner Banham'. Kath Shonfield to Muf, 2000.

Architecture projects are often at first dependent on wild claims which are in turn followed by a set of procedures to achieve certainty – risk assessment tables, the insistence on using proven materials and techniques, everything put into writing. Did someone once write a book called *Entwurf und Utopie*, i.e. *Project and Utopia*? The experience of public realm projects is closer to *Project and Reality* – but it sounds better in German because *Entwurf* sounds like you are throwing something out into space and seeing where it will land.

Relationships need nurturing; their development is unknown at outset. Art practice is predicated on not knowing its resolution.

The Muf manual was in part a series of ambitions, of wild claims, of assertions, of promissory notes stated in good faith – assertions which are now being honoured, met and tested through putting those early claims into practice.

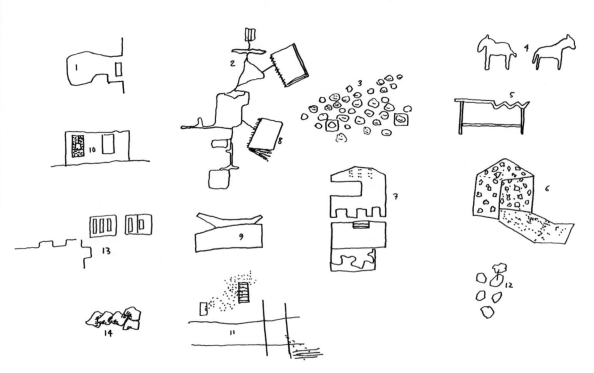

16.01 – A pictoral glossary of Muf projects, including the research project *The Horse's Tail* (4), and the corresponding design for the community garden / park (7) and the installation of pumpkins at the Urban Summit 2002 (3).

The first project we present is the design for a community garden/park in Tilbury (completion 2004) and its companion research project, *The Horse's Tail*, a short research project to investigate the cultural and emotional claims to the land expressed by the people of Tilbury by the semi-legal practice of grazing ponies on it. The second is a 5000-word text by Katherine Shonfield prompted by *Pumpkin Logic*, a video piece, pumpkin soup and the delegates of the Urban Summit Birmingham 2002.

Tilbury: A Community Park 2002-2004

Tilbury Park and *The Horse's Tail* are two interlinked pieces of work, a design for a park and a piece of artist-led work. The theme of both is contested space.

A landscape project was developed with the residents of a housing estate in Tilbury. The garden acknowledges and makes space for the diverse and contradictory demands made on limited space. The starting point for the design for the park was the observation, on the first site visit, of horse dung amongst the stray play equipment in the middle of the site, a barren stretch of grass land surrounded by housing tenanted in the main by temporary residents. The bleak open flat windy space was used by children, dogs, and joyriders dumping cars and sometimes torching them. It was not used by the old or the very young. The horse dung was from horses that belonged to some of the tenants. These horses had not been mentioned in the brief and the land was not for grazing. Once recognised (a photograph of dung beside a swing) and represented (a client interview), the horses were official. They existed – as transgressive and also as a source of pride.

In Tilbury public space is vulnerable and contested. How do you make a park that is notionally for the community, really *for* the community? Can it be robust *and* bucolic?

The scheme

An undulating landscape of made ground is laid over the site, first as a meadow, then banking to form windbreaks as boundaries to and platforms for activities, then transforming itself into a cluster of hills and shoring up at the edges to secure the site against joyriding – on car, bike or pony. Cut into this landscape are a dressage arena for horses, a scented garden, individual alcoves for play equipment ranged off a path, 16-metre-long south-facing granite steps as if appropriated from the front of a town hall, a lawn big enough for football but not identified as such and, at the opposite end to the meadow, the cluster of hills inset with slides and swings for the under-fives. The embankments separate uses from one another but planting (indigenous decorative almost weeds) overspills and overlaps these shared and discrete spaces. The project is currently on site; whether it will be used as we have imagined will only be demonstrated in time. By June we will see if the young men that gather on the corner will sprawl instead on the granite steps or if horses will exercise in the dressage arena. If the sense of who we are is in part dependent on where we are, then does being in a place, however transitory, generate a sense of ownership of that place – however momentary?

16.02 (top left) – Tilbury steps under construction
16.03 (above) – Horse arena
16.04 (right) – Tilbury gymkhana

The Horse's Tail: a research project, Tilbury 2003-2004

The Horse's Tail began with a group of secondary schoolchildren documenting the presence of ponies in Tilbury through photographs and stories gathered and mapped in layers onto a digital archive. A group of primary schoolchildren started fabricating horse heads and bodies out of card and fleece: costumes for acting out these stories in their literal setting. A horse (with two children inside) walks across Tilbury. The horse is photographed performing along its route and made into posters that are displayed at bus stops across Tilbury (see Figs. 16.05 & 16.06), questioning people's relationship to their surrounding landscape.

The ponies represent a desire for a relationship to the land that exists outside conventional organisation of social order, emotional claims that test regulated/prescribed definitions of land use.

Rights of common can include:
• Grazing of sheep or cattle (herbage)
• Taking peat or turf (turbary)
• Taking wood, gorse or furze (estovers)
• Taking of fish (piscary)
• Eating of acorns or beechmast by pigs (pannage)

A removal policy threatens to remove horses that have wandered onto the common – though ownership and definition of this land (like those of the horse) remain ambiguous. Is land borrowable?

Dealing with the proper place and function of things in a place... where ownership of a place is always legislated. But how do you lay emotional claim to a place that isn't yours? Can you still belong to a place that you move through?

16.05 & 16.06 – Posters from The Horse's Tail

Sometimes projects stay unresolved: you start out with a set of preconceptions (to investigate the historical relationship between the legacy of a transient population and their connection to the landscape through the ponies) but you meet people who draw your project aside and experience the frustrating delight of meeting someone who encapsulates the project when time has almost run out, and realising that the person you most want to speak with is the most reticent.

Sometimes outcomes remain open-ended or turn in on themselves, circuitously, so that you find yourself, in some ways, back where you were.

Maybe a dressage arena specified for horses will end up as a space for riding mopeds, where for lack of 'owned' horses a designated space for ponies becomes a borrowed space for adolescent masquerade – moped dressage.

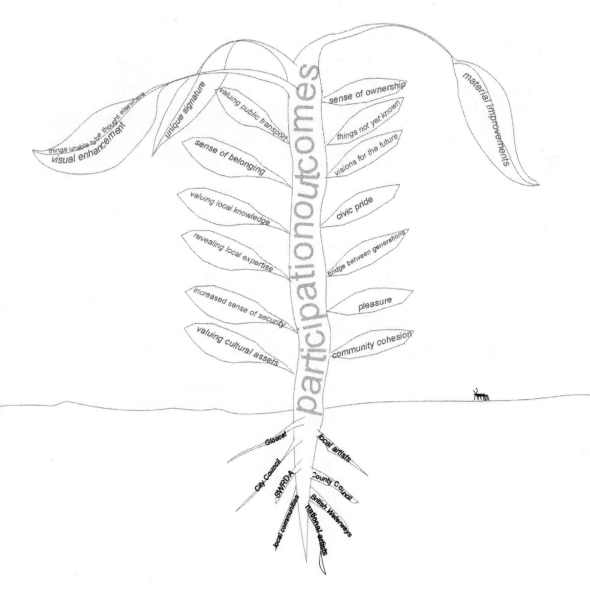

things unable to be thought elsewhere

visual enhancement

unique signature

valuing public transport

sense of belonging

valuing local knowledge

revealing local expertise

increased sense of security

valuing cultural assets

participationoutcomes

sense of ownership

things not yet known

visions for the future

material improvements

civic pride

bridge between generations

pleasure

community cohesion

Glosca

local artists

City Council

SWRDA

County Council

local communities

national artists

British Waterways

16.07 – 'Participation Outcomes' – Muf's diagram for
Gloucester Docks Art Strategy.

We need artists' ways of doing things: a critical analysis of the role of the artist in regeneration practice

1
Editors' note: The International Conference
Centre in Centenary Square, Birmingham,
was the setting for the 2002 Urban Summit.
This event was organised by the UK Office
of the Deputy Prime Minister to articulate
its urban regeneration policies. The
pumpkins were an installation by Muf Art
and Architecture; they were commissioned
by Midlands Architecture and the Designed
Environment (MADE), Public Art Forum
(PAF), and Public Art West Midlands
(PAWM). This chapter was first published
in a report issued by these three partners to
coincide with the Urban Summit. *If you
always do what you've always done – the future will
look a lot like the past,* Birmingham: Public Art
Forum, 2002.

Spaces deliberately set aside for conviviality and human interaction, such as Centenary Square Birmingham,[1] beg their opposite. It is as if you have paid for every concrete pavior twentyfold in tarmac in the rest of the city; for each bench 'set aside' at Centenary Square, there are impossibly narrow pavements where you are hemmed in by boarded-up shops and clapped out galvanised steel barriers. To all Centenary Square's ticked boxes of graffiti-free, fancy pavement, planting, sculptures and water you can add quietly civilised conference delegates going about their lawful business.

In such a place, what could be an appropriate artwork to bring to the attention of those delegates the role of artistic practice in regeneration? – 200 pumpkins, carved with faces, placed directly on the ground outside the back entrance to the Urban Summit.

- They arrive on the morning of the first day, and their public removal is invited at the end of the second.
- Some smile, some frown and some are non-committal.
- The stalk lid of the pumpkin is removable.
- Inside they have snap lights, which illuminate them at night for some four hours.
- They are bright orange and not grey.
- They may not be art as they have apparently jumped off their plinth.
- By landing on the ground the pumpkins may have turned from art to something unwanted in the city, like litter.
- They are crafted and sculpted, not mass-produced from a mould like their precast concrete surroundings, so maybe they are art.
- They will rot and grow mouldy in a matter of days, so perhaps they are not art.
- Unlike the people going past they do not move.

Hot pumpkin soup is served; driftly tranquil classical music is played. On examining a video of the event it is clear that one thing has become an unspoken point of honour. If you are carrying a bag (but not plastic) and are dressed in dark colours you may only glance for a matter of one quarter of a second at the pumpkin heads. Alternatively the pumpkins' irresistible gaze may provoke a discourse. By the simple act of placing the pumpkins there, an unseen authority has intervened, challenging the designated response. The question remains – how far are we ever prepared to deviate from our self-imposed curtailment of experiencing the world?

Still, if temporary, it is nevertheless remarkable how these 200 vegetables are a major irritant.

17.01 – 'If you always do what you have always done'. Temporary installation.

The magic of corporate architecture allows the pumpkin heads to instantly be reflected in the windows and appear as if they are now inside and have taken their place in a plenary session. Has a transformation occurred and are the delegates now a bunch of carved-out vegetables; are the pumpkins a static, voiceless constituency within the conference; or have the pumpkins joined the mainstream, which is now well able to embrace their limited peculiarities?

Meanwhile, within a real, not reflected, interior space, two monitors show pumpkins talking about art: with a loudly insistent Birmingham voice. In a place where anxiety levels about measurable outcomes are reaching fever pitch, what the pumpkins say isn't precisely welcome:

• 'Art is not good at doing what it's told.'
• 'Society needs the artist's way of doing things more than it needs the things they make.'

- 'When art doesn't represent anything else, it can equalise difference.'

Two groups of people in particular generally react and explore spontaneously. These are children and elderly people. Children are delighted by the spectacle of the pumpkins: they dance round them, between them, take their lids off, and run off with them. The elderly allow themselves a good look and to pause with open

17.02 – 'If you always do what you have always done'. Temporary installation.

puzzlement. Such groups have an affinity with those in the city who are to be 'regenerated': whether they like it or not they have the time to ponder. Their wholehearted engagement suggests the possible pitfalls of the absence of such unrestricted, undirected time and thought in the lives of the decision-makers.

Commentary

The Urban Summit event raises a number of possibilities for what artistic practice can bring to regeneration. This can be set in the context of public art practice in general and its particular relationships to regeneration.

The one-off public art commission

Valuable object: valuable context
At the other end of the spectrum to the perishable, disposable pumpkins is the one-off piece commissioned from a well-known

artist. At its most successful – as in Gormley's *The Angel of the North* – this takes the form of a recognisable, possessible object, familiar from the art gallery, but set in the realm of the public. Such a piece is directly relevant to the aspirations of urban regeneration in a number of ways. As a precious and valued object, it can transform its setting. The successful one-off commission can render its context precious; it is upgraded simply by virtue of the piece's presence. This effect can be virtually instantaneous and hence potentially easy to quantify.

Positive identity
The one-off piece can become the single most identifiable image of a place, offering huge marketing potential. This marked identity, at its most powerful, can become synonymous with a particular place. Once that has happened, the more intangible definitions of what makes that place different and special, that are essential to regeneration, can blossom.

Art success: herald of regeneration
By the way such a piece can uplift a sense of what an entire area is about, it both allows and provokes discussions to broaden over what kind of regeneration a place can aspire to. The very presence of a successful piece of public art allows belief in the process: that regeneration initiatives can and will have a positive outcome.

High stakes: high risk
The strong identity can, though, work two ways. Its downside is that such an artwork can work as a kind of badge, signifying that an area is run-down and in need of regeneration, and so potentially undermining already successful endeavours. Such a single commission requires an enormous act of faith just to acquire the necessary investment to get it off the ground in the first place. This means that not only is this version of public art unsuitable in the majority of cases, it's also untenable.

   The high profile, high investment art commission carries failure stakes equal to the potential of success. When unsuccessful, such projects risk the Millennium Dome effect. The visibility of questionable investment means that unsuccessful commissions may actively blight possibilities for urban regeneration. While clearly less cataclysmic than investment in the equivalent building project that flagships regeneration – usually a single large-scale cultural building – the prominence of the less than successful one-off commission means further acts of investment are likely to be questioned for the foreseeable future.

Active regeneration by the community

While the driving creative force in the one-off commission is the artist, community arts practice is about collaboration. The driving force is the community itself, aided and abetted by the artist. It is the community, combined with the momentum, inspiration and orchestration of the artist, that develops the subject matter and means of artistic creation. As such, community-based public art is one of the only deliberate acts in the regeneration process which simply cannot take place without the active involvement of at least some of the general public – the very people regeneration is for – in the physical transformation of a place.

Process as regeneration

Others agencies concerned with regeneration – for example, business investors or architectural rehabilitation schemes, propose or set in motion regeneration at a future date. Community art practice has a different quality in that the process of involvement of the community in the making of a work itself immediately begins the regeneration process. The regenerative aspect of community arts practice is as much about the transformation of the community itself through its empowerment to change its own surroundings, as it is about the final product. The success of community arts practice differs from the one-off commission in that it is not to be judged only by such a final product, but by the process of creation itself. This is underlined by the way such practice may encompass an event or a temporary piece as much as a permanent artefact.

Evaluation and the traditions of critical art practice

Investment-based and architecturally driven regeneration initiatives mean that the particularities and specifics of a community are conceptualised using preconceived forms and trajectories. This is essential in order that the substantial amounts of money involved can be spent on the safe basis of informed predictions. But such preconceptions mean that analysis of a special place takes place at some remove from its unique day-to-day reality. The artist, on the other hand, is completely free from the need to interpret this reality via predictable analytical categories. This can mean that the response to a place that is the product of collaboration between a community and its artist has the potential to be particularly precise and honed. The community artist is in at the hot end, involved in the literal production of change. Their evaluation of the project's success or otherwise, while avowedly subjective, has the advantage of being both continuous and immediate. Other agencies involved in urban renewal continually question how they can evaluate the elusive added benefits their investment in regeneration projects may bring. For the artist the assessment of benefit is more straightforwardly determined: it is 'whether they can sleep at night'. It is here that the benefits are reaped from the happy, if fortuitous, marriage between the habitual self-examination that is part and parcel of contemporary art practice, and the role of the community art process within the regeneration process. The contemporary artist will subject their work to constant examination and criticism. This allows for an ongoing commentary on, and understanding of, the process the community is undergoing: it is gives an automatic space for reflection untrammelled by the imperatives of outcome.

Reframing the terms of regeneration

It often happens that the community artist gets what you might call the hard bits of regeneration: confronting everyday people's alienation on estates with the highest unemployment, the greatest drug-use, the most derelict physical fabric. However, because artists aren't social workers, maintenance officers and drug counsellors, they are liberated from the necessity to see these 'hard bits' as a problem in the same recognisable terms as the other teams involved – indeed they may not frame them as a problem at all. And so, uniquely amongst those concerned with the quality of urban life, artists are not required to produce solutions. This gives artists working with the community an exceptionally important role – one of authentically and necessarily thinking 'outside of the box'. The presence of the artist on the ground can, because of this, be exceptionally valuable in opening up to all parties' diverse outcomes and possibilities that are important precisely because they could not have been predicted at the start of the process. So in this way the community artist's practice is not just different to others in regeneration: it can also be contrasted with the one-off public art commission where successful outcome largely depends on its predictability from the outset.

Value for money

The economics are important. Because of the exceptionally low outlay involved in their commission, it is realistically possible for the community artist to allow for work to develop in such less predictable ways, ways that would be too risky if applied, for example, to a large-scale redevelopment project. The community artist's way of working means they can assume the role of the 'canary down the pit': they may both guage the atmosphere, and assess the creative potential of a community. Moreover, artists are unusual among regeneration agencies in that they can formulate and then present back to the community its own ambitious expectations of what might be achieved. Such expectations emerge from within the collective unconscious – again, this is unlike other initiatives at work in this field, which are essentially introduced from outside. This emergence from within gives the completed community arts project a different status within the community to other physical manifestations of regeneration. When successful, it means there is a sense of individual identity and possession embedded not just within the work itself, but in the collective experience and memory of its creation.

Socially aware art practice?
Some implications of the Urban Summit event

Questioning detachment
Our habitual social activity is geared to ignoring urban zones that are depressed, dangerous and run-down, and to remain equally oblivious of the people therein. The standard tools of regeneration – statistical analysis, flow charts, timetables, etc. – tend to engender similar distance: at the very least they don't actively challenge it. By making its audience willy-nilly enact their distance or their positive engagement, the pumpkins forced the pitfalls of such detachment to be acted out, as it were, before our eyes.

The Rod Hull, Emu and Parkinson technique
This kind of art can be called socially active in that it makes active demands of the viewer. To be appreciated properly it needs the viewer, or at least the imagination of a viewer, to be present. The set-up – temporary, accompanied by the sensual assaults of beautiful sounds (music) and beautiful smells (soup) – and its obviously fun character mean that even if you ignore it, your indifference looks too studied: you are revealed as equally engaged as the most enthusiastic of participants. Like Michael Parkinson trying to have a serious interview with the glove puppet Emu, the more you stand on your dignity, the more the art disarms you.

The Silence of the Pumpkins
The dumbness of the exterior pumpkins was a symbolic constituency of the unheard those-to-be-regenerated. The interior pumpkins by contrast were given the most insistent voices: articulated by the artists involved.

The power of cheek

The cheek and humour of the pumpkins, as it were, bullied the audience into this response. They have the annoying, grudging, legitimacy of Halloween about them. Like when 'trick or treat' is demanded: you either have to respond in the terms set by the trick-or-treaters or be labelled a fun-free curmudgeon.

The light touch of the temporary

At the same time the clearly temporary nature of the installation – given the fragility of the vegetables – meant that the contrast between the pumpkins and the delegates was light-hearted. The piece was clearly not going to last for ever, but it was going to go away once it had made its point. Its temporary character underlined the fact that this was a thought piece. What remains is not the work of art but its memory: how it had made you think.

The Urban Summit event's value rested precisely in its ephemeral quality – 'you had to have been there'.

Conclusion

It is clear that different kinds of trust and clarity are needed when commissioning public art. In the case of the one-off commission this is more simple: a mutual understanding of what the work will be and how it is to be produced.

In commissioning socially aware and community-based art it is essential from the outset to be conscious of three things: first, that such practice will articulate formerly silent voices, and that not all of these will be welcome. Commissioners should stand firm by decisions made, and make it clear that retreat isn't an option. Community art is so important to the regeneration process just because we know we will hear that rare thing: the authentic voice of the community. Second, sometimes the absence of a strictly defined outcome by commissioners can allow new points of departure and unpredicted positive possibilities for regeneration to emerge from the community itself. And third, when successful, community arts practice draws together different aims: the material tangible improvements desired by the community; and the artist's own desire to get to the essence of what kind of creativity is necessary both for regeneration and their development of their own practice. In other words, agendas can cross: they can be successful yet not the same.

Regeneration normally implies the implementation of a linear set of processes – indeed, presumably the real rationale of the Urban Summit has been the honing of such process so that successful outcomes are more likely. In the midst of this, community-based arts practice and socially engaged arts practice remind us of regeneration's ultimately intangible quality. By allowing space for thought and reflection to happen for all involved, most especially those 'being regenerated', it also allows the reality of regeneration's complexities and contradictions, in contrast to the occasionally less than helpful imperative of good intentions, to be articulated. Going even further counter to the received wisdom of regeneration, the implication of this is that the material object, the assumed product of public art, is not necessarily its most important outcome: the process of creativity itself regenerates communities.

In the confrontation of the fragility of the individual with the robustness of policy, much of the peculiarities of existence, which form a large chunk of the subject and form of art, are filtered out. And hence, paradoxically, it is policy, which sometimes presents a less than real view of the everyday world, the word urban regeneration directly addresses. Art is special in that it can both sustain and contain these peculiarities; for art there is no particular point to be proved, no constituency to be won over. For art, the success of an endeavour can be the net effect of recognition and acknowledgement of peculiarity. For strangely, such acknowledgement makes people in general feel a lot less peculiar and therefore, a lot more empowered.

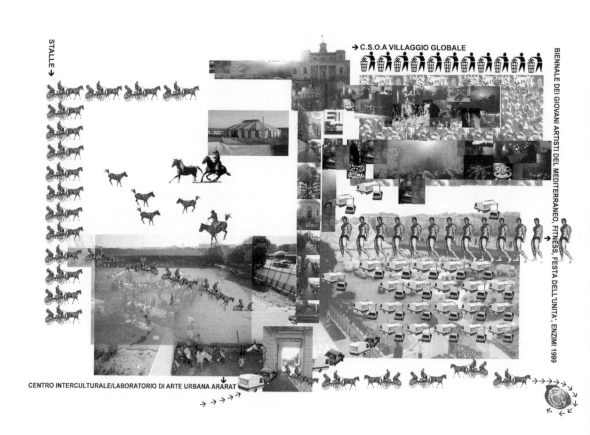

STALLE →

→ C.S.O.A VILLAGGIO GLOBALE

BIENNALE DEI GIOVANI ARTISTI DEL MEDITERRANEO, FITNESS, FESTA DELL'UNITA', ENZIMI 1999

CENTRO INTERCULTURALE/LABORATORIO DI ARTE URBANA ARARAT

18.01 – Campo Boario map.

Stalker
and the big game of Campo Boario

Stalker is not a group: it is an interrelated open system, which is growing and emerging through its actions and through all the individuals that operate with (for and among) Stalker. It is a collective subject that engages in actions and research to catalyse creative motions in time and space, to produce self-organised places, environments and situations. Stalker does not have a physical body, not even those of the persons who gave life to it. 'We' has always been an entity including 'others', who, without pretending to be us, participated in the activities, becoming 'us' in their/our actions.

After exploring 'actual territories' for a few years, in 1999 Stalker – Urban Art Lab[1] has begun to interact with the nature of spaces and with their inhabitants in a more structured way. The work has developed through a phase of observation and listening, which has brought us to assume responsibility for the transformations of these spaces, and to research into methods and operative tools in order to care for and bring about the spontaneous transformations that characterise them. This new experience was carried out in Campo Boario in the premises of Testaccio's former slaughterhouse in Rome, an area with no land use designation since 1975. Since then, the sedimentation of time and the absence of any kind of design project have made this area an example of self-organisation through the cohabitation of different cultures. The slaughterhouse lies in the central area within the ancient walls of the city, but it is hidden by the River Tiber, the railtracks, and an ancient dumping place of Roman amphorae called Monte dei Cocci. It is the perfect cul de sac where uncertainty and instability have prevailed, cut off from public view. Campo Boario is a rectangular courtyard measuring about three hectares. Here different communities, extraneous to the 'normal' life of the city, live together: in this large space, the caravans of the Rome Calderasha community are settled for almost the entire year. They are an Italian nomad community, who specialise in working raw metals, and they have been present in the area since 1500. The stables are occupied by the *cavallari* and their three hundred horses. These are the drivers of the horse carriages which allow tourists a different perspective of the city of

1
To read more about Stalker see: *www. stalkerlab.it*; Jean-Michel Place, *Stalker attraverso i territori attuali*, Paris :2000; *Stalker /Ararat*, Librerie Dedalo, Rome: 2000; L. Romito, 'Ecouter, regarder, interagir', in *Mutations*, p.136, Centre d'Architecture Arc en Reve de Bordeaux/Barcelona: Actar, 2000; P. Lang, 'Stalker', in *Suburban Discipline*, pp.130-41, New York: Princeton Architectural Press, 1997. Also see: F. Careri, *Walkscapes: Walking as an aesthetic practice*, Barcelona: Gustavo Gili, 2001; F. Careri, *Consant/New Babylon. Una città nomade*, Turin: Testo & Immagine, 2000; F. Careri, 'Rome, archipel fractal, voyage dans les combles de la ville', *Techniques and Architecture*, 427, 1996, 84-7.

Rome. On the opposite side is Villaggio Globale, the most famous Roman social centre, which has been occupied and self-managed, housing intercultural activities throughout the year. Other parts of the space are inhabited by different foreign communities, especially people from Senegal and North Africa, by Italian homeless men and women, and by anyone else unable to find a place elsewhere. The result is a strange cosmopolitan and multicultural universe evoking the surreal city of Pasolini and Fellini, a universe that no one would expect to find in the centre of modern touristic Rome.

Stalker was invited to participate in the Biennale dei Giovani Artisti in May 1999. The art exhibition took place in an area adjacent to the Campo Boario. On that occasion, Stalker proposed to integrate the Kurd refugee community arriving from Turkey into the existing multicultural context of Campo Boario. The Kurd community had arrived in Rome when their leader Ocalan came to Italy to ask for political asylum. They offered the chance for an unforgettable encounter between their culture and the city of Rome, whose citizens showed solidarity and welcomed the Kurdish community, as had never before happened in Rome. After Ocalan was arrested, the Kurds who remained in Rome built a small paper village near the Colosseum; the village was called 'cartonia' (in Italian *cartone* means paper). Cartonia was a place of encounter, where the citizens of Rome were always welcome. It had a short life, and it was soon dismantled. The Kurds were then dispersed to different locations throughout the city.

Stalker organised a workshop entitled 'From Cartonia to Piazza Kurdistan' which involved the students from one of Rome's Schools of Architecture, the organisation Azad and the Kurd refugees. During the workshop Stalker decided to occupy and restore the building which had housed the veterinary surgery of Campo Boario in the past. The building was named 'Ararat', which is the name of the sacred mountain where Noah landed after the flood. During the following months, Ararat became the gathering place of the Kurd community and a working space for artists, architects, researchers and citizens, who were invited to share the experience of such a space. Ararat is the ideal lookout place on Campo Boario, presenting an entrance door to a space that many would otherwise not have entered. It is a place which invites people to comprehend the complexity of its dynamic changes and allows them to pass across the physical and cultural boundaries that enclose it.

Without any public finance or any help from the city administration, the space in front of Ararat was transformed into a giant playground, a blackboard on which actions and interactions among the different communities who live around it could be inscribed.

During three years, from 1999 to 2002, the large asphalt space became the playground for big collective games: the *Carta di non identità* (Non-ID Card) which was distributed to all the inhabitants in the occasion of the Clandestino Day, the *Pranzo Boario* (Boario lunch), a big circular dining table where Kurdish food, gypsy goulash and

18.02 – 'Pranzo Boario' (Boario Lunch).

Japanese seaweed (cooked by Asako Iwama, Japanese artist and architect) were served together, the *Global game*, during which two thousand soccer balls were thrown and then used to write and collect stories of Campo Boario; the *Transborderline*, a spiral space which represented symbolically a permeable and habitable border, which was then illegally installed on the Italian/Slovenian borderline; the *Tappeto volante* (flying carpet), an itinerant ceiling which traced a representation of Palermo's Cappella Palatina for a travelling exhibition entitled 'Islam in Italy', by using ropes and copper. Many other games and actions without names were played and left no traces, but surely contributed to the transformation and emancipation of this space. This asphalt blackboard has also been the site of workshops, parties and interventions by artists and architects.

Today Ararat is a mandatory stop for all Kurd refugees who pass through Europe, and there have been more than 3000 so far. It is the main gathering place for the entire Kurd community in

Rome. After negotiations with the Cavallari, part of the asphalt has been transformed into the Ortoboario, a public garden where sunflowers and fruit trees were planted. In the common space the Newroz celebration takes place every year – the New Year Kurd party where the entire community gathers around a fire and dances to remember the time when Babylonians were chased out of the territory of Kurdistan, and to remember today's liberation fights carried on by fifty million Kurds who live divided between four different nations, the largest stateless people in the world.

18.03 – Kurdistan imaginary map becomes a garden in the Campo Boario courtyard.

Much time was needed and much energy spent to be able to get into Campo Boario, to find the right way to relate to its inhabitants and to the Kurds, who shared Ararat with Stalker for a period of time. The first step was to overcome many cultural barriers, to open up what seemed difficult to comprehend, to overcome fear and ethnic prejudice, to find peace and serenity, to avoid making judgements, to steer away from determination and certainty. We had to change our usual point of view and look at the world as an inhabitant of that particular space, to share in the illegal conditions of the occupants of the space, to take on ourselves daily responsibilities, to comprehend and observe the equilibrium, the rules, and the visions. We realised and recognised, from the inside, the ability of the space and its inhabitants to organise themselves. There were no laws or written rules, every situation being managed by negotiations between communities and individuals, even though everything seemed to be abandoned. In every corner were invisible boundaries, never marked and always open to change. Everything lives in equilibrium, an unstable state that has developed in time through the history of the space, where no one is the owner, and no one has real rights. This equilibrium has been found in time through temporary negotiations, which never caused deep traumas, persisting through arrivals and departures, across borderlines and despite new passageways.

Stalker was at first received with indifference, as the last to arrive there, but this behaviour soon changed and a curiosity grew to understand this strange tribe of artists and architects who didn't want to draw or design and create something, who were neither political activists nor social service or public institution representatives. This ambiguity of roles was the key for Stalker to become the organiser of collective games and to generate involvement of the inhabitants in play, challenging one another through playing. Stalker has slowly found the way to operate and to become part of the evolving transformation processes, trying to propose playful activities and methods to discover and activate the complexity carried by the space, instead of proposing a 'participative project' in the worst sense of the word.

Campo Boario is an urban area produced by the globalisation process, like many others in different cities and countries of the world. These are areas that seem extraneous to our culture, even though they are part of it by now. They are beginning to emerge in the way we perceive our cities, in our mental maps. In these places the city forgets all its masks and becomes naked, showing what the city itself does not know. No traditional projects are accepted, the energies and the intelligence to redefine itself are found in its ability to self-organise, to invent new and different intercultural rules and relationships in space and time. Here architects can leave behind their certainty and their projects, finding the way through unknown processes, which involve many different actors, many different levels of perception and many kinds of action. New possibilities open the way to transformation of public spaces and to innovative urban experimentation, preserving multiple identities. Here we are beginning to define new tools and methods to let these realities represent themselves, producing neither objects nor projects, only paths and relationships. The discipline becomes hybrid, moving on from architecture to public art, something we can start calling 'civic art'.

Campo Boario needs neither art works nor public architecture to clarify its identity. Its very characteristics are the uncertainty, indefiniteness and the self-organisation of its own physical and relational spaces. The challenge is to produce a public space starting from these premises. In fact, the interest in operating in these areas consists in trying to involve the inhabitants' creativity and inventiveness to share areas emerging from a real melting pot of cultures, where the culture of architecture and urban art is only one of those at stake. I do not mean that we have to ask those who have different problems to turn into urb-artists, but they should be prepared to assume an active role within a transformation game where everyone participates in establishing rules and shares the general aims, trying not to waste any competence or human quality.

The aim is to achieve a meeting point where different identities are prepared to take the risk. Even this action, as a means of overcoming the first barrier, is far from easy. Like any scientific experiment, it is an experience that involves a series of unsuccessful attempts, miscalculations or wrong approaches, but also unexpected and sometimes inexplicable successes. The real difficulty is, in fact, to find a way of building up the right interactions and of asking the right questions, to be able to define the transformation processes in progress.

This creative process is very similar to a biochemical transformation where differentiated forces work together. It is necessary to catalyse the developing transformation processes, trying to eliminate idle prejudice and conflict, directing useful energy towards change by means of playful devices – the heart of the design process and activity – and seeking the definition of new configurations of sense and space by means of the self-defined relationships which emerge in the process.

Being 'present' is often necessary to operate as described. To be

2

F. J. Varela, E. Thompson, and E. Rosch, *The Embodied Mind: Cognitive science and human experience*, Cambridge, MA: MIT Press, 1991. H. Maturana and F. J. Varela, *L'albero della conoscenza*, Milano: Garzanti, 1992.

present means to observe sympathetically, to suspend judgement, to pay attention to the processes. One tries to read and interpret the dynamic emerging sense and the creative definition of relations, leaving behind competition and conflict. Being present activates a unitary process that binds the observation of the world and the contribution to its transformation. According to this conception,[2] the knowledge of a place is the coexistence with, and participation in, the transformation of the analysed realities, being part of the system of relations that are present in such realities, contributing to their development and evolution. This evolution is an unpredictable process: it cannot be foreseen. For this reason any planning activity cannot be structured on the definition of a clear objective, because the activity instigates a change in perspective of reality, trying to upset any equilibrium by means of '*detournements*'. This creative restlessness forces all involved actors to redefine their own positions, their own vision of daily life, by *playing*.

3

F. B. Bifo, *Felix, narrazione dell'incontro con il pensiero di Guattari, cartografia visionaria del tempo che viene*, Rome: Luca Sassella Editore, 2001, pp.20–3.

In this way Stalker could be anyone. Stalker is a desiring community where no one belongs and where individuals encounter each other. It is an unstable entity, 'a temporary community which is founded on possibilities, on desire, on intention, on promise and waiting'.[3] Such desiring power is Stalker's hypothesis; 'transgressive excitement, tension in motion, energetic investment in the future'. Stalker will always generate a dissipation of energies drawing a dynamic vital geometry, in order to make this power come to life without any determination. Such entropy, this flux of energies, will generate vital negentropic and creative fluxes, in order to avoid the dissipation of available energies into depression. Stalker will then come to life, without consuming its own desire, without losing it, and become something else, an autonomous entity, living away from chaos. It will be generated by desire itself and not by determination. In coming to life it generates a space, which is an ethical, political and aesthetic space, a real, autonomous, living space, a territory made up of environments, situations and places, which have been taken away from chaos, from rigid and ratified dominions, finding its way away from destruction and destructors, re-establishing a creative circularity which has been stolen from us by the transformation of life into merchandise.

This is Stalker's necessary ethical, political and aesthetic approach. Without these premises, Stalker's games run the risk of turning out fixed games...

Translation by Barbara Galassi

Chapter 19

Raoul Bunschoten [1]

Points, spirals and prototypes

1
This text is based on the transcription of a lecture given by Raoul Bunschoten at the University of Sheffield, 12 March 2002. The lecture introduces work that has been conducted in parallel with CHORA/Raoul Bunschoten's book *Urban Flotsam*, Rotterdam: 010publishers, 2001, which outlines Chora's methodological basis.

We open with the key word 'participation'. Participation is extremely important; it has been important for myself over a long time, but it has become even more important recently because you have to win people over to get involved in experimental projects, to participate with you, with your team and the structure you are setting up. I will introduce quite a few things on the topic of relationships, interaction and participation with different kinds of people, or what we call actors and agents; roughly speaking, 'actors' being those who have desires for projects and 'agents' being those who have interests in projects. The centre of this mostly urban work is a key concept: the *prototype*, which somehow links the participatory activities.

19.01 – Signs on the narrow gate. Cardonagh, Donegal.

Cardonagh, Donegal: signs for the Sacred Heart

2
The signs reproduce quotations from *New Jerusalem Bible*, London: Darton, Longman & Todd Ltd, 1985. The quote was introduced by Gary Doherty, then working in CHORA.

We will start with an image of a quote from the Bible,[2] which we used in a small commission we were asked to do by a church in Ireland and where we wanted to bring in the people to create a participatory space for those around it. It is actually a traffic sign which sits on a wall. In this wall there is a narrow gate which people from the parishes of this small town in Donegal, Northern Ireland, use. We had this commission to make signs but we didn't really want to make arrows because we wanted to draw people into a debate for these reasons: the fact that the church emanates out into the town, which is obvious, but also the fact that we can do some things, we can change stuff, we can change this form of emanation from the church. We can try to change this impression and try to make it a bit more common. So we have made several of these traffic signs, an original idea by Gary Doherty, some of which have now been installed around the church.

'It's an evil and faithful generation that looks for a sign.' It took a while for the priest to absorb this, and it has not been mounted. The path and signs go on:

3
Matthew 12:39

4
Hebrews 12:13

5
Ecclesiastes 12:7

'...the only sign it will be given is the sign of the prophet Jonah.' [3]
'...and make your crooked paths straight.' [4]
'Thye dust returns to the earth from which it came and the spirit returns to God who gave it.' [5]

It is a very tiny project, very small but very interesting because it is a way of beginning to interact with the population, which is mostly Catholic and has a deep tradition while at the same time the town is radically changing. There is a lot of funding going into this area. Irish people are returning from the States, there is a big cultural shift taking place. I was working as an outsider, and at the same time I was working with an insider, a local person, Gary Doherty. Through him we began to build up relationships with people around another project, a community centre in the area.

But what we were inspired by was really something else. Cardonagh is a little town in County Donegal, at the very north tip of Ireland. Amongst it, there is the church. The signs now sit every-where. We had been inspired by something already there. We wanted this thing with the signs to be a prototype that would make people think and somehow make them have new postcards from the town. It is only a small town and has declined, as have a lot of places in Ireland. But what I want to talk about briefly is the initial proto-type. Prototypes are inventions; they are organisational structures that link different programmatic layers. But they occur naturally as well. That is the best way you can see them, the best way you can find them.

When we started working there, there was somebody who had just painted his house red. He'd just finished it. The week after when we went back, there was somebody else who had acted on this and painted his house also.

Then two weeks later when we went back, there was another person who had taken the same red for his house.

And so on, several more houses were painted red. And eventually they make it to the main square of the town. So if you drive now through the town, it is something like 30 per cent red. This happened very quickly, in only a few months.

And then, we did a proposal in which we acted on the 'red'. We proposed a series of signs that went up to the entrance of the church. What's important here is that this 'red' is now an identity. Somehow, one person who painted this first house red, the others followed; they created a natural prototype which you could map. We made crosses and dots at times when the houses had been painted red, but now they are so close that we can see that the red would be the dominant factor of the town. They create a form of branding, a new form of identity. This is something I am very inspired by and I try to use it in urban projects, this natural force. You can ride piggyback on that natural force, something that we are trying to do in different ways. The clerical committee of Ireland voted these new proposals down – the signs were too big – but we tried to claim that there was a whole tradition of murals in the north of Donegal.

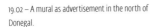

19.02 – A mural as advertisement in the north of Donegal.

We wanted to recreate these murals with signs. Of course the signs are based on the recent or perhaps still ongoing war, depending on viewpoints. There are very direct messages coming from the walls to you and we said that we wanted somehow to continue that tradition, to shift and mutate it.

After this recent war, the environment can be very territorialised with signs. But these can start to mutate as well; they start to shift. For example, an entire mural is used to form purely an advertisement (see Fig. 19.02). There is a kind of benign shift that is happening now with the murals in Derry.[6]

6
On good days you can now fly with Ryanair for fifty pence from Stansted to what can now be called 'The City of Derry'. Basically, Derry is now on the outskirts of London. That is why it is possible for us to go often. The geography of Ireland is changing; the cheap flights are but one symptom of this. It is a very strange country: there are six million tourists each year next to a population of 3.7 million people.

Lough Foyle spatial development plan

Interestingly we have been asked to develop something else too, on a larger scale, called *Urban Gallery*. It is a kind of planning instrument that we would introduce into this cross-border area. It takes in both landscape and other elements. The map of Lough Foyle area was produced with four politicians in a pub, including a MEP, and was about a wish for £60 million for development of different harbour facilities in the area. The main discussions over those months took place in pubs in very informal ways. Now this is where we get into the participatory process. How do you handle this? Just to give one little example: we brought this map and showed it to the politicians. One of them, the MEP, took a pen and made a line across Derry. I thought that this was a little fussy, already getting into the planning of a third bridge. This is only an anecdote, but what happened of course is that we'd taken this map with 'Londonderry' on it. The first action has been to cross out the word London from the name.

19.03 – The map of Lough Foyle.

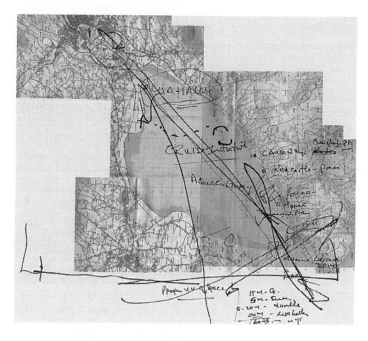

So this is the type of situation you get into. You go there and you realise then that you are walking around on the ground that it is never quite solid. You realise that there is a lot more that meets the eye. There is deep history close to the surface. And the planning of anything here, be it the clarification of the area, be it ecological processes, be it the facilities for tourists, touches this history. Cross-boundary commissions will take a lot of participatory processes. We are going to have to be very inventive because it is very tricky. You get a lot of resistance. This is also very exciting because you get real challenges here as architects and planners. Not just with the design but with the design processes that bring people together.

We are talking about these flows that are creeping around the earth's surface and where, if we are working in the area, we have to take something significant out of them. We have to somehow begin to understand something about the interaction of flows, of these forces. We call them *proto-urban conditions*. And what do we have to do? We have to take them apart and somehow reconnect them. So what I'll be speaking about with *Urban Gallery* is all this business of connectivity and how you reconnect the flows. How you can get one part here and another part here and start separating them, then reconnecting them.

Urban Gallery

One of the tools we are working with is the *Urban Gallery*. It is a planning tool but it is also a virtual building. I am more and more trying to portray this like a house, a house with floors, in a way like an art gallery. We use to link it with the concept of curation, although the link is not so direct. But you know it is architecture, it has floors: a virtual architecture. You need to see it like this to understand the connectivity in a three-dimensional way.

So this building, this virtual building, has storage space for comparative models. It has floors of speculation and stimulation. It has a floor for managing connectivity and decision-making. It has a floor for implementation, which is going towards a manual of use. So more technically speaking, it is a *database*. It has prototypes, scenario games and action plans.

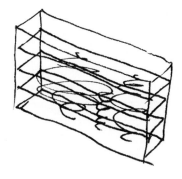

19.04 – The four virtual floors of the Urban Gallery; the top floor is branding, and below this are earth, flow and incorporation.

7
See *Tokyo Story*, *www.chora.demon.co.uk*

Tokyo Story

The first model for the *Urban Gallery* is called *Tokyo Story*, and it was built up according to the four layers: the database, the prototypes, the scenario games and the action plans. It is a web-based instrument.[7] You can see this as a prototype for a web-based version of this tool. It shows the four layers and how we begin to draw in both things from the ground, as it were. At the same time we are trying to structure them and allow them to become a kind of game. Within the database in Tokyo, we took a kind of strip in which we carried out fieldwork at various foreign points. On these we applied four basic processes. We look at one point; let's take one randomly in which the four processes – erasure, origination, transformation and migration – have been applied. For example, erasure: in the year 1650, the priest has turned the slope of the hill into a street. The wooden signpost gives us some knowledge of the history at this point. A change in time is called origination. Our awareness of how our imagination changes the relationship with the street is called transformation and the last one is called migration. And so the narrative memory of the place is stored in our brain.

We call this a *mini-scenario*. It is a very quick kind of proto-mapping of the processes active in that site. Mini-scenarios are necessary because they communicate something very quickly about the site and at the same time, it is the beginning of the description of that site. What happens in the second column is something that has only been developed recently: it is what we call *operational fields*. Here we begin to meet the actors and agents: the workers, the residents, various companies and so on. We begin to see who is there, who is doing what, who is local, who is coming in from the outside. We are now developing this much further as a kind of basis. Doing enough of these, you get a random database, but at the same time you begin to get an encyclopaedic density.

In this case, we brought three schools together: the Architectural Association, the Berlage Institute and Tokyo University. The students, like travelling salesmen, brought along prototypes. For example: 'building light structures onto existing buildings', which is an idea based on the way advertisement companies work. Saatchi & Saatchi was taken under the microscope because they cover so much visual space in cities, that in a way they become planners. They are not accountable to anybody but they influence so much public space. How can we regulate the surfaces to occupy? The idea is that prototypes are innovative organisational structures but are also applicable throughout the world. This is because these forces that we are looking at are global forces. They don't always look the same, but they are acting in a similar way.

Then, we bring the urban actors together. We put them together around tables. This involves people from cities, from authorities and companies. At the tables we play scenario games. The game has four players and one animator, a table, four chairs. Each player has a role: erasure, origination, etc... You start from one 'bean-site'[8] and keep going round as a process. You get for example, an actor from 'bean-site' 272. If in the second round, you feel time is appropriate, you import prototype 4, for example, the 'estrange' room. It involves a hotel room, making love ... and so on! The aim is to create the conditions for a particular prototype. You can invent something, you can build a house, but with prototypes it is a bit more difficult. When are the conditions right? And are you able to influence these prototypes?

Here's a scenario that started in a funny way: in this scenario we had four players, but half-way through the scenario we had

8
For description of a bean-site, see p.241.

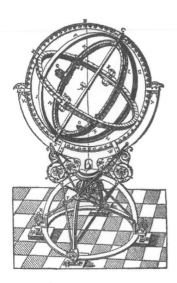

19.05 – A brief excursion about instruments: Tyco Brahe was a scientist, a kind of all-round scientist who lived in the 1500s in Denmark. He built these instruments and instantly became a global success, like these astronomical instruments in Beijing. What I love about these instruments is that they are both things with which to measure the world, as well as tools which represent the world, this spherical earth. Here you see, still in Beijing, the tools have a plastic presence themselves.

Talking of the building of institutions, the King of Denmark gave him an island. He was kind of restless and didn't want to accept a castle. Here he started to develop the first scientific institution in the world. It was the first institute for scientific research where they developed all kinds of representations of the universe and the way bodies moved through the universe. But more interestingly, he began to develop all kinds of new methods that were outside of astronomy. He started to invent a form of cartography. This enabled him to measure the place where he was in relationship to Copenhagen. He started to create with his institution a sort of network of people across Europe and other parts of the world. If you look at anybody who was important at that time, who built atlases or produced text on this subject, they have all at some time been on that little island just outside Copenhagen. So that was all about institutions and interventions.

I always speak about this although I speak about urban work; never forget that it is about plasticity. If you cut a piece of air out of a city, it is always plastic: all these forces working on the city. And so, we keep making models of these forces, just to understand that they have to touch each other and interact with each other.

some guests coming in. They were the director of the largest development company in Tokyo and the son of the governor of Tokyo. They shifted the meaning of the scenario away from strange and incidental things towards quite big planning problems. Cemeteries in the bay of Tokyo, for example, or the changes that occur due to the national airport changing into an international airport. You can play with reality very quickly and very loosely this way. It's a way of playing with reality in order to create conditions to change the reality. Then, we get to action plans, which are based on the use of the knowledge of mini-scenarios and prototypes. We know that and if we combine these two things we could actually achieve this kind of 'product'.

We often start by creating random knowledge. We throw beans. Now these random points have their own name: 'bean-site'. It is crude but it has to be crude to create a narrative. We do that so we look at things we otherwise don't know, that we don't see. This graphic image shows how this game works: a kind of spiral in time on which, at one point, you try to implement a prototype. I believe more and more in urban situations where you have to work like that; you can't make fixed plans and fixed master plans. We have to work with the dynamics of the environment. These games we set up are about participating, about making different actors participate and creating a kind of ritual in which this play happens. Only during a game like this do people lose their inhibitions and direct aims and begin to mix their interests and desires. Of course, you have to have props, you cannot be 'naked', and therefore have the bits and pieces with which you play with and a map. Then to translate it. But you can never forget the architecture. This is the architecture of the site: the database, the prototypes, the scenarios, and the action plan. These are the actual links and this is the topology of one project. It's about the connectivity between different parts, different components of the whole structure.

A new suburb: Høje Taastrup

Recently we entered a competition in Copenhagen and won second prize. The site is a suburb of Copenhagen. It is a typical place: if you look at it, it looks like anywhere in Europe, at least, with a shopping mall, a church, a village square, a pond, a school run, a passage under a motorway, a field, a newspaper. We have quite a mixture: a big railway to Copenhagen, a national research institute, farms sitting in a city, an old village, a bit of everything. We had to deal with this. So we said okay, we want to set up an instance in which the *Urban Gallery* can be applied and used. At the same time we began to build: we added a symbolic game structure to the existing situation.

Over many years, I have been inspired by this notion of a garden and attractor points: if you look at the attractor points you begin to move beyond the dynamic environment.

19.06 & 19.07 – Høje Taastrup.

We treat the site like a game board, literally. The goal is to create communities and the product is a dynamic master plan. We said there's no topology whatever, no significance to anything. We may as well put a game plan there. We look at what's there and, as a result, choose specific points: the centres of the community. Then, with these specific points, the *Urban Gallery* generates a dynamic environment with centre points, which have a name and a certain development based on the engines of five or six prototypes. They are not unique to any one of these; they repeat themselves over different places. This is the 'genetic code' of one centre: the anchor point, a name, a prototype number, a space for the development, though not necessarily the form of the development, and some kind of built environment. The result is a kind of mix between landscapes, density, mixed use, sports facilities, etc. Some prototypes are very concrete: housing, cultural centre, playground. Others are more about rules: rules about density, rules about landscape, rules about open space, rules of how to deal with the waste that you make in this town. We make programmes for prototypes, and the criteria of when a prototype is effective. When you have a whole collection of them – a performance cube, machines for living, plug-in infrastructures etc. – you get to something like a three-dimensional version of the *Urban Gallery*.

Project W, Sector E, the Netherlands
This method is now being applied at a large scale: in the Netherlands, in Project WW (it stands for a lot of things, water and so on), an experiment set up by the Dutch government and several ministries. The test has to do with one of the densest areas in Europe;

the area between Rotterdam and the Ruhr-Rhein metropolis. There are so many actors and agents that it was impossible to plan something clearly. We were debating with the government on the study of the flow of goods from one of the largest ports in the world into the rest of Europe. And of course, Europe is doubling in the next few years and the markets are doubling. The flows of goods are doubling because people want to consume more or do more. There is an enormous change happening in this area, and we've been asked to bring this instrument into this context, but because this area is too large to deal with, we are only focusing on one case study.

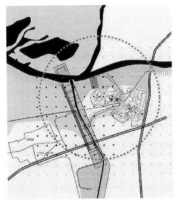

19.08 & 19.09 – Project W, Sector E.

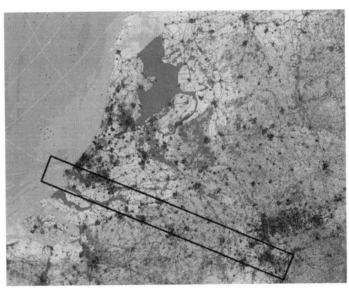

London and Paris are very large centres, but overall the Netherlands is larger and very dense. It sits in the centre of a web of connections with the rest of Europe. Here we used the Urban Gallery and applied it to the whole zone while, at the same time, we took one of our favourite forms – a line – connecting A and B. We are looking at it now as a 'zone'. On this project, I worked with students at the Berlage Institute. They threw four thousand bean-sites in the area. With a consortium, we focused more on one case project. One point shows how we can begin to link all the different flows while at the same time do a test project for the *Urban Gallery*, testing it before it is applied for conducting a lot of things happening in the whole zone. These frames are useful: they are crude devices, but they are useful because they are virtual spaces linking things together, they are all in a frame so you can start recognising connections and draw lines. It simply makes you see things.

At the same time, the whole thing is a 'bar'[9] of conflicts. There are a lot of conflicts emerging because of the increase in the flows of

9
The bar is a term used to denote a strip taken across the urban or rural fabric, effectively sampling a given area (editors' note).

goods and people. The prototypes we are developing in this city called 'W' apply also to various other conflicts. Due to the brief, we need to know about these conflicts to develop the test case. We have to divide the whole bar; we are now doing the test on four thousand bean-sites and have an agreement with the institute to work collaboratively.

19.10 – Prototypes developing.

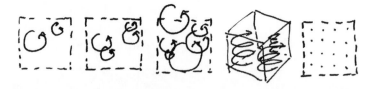

We are doing a case study that is based on trying to reintroduce activity into the infrastructures of water, which at the moment are barely used. There is a very banal level: the clogging up of the roads in the Netherlands. But also, when we started to look at this area other things popped up: for example, the problem of the landscape not being productive. Much like here in England, it is heavily sub-sidised and is there to be an open space. At the same time, we have the Dutch version of Enron: one of the power stations in the Netherlands that is in trouble juxtaposed with nature zones and nature monuments. We had found the factors to create the kind of conflict we needed to prove and to demonstrate the working of this instrument.

In the south is one of the very big rivers in the Netherlands, a typical highway net. We are setting up a kind of fieldwork camp. Take a mini-scenario about a sheep used for kebabs eaten in the city. Of course, looking at the kebab has to do with the meat industry, the way it is changing because the population is changing. We go from very simple to quite complex. Suddenly this whole thing works like a machine, it has an input and an output and we are to reorganise those inputs and outputs. We try to see it like a machine, which connects and adds value because of this connectivity. However, we are dealing with very big players. We began by looking at a competing harbour up the river and new types of prototype ships to take all those containers. Its all about containers these days and harbours up to the rivers. But at the same time, we took this project over and said that we have to create cities that are much more mixed. All these conflicts cannot be solved only at the techni-cal level. This is a cultural and not just a technical problem.

We produced a lot of 'products': in the beginning we produced a small agenda for the consortium we are working with, including several ministries and large firms. This is quite a unique step in the

Netherlands. To go more abstract, we needed a layer for the individual members of the consortium. This is called the 'Community of Practice' for the consortium, and then we have the *Urban Gallery* with which we will regulate them. At the moment we are dealing with the management of the process; at what time each layer is activated and how it gets back to the consortium.

As architects, we are also *process managers*: we have databases, prototypes. All the stuff will happen here but it will be quite real.

The first sketch of the dynamic master plan we are working on includes places where we propose centres for communities. Each will have a different set of actors and agents that will participate in the development of building projects in the area. We need to have all the elements of planning there: from the harbour people to the ecologists to the new immigrants and so on. It's an enormous mix.

So we are trying to create a kind of mix, but it is not only about mixing. It is a dynamic tuning of different programmes. We go through the whole range again: open spaces, the prototype boxes etc., trying to compete with the area next to the harbour. We want to break the 'rules', the 'law'. We believe we can have a total mix between industry, landscape and city. This is in effect what we are trying to do: a reaction to the working city. It is very strange to be involved in something of this magnitude. But that is part of the society we are in now. In the consortium, we are trying now to discover which are the prototypes that can be tested out. We have a logistics expert, a system management person. We're looking at the area where we could actually start, the higher density area. Of course, we can begin to look at special arrangements between different problematic conditions. But at the same time we are like caretakers. We have to say: 'Hold on guys, this is not only about the harbour'. There is a big tendency in Holland to create more building and to give this useless, agricultural land back to the ebb, the flow and the tides of the river. As architects we can act as caretakers of these trends and we are trying to build them into this environment. There is a big cultural shift going on in the Netherlands at the moment. And it is effective, because most of the land is below the sea level and it is very easy sometimes to cut a dyke and be there.

At the moment we are dealing with the biggest actor, the Dutch version of Enron. They are a very powerful player who is in trouble. We are beginning to negotiate with them on how they can be the main player within this working city. We thought of how to link the new types of agriculture to the production of this power plant. I was very scared at the beginning; scared to touch them. But then I approached them and they were quite keen to become partners in the whole thing. I realised that we actually have a role to play: as architects, in fact, you have a part to play with such actors. I think they need people like us, because they don't know how to move in the changing society. The buildings in which they are making vegetables have nothing to do with the sun or the earth. We can give them some very simple steps, in the beginning, to linking new types of agriculture with the power plant.

At the moment, we are also involved in building up a new web site. In fact, it is not only a web site. It is a knowledge management tool that is based on some of the things that we are developing. This knowledge base will be developed as part of the tool in order to get as many people to participate in the whole thing as possible.

We try to separate things out in layers, but we always look for connections between them and, of course, the people that are related to these connections. A prototype connects things into what we call operational fields. The typology of the prototype interweaves between different operational fields. The key is adaptation: a prototype must always be adaptive. It has to be adaptive from [01] into [02], or more, such as [02] into [03], etc. There is an endless proliferation in a larger area. It is a kind of stitching. Then we begin to link that to imported phenomena, to juxtapose it with existing phenomena that create dynamics. The prototype regulates and interconnects dynamics of layers. This is the issue of complex dynamics, this kind of handling, the adaptation and proliferation of prototypes in a particular environment.

To stir a city you have to first get its ingredients sorted out, then feed them into the cooking pot one by one, each one prepared in the manner that gets the most out of them. Urbanism needs to be treated more like cooking, or another creative art in which we mix many ingredients and then manipulate them. But cities have minds of their own, and that is where things get both exciting and challenging: which way will trends move?, where will conflicts emerge?, where will new opportunities arise? The real skill is to move inside it, with it, and to be outside it at the same time, in a kind of meta space in which its dynamics are reflected, drawn upon layers, distilled into recognisable configurations, delineated into a rarefied plastic space in which the hand can touch each evolution and intervene in it with immediate effects in the real city. Luckily it is not that simple, and there are many obstacles to be surmounted and steps to be negotiated.

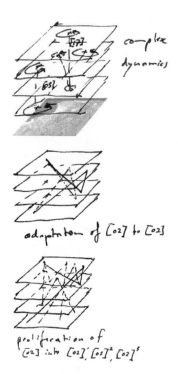

19.11 – Prototype layers.

Your place, or mine..?
A study on participatory design, youth, public space and ownership

The scenes
- Preamble
- Place
- Project
- Players
- Products

The cast
- A visionary man from the local authority
- A couple of people from Fluid, teaching at London Metropolitan University
- Some architecture students from said university, one of whom later joins Fluid and two of whom provide accounts in this chapter
- A few young people from 8 to 18 years of age, not all of them local
- Two youth outreach workers from the Clerkenwell Detached Youth Project
- A university Reader in Urban Policy, who is also a local resident
- A well known and highly respected engineer
- A quantity surveyor
- Ken Worpole (a brief walk-on, but very significant part).

Preamble
In this chapter we will reflect on issues of participatory design, patterns of ownership and the nature of contemporary public space, with reference to a small project for the design and delivery of two youth shelters in Clerkenwell in the London Borough of Islington. We will look at the social and physical make-up of our site, explain the nature of the project, introduce the key players and accounts of their experience of and contribution to the project. We will then discuss the products (the shelters) and some of the by-products, for instance, 'social cohesion'. In other words we'll use a small project to test some big ideas.

      This preamble includes a brief review of urban youth, one of our new 'hard-to-reach' groups. It discusses issues of belonging, exclusion, branding, criminality and consumption.

Your place, or mine?

Possession, some say, is nine-tenths of the law. Others, including the influential social and political philosopher, John Stuart Mill, says it is theft. But beyond the 'mere' status of direct ownership, whatever the shaky nature of acquisition, lie further, subtler questions about the nature and ownership of place – its design, image, necessary protocols and 'brand', and how these characteristics include some and exclude others just as surely as a good 9" brick wall or cast-iron title deeds. Of all those excluded from any given urban territory, youth surely form the greatest subset. They are excluded on the grounds that they are not yet adults, that they cannot pay, that they are trouble-makers, that they will break the law, be noisy, or frighten other, paying customers away. A 2002 survey discovered that around 28 per cent of English people believe that 'teenagers hanging around on the streets' represent a problem, a figure that grows to 40 or 50 per cent in areas of multiple deprivation.[1] This is far from being an aberrant finding and in fact just scratches the surface of what appears to be a deep and growing level of resentment against young people. A 1997 MORI poll[2] found that an astonishingly high 75 per cent of the adult population supported a legally enforceable evening curfew on teenagers. Ken Worpole suggests that coercive restraint of young people is not only widely supported by the adult public but is also gently reflected through government structures:

> It is telling that the Minister for Children and Young People also doubles up as Community and Custodial Provision Minister, based at the Home Office rather than being a minister located within the more permissive and developmental settings of Health, Education or even Culture, Media and Sports ministries.[3]

It is often forgotten that young people are themselves afraid of 'public space', and are more likely to see themselves as victims of, rather than perpetrators of, violence. Such fears are echoed by research conducted by Newcastle City Council, which sought the views of some 300 children and young people in the city about their attitudes towards the use of open space. It found that many chose not to go out or to use parks because they were afraid of getting bullied or worse.[4] A recent survey[5] carried out by the EC1 New Deal for Communities project in London (the organisation which co-funded the youth shelters discussed in this chapter) reveals the perspective of the young people who said that 'adults are aggressive and horrible to us', they 'think children are the scum of the earth', and that 'we are always being complained about'.

20.01 – 'Youth'.

1
General Household Survey 2002. UK National Statistics Office. The percentage is those for whom 'Teenagers hanging around (is) a very or fairly big problem.'

2
www.mori.com/polls/1997nfmo2/shtml

3
K. Worpole, *No Particular Place to Go? Children, young people and public space*, Birmingham: Groundwork UK, 2003, p.9.

4
L. Holland, *Newcastle Parks and Green Space Strategy: Draft background report*, Newcastle: Newcastle City Council, 2003.

5
Community Safety Audit, London: EC1 New Deal for Communities, January 2003.

Such complaints, however vague or ill-founded, may point the finger at anti-social behaviour (ASB), a misdemeanour that is nowhere clearly stipulated yet serves as a cause for forceful action. In effect, ASB is a kind of trip switch between the two poles of bottom-up involvement and coercive control, the carrot and stick of current policy. It is reflected in the chemistry of 'Acceptable Behaviour Contracts' [6] originally piloted locally by Islington community officer Paul Dunn, who discovered that many parents were unaware of what their children were up to when they were out of the home and had little understanding of the impact that so-called anti-social behaviour has on communities. The young people themselves often simply did not understand what by most standards constitutes acceptable and unacceptable behaviour. Dunn introduced a new approach 'to adjusting the behaviour of young individuals over 10 years of age' through a form of policing that involves not just the police force, but the Local Authority's housing department, the young person and their family in agreeing what those standards are. The scheme takes the form of a contract, an 'Acceptable Behaviour Contract' (ABC), which is drawn up by the youths in question in the presence of their families, a police officer and a housing officer. The intention is, in the first place, that all parties understand the impact that the young person's behaviour is having. The seriousness is brought home by the implied threat that a serious breach can lead to the eviction of the family. Thus the 'family is brought into the loop of responsibility for the child's behaviour and the child has to face up to their responsibility to their family'. Those who breach are not automatically punished; it is acknowledged that young people will test the boundaries. However, in the rare case of repeated breaches, the ABC can be replaced with an Anti-Social Behaviour Order (ASBO) that can bring up to a five-year sentence if flouted.

The binary nature of policy responses to youth justice, the carrot and stick of inclusion and detention, is not constrained to the UK, but is evidenced across all of Europe. At the same time there appears to be a growing awareness that crime has to be dealt with not so much through punishment meted out by a remote system, but locally, with and through the agency of active community. As Lode Walgrave and Jill Mehlbye note:

> Every country has developed its own system for dealing with juvenile crime, and is struggling in its own way with the tension between two opposite accents in it: offering support, assistance, education and assuming that this will bring about more commitment to social values and norms, versus controlling and punishing, while safe-

guarding elementary legal rights. There are nevertheless some general lines discernible. As public pressure became more strict and defensive, authorities had to take more seriously public security on a short term. In prevention, as well as in juridical reaction, two key words seem to become more and more apparent: community and accountability. Community is involved in all kinds of preventive initiatives, for giving support as well as for providing informal social control. Accountability is the essence of the emerging attitude towards juveniles who offend. Increasingly, the way they have to account concretely for their acts is focused on restoring in community. Their offence is considered as an intrusion to life in community, with the concrete victim and with the broader environment, and they have to do gestures of restoration towards them. It may announce the emergence of a broader tendency in dealing with crime, the restorative justice approach.[7]

7
L. Walgrave and J. Mehlbye (eds), *Confronting Youth in Europe: Juvenile crime and juvenile justice*, Copenhagen: AKF, 1998.

Whatever the responses to issues of social justice, the wider problem of the deterioration of our public realm has yet to find an adequate solution. At government levels this problem appears to be compounded by a lack of clear understanding about the role of public space:

> For some politicians and civil servants, public realm issues seem to be regarded principally as a crime and disorder matter, for others an issue of environmental quality, while yet another group see them as being principally about tourism and consumer-led leisure and regeneration (as in the Select Committee Report on The Evening Economy and the Urban Renaissance 2003). The concept of 'public space' has never been so popular but never so poorly conceptualised or understood, especially in its use by children and young people.[8]

8
Worpole, 2003, p.9.

In areas such as our Clerkenwell site where there are multiple levels of deprivation, for instance, where poor education, low employment, poor health and substandard environments combine, the public domain gets further problematised and stigmatised through steep escalations in perceptions of fear based on real, but often undramatic evidence of higher than normal crime rates. In response, whole neighbourhoods retract into themselves, voiding public space, emptying out streets and isolating 'public' facilities, all further severing the suffering neighbourhood from the surrounding city. A range of studies carried out by the Joseph Rowntree Foundation discovered that real and imagined barriers had both to be overcome if disadvantaged neighbourhoods were to be healed:

The studies found both physical barriers, such as lack of adequate transport, and psychological barriers to reconnecting disadvantaged neighbourhoods to the urban areas of which they are part. Better transport links to the rest of the urban area are an essential requirement in this respect. But more fundamental was a need to break down the psychological barriers to integration.[9]

In attempting to deal with one of these psychological barriers through repopulating public space a recent regeneration project in Glasgow tried to reintroduce street games, but discovered that most of the local young people did not know how to play them. Hopscotch was as relevant to them as 'pall-mall', a Victorian street game now only commemorated by a London street name, though it is perplexing how quickly social traditions can get erased and forgotten. However, surely we should have learned by now not to expect handed-down solutions to work? The proposals have to come from a more informed reading of places and people. Participatory design offers one avenue, and it is an avenue that can lead to more than just a physical or spatial solution. With a little forethought, design can extend to and stimulate social interchange and the repositioning of perceptions of a neighbourhood, and particularly its public spaces. This applies to young people as much as to adults:

> Creating a sense of 'ownership' of public and community spaces is a pre-condition of successful use, care and maintenance. The key stake-holders in a secure public realm are the public themselves, including children and young people, and their involvement at all levels is essential.[10]

The fabrication of youth culture

In *Hiding in the Light* [11] Hebdige asserts that 'in our society, youth is present only when its presence is a problem, or is regarded as a problem'. In fact the whole category of 'youth' as articulated in the ethnographic research of Robert Park and his colleagues at the University of Chicago in the late 1920s identified youth with trouble: 'The high incidence of juvenile crime in inner city areas and the significance of group bonding in distinctive juvenile gangs' was explained through the metaphors of 'social pathology, urban disequilibrium and the breakdown of the organic balance of city life'. This tradition is largely responsible for establishing the equation, by now familiar in the sociology of youth, between adolescence as a social and psychological problem of particular intensity and the juvenile offender as the 'victim of material, cultural, or moral deprivation'.[12]

9
Social Cohesion and Urban Inclusion for Disadvantaged Neighbourhoods, Joseph Rowntree Foundation, April 1999.

10
Worpole, 2003, p.30.

11
D. Hebdige, *Hiding in the Light: On images and things*, London: Routledge, 1988.

12
Robert Park, E. W. Burgess, R.D. McKenzie, *The City: Suggestions for the investigation of human behavior in the urban environment*. Chicago: University of Chicago Press, 1925.

So far as recent social history is concerned, the condition of youth and the specific transition from childhood to adulthood remained 'concealed' within the militaristic regimes that pervaded Europe for the first half of the twentieth century. Thus it was only on the demise of militarism in Europe that young people were given the opportunity of free expression – and then, in a highly industrialised world where they were brought into contact with marketing and media forces on a scale that had never before existed. In the absence of accepted rituals, contemporary rites of passage were about to be rewritten. By the late 1950s the teenager had truly arrived, whilst conscription, in most European countries, was fast disappearing. The unruly and rebellious nature of the teenage condition, something that was considered inherent, was celebrated in cult movies like *The Wild One*, starring Marlon Brando, and *Rebel Without a Cause*, starring James Dean, or in novels like Jack Kerouac's *On the Road*, or Alan Sillitoe's *Saturday Night and Sunday Morning,* later themselves translated into film. As with the protest songs of the 1960s, or still further with rock and roll, these forms of mass media dealt with a highly symbolic yet nevertheless deeply felt rejection of the values and lifestyles associated with capitalism.

The penetration of marketed models – say, for instance, rap music in the UK and northern Europe, which refers not just to the consumption of music but to the acquisition of 'attitude' – is sharper and harder than at any previous time. Marshal McLuhan noted the inherent conflict between media figures and the authority of the family many years ago.[13] The intensity of this conflict has, if anything, increased. According to European-wide consultation, only 15 per cent of youths aged between 18 and 25 consider political parties and religion to be very important versus 44 per cent who see television as very important. The depoliticisation of youth is a measurable long-term trend.

This depoliticisation goes hand-in-hand with the branding of youth culture. The consolidation of corporate power in the global economic system that emerged after the collapse of the USSR has led, amongst other things, to the domination of media and information systems by an ever-shrinking number of multinational media corporations. Time Warner, Disney, Bertelsmann, General Electric, TCI, Viacom, and Rupert Murdoch dominate global media in a manner that would have been unthinkable only ten years ago. One aspect of this has been the emergence, over the last decade, of an apparently borderless youth culture. In her evaluation of youth culture, Naomi Klein[14] cites the 'New World Teen Study', which revealed that the single most significant factor contributing to the shared taste of the middle-class teenagers it surveyed was TV – in

13
M. McLuhan, *Understanding Media: The extensions of man*, New York: McGraw-Hill, 1964, especially the chapter: 'The medium is the message'.

14
N. Klein, *No Logo*, London: Flamingo, 2000.

particular MTV, which 85 per cent of the sample group watched every day:

> By identifying with deeply cherished parts of a 'manufactured' culture, corporate brands approximate a transcendent quality. A transformation has taken place from advertising agencies and media companies as marketers of products to 'meaning brokers'. They no longer just sell goods, but a way of life. It is a way of life that knows no barriers.[15]

15
Ibid.

16
Societal change and change in value systems.

On top of the artificial pressures brought to bear on young people through marketing, media and branding, it is clear that today's youth are also exposed to high levels of churn.[16] In highly deprived areas, few adults are in a position to act as role models or mentors; their own exclusion through lack of education or employment all too often precludes effective action. The loss of respect for symbols and actuaries of authority is a natural corollary of disaffection. In areas of high deprivation this lack of respect can be seen to spread beyond the family towards teachers, policemen, political figures and, in effect, most paternalistic systems. If political figures are unable to enter into discourse with youth, then it is possible that the needs and desires of young people will remain invisible. As youth are 'without power' and appear indifferent to party politics, they cut themselves off from formal systems of representation. Could this self-exclusion partly explain the prevalence of youth violence?

It is generally assumed that there is a causal relationship between long-term unemployment and opportunistic juvenile crime in a given area, but crime statistics indicate otherwise. For example, the North-East of the United Kingdom, with the highest unemployment rate, has one of the lowest juvenile crime rates. Equally, there is no direct correlation between the incidences of juvenile crime in relation to adult crime; the UK has by far the highest incidence of juvenile crime in the EU, but is not at the top of the adult offender league tables. This points to the conclusion that trends in youth culture follow patterns outside adult norms, and are affected by a series of issues that are particular to the youth sector. What became apparent from both our readings and our observations was how carefully any approach to user groups should be orchestrated, and how one had to dismiss the normal clichés and labels (youth with hood = bad). Instead we had to enter with our eyes open to the experience of the users, and how this was culturally and socially defined in ways beyond their immediate control.

Place

17

S. Murdoch and S. Thake, *Exmouth Market: Building a shared vision for the future*, London: UNL, 1997.

Stephen Thake, a Reader in Urban Policy from London Metropolitan University, mapped the changing fortunes of what had once been the borough of Finsbury in an earlier study.[17] These maps tell the tale of change from a thriving place with strong business links to the City; a place with its own Town Hall and 30 Councillors, Sadlers Wells Theatre, the local Church of the Holy Redeemer with a congregation in the high hundreds, the nascent City University and its swimming pool (then open to local people), and big local employers including the largest postal sorting office in Europe, the headquarters of the Metropolitan Water Board, Booths and Gordons Gin Distilleries (drawn in by the spas and rivers of Clerkenwell), lens grinders, book binders, printers, jewellers and watchmakers.

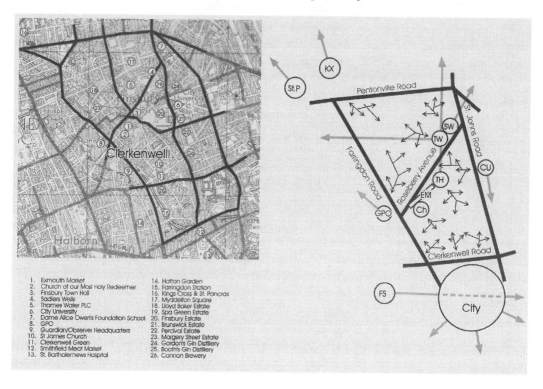

1. Exmouth Market
2. Church of our Most Holy Redeemer
3. Finsbury Town Hall
4. Sadlers Wells
5. Thames Water PLC
6. City University
7. Dame Alice Owen's Foundation School
8. GPO
9. Guardian/Observer Headquarters
10. St James Church
11. Clerkenwell Green
12. Smithfield Meat Market
13. St. Bartholomews Hospital
14. Hatton Garden
15. Farringdon Station
16. Kings Cross & St. Pancras
17. Myddelton Square
18. Lloyd Baker Estate
19. Spa Green Estate
20. Finsbury Estate
21. Brunswick Estate
22. Percival Estate
23. Margery Street Estate
24. Gordon's Gin Distillery
25. Booth's Gin Distillery
26. Cannon Brewery

20.02 – Clerkenwell, past (left) and Clerkenwell, present: reorientation and disorientation (right).

Over a period of something less than forty years between the mid-1960s and the present day this situation has changed dramatically. The old borough was absorbed into Islington, with the loss of use of the Town Hall (rumoured to be on the market for conversion into private housing). Of 30 councillors, only 6 are left in place. The Church, though still highly active in the area, has a congregation that is a fraction of what it was. City University, once highly used by locals, has turned its back, whilst the City now trades globally, and neglects the 'city fringe'. The Metropolitan Water Board has been absorbed by Thames Water Utilities who have moved the HQ and left only a skeleton team at the site of what had once been the 'New River Head'. The postal sorting office was downscaled, the distilleries moved north as the local waters became polluted, and the lens grinders, book binders, printers, jewellers and watchmakers have mostly gone. Finsbury Health Centre, once the pride of the borough, had, through interminable battles with English Heritage,[18] failed to keep pace with health care needs and had been marginalised as a local, 'dysfunctional', clinic.

The site of our project lies between what are now the deprived estates to the east and the newly gentrified and media-dominated enclave of Clerkenwell to the west. Exmouth Market to the north, once a functional street market, has been replaced by branded bars

and eateries that tend not to be affordable by many of the area's long-term residents. To the south is the 'cultural quarter' full of young architects, media companies and schools converted for business use. One has also to factor into this shifting picture the growing unease between the area's white residents, and its relatively modest scattering of ethnic minority groups. Sitting in the middle of all this is the small but well-used park of Spa Fields (Islington is the third worst London borough in terms of the amount of public open space). Taken together, the site can best be described as a kind of socio-economic, historical and spatial fault line, a place of great tensions and inexorable drifts.

The park itself is a fiercely guarded territory as it is the one place that all can afford. This weighs heavily in lingering local perceptions that the park might go the way of the Town Hall, the swimming pool, and other facilities that are now either sold off, closed down or out of reach. Spa Park sits in the shadow of Michael Cliffe House, a twenty-storey landmark, known locally for the

18
Finsbury Health Centre (1938) by Berthold Lubetkin and Tecton is a listed building.

20.03 – Aerial view of Spa Fields Park looking west, taken from Michael Cliffe House.

twenty-two rooftop suicides it has witnessed over the past two decades. It stands over Three Corners Playground, a facility managed by Islington Council to provide monitored play for five- to twelve-year olds. The park includes two five-a-side football pitches and two tennis courts. But most edges of the park are defined by rear elevations, leftover spaces generated by the imposed footprint and anterior logic of estate master plans, or dark institutional buildings generating a dim and dangerous void at night.

20.04 – 5-a-side football pitch in Spa Fields Park. (Photograph: Jeff Forbes.)

19
Places where kids congregate – they tend to be distributed and diffuse in use rather than fixed and regularly used.

Wilmington Square bandstand, 200 metres away from Spa Fields, is one of a number of 'youth plots' [19] in and around the park. It offers shelter and focus, but local (and mainly middle-class) residents of the Georgian Square have already succeeded in moving on the previous tenants of the bandstand, the Wilmington Square boys. They are on the lookout for new plots.

20.05 – Elsworth's route and occasional 'plots'.

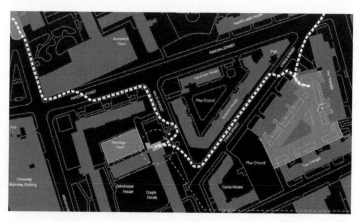

The Clerkenwell Detached Youth Project aims to gently intervene in the lives of the youths who use the park and its surroundings, entering their spaces only when trust and respect have been

20.06 – One of the 'plots'.

gained. They offer activity, advice and direction in terms palatable to the youths. Elsworth, a CDYP youth outreach worker (see p.265), follows a route through the Clerkenwell Estates twice a week, gaining and using intimate knowledge about youths' use of various places and spaces. Parks are a big hit for the youths as they are rarely patrolled by the police and wardens are a thing of the past. They are free here and unobserved. In the centre of the Spa Green Park, hidden from view by bushes and shrubbery, is their 'hut' and sometime centre of operations. It is the meeting ground for many of their transactions with CDYP. It becomes important to us later.

Project

In the Autumn of 2002 we were finalising a site for the year's project to be run in 'dip5' – the diploma architecture unit run by Fluid at London Metropolitan University – to look at issues and ideas of play in the city. We were drawn to Spa Fields for its curious and intense history, its strange existence, and its location on the fault line of a socio-economic divide. Over time, and in collaboration with the London Borough of Islington's Greenspace Department, the Clerkenwell Detached Youth Project and EC1 New Deal For Communities, a brief was agreed for the collaborative design and delivery of what was originally one youth shelter, to be located somewhere in the Spa Fields Park. A budget of around £12,000 was agreed for all capital costs, with the design and construction of the shelter to be delivered free by the students who, in return, would gain hands-on experience and a break from the tedium of infinite possibilities. Fluid would act as the project managers, and field the necessary professional indemnity and public liability insurance. The university would underwrite the site insurance. The rest would be down to the teaching process, the resolution of the students, the input of the local youths, and the determination of Jamie Dean, our key contact at Islington Greenspace and the main project champion.

Though a tiny structure was envisaged, it was clear that planning consent, building regulation approval, a clear Health and Safety plan and a fully costed specification would have to be negotiated and delivered. There would also have to be intense negotiations between the borough, EC1 NDC, CDYP and the main users – the area's young people. For a small project, it asked for a lot.

The students initially worked in four competitive groups. Each met regularly with their users who were themselves split into two groups (nominally those up to, and those over fourteen) at the local CDYP HQ. At other times 'consultation' happened at night in the park, though this most often boiled down to 'getting to know you' sessions, to reduce the risk to life and limb of the uninitiated (essentially, architects, their students and other professionals whose knowledge of the use of space is often not equal to their knowledge of 'space' *per se*). A preferred design was to be chosen by the 'kids' and a panel of representatives drawn from the main players. In the event, through the perhaps slightly dubious method of having the funders rather than the youths themselves vote, two schemes were chosen, resulting in twice the headache for the students (and for us). One was to proceed immediately on a site that CDYP were keen to see adopted, taking into account the ideas of the three other groups, but essentially formed around the strong design armature of one particular group. The other was to be situated in the eastern spur of the park, following the advice of the Greenspace man. The first scheme was named *Zorro*, the second CU (pronounced 'see you'). On deciding the schemes, all students joined one or other group to work up the ideas, sort out the constructional drawings and generally get on with it.

Getting on with it took a lot of doing.

Players

The following accounts describe the interests and contributions of each of the players from their own perspectives.

A visionary man from the local authority:
Jamie Dean, Islington Greenspace

'Many planning devices still seek to address the industrial city; prescriptive densities, front-to-front distances and a desire to preserve and create public open space (POS). This position is generally supported by the general public despite a recent Mori poll (2002) suggesting 38 per cent of people are too frightened to enter urban parks and that open space management agencies struggle to maintain their existing POS as socially functional space. So by protecting open space from encroaching development, what does the single use POS designation deliver for the adjacent neighbourhood?

The neighbourhood around Spa Fields Park, along with the rest of London's City fringe, has witnessed radical social and physical restructuring following London's globalisation/deindustrialisation. The existing social infrastructure has struggled against this change. Many of the economic opportunities and social structures of the past are no longer in place, leading to considerable social exclusion. Conversely, an emergent, virtual neighbourhood, the 'Creative' Clerkenwell, converts and reuses redundant buildings and spaces to meets its needs.

Spa Fields Park is defined both spatially and socially by this

20.07 – Jamie Dean.

condition. Exmouth Market with its fine grain building plots and adjacent former warehousing contains and services the 'Creative' Clerkenwell. The Finsbury Health Centre, a valued piece of architecture/public health infrastructure, backs onto the park, and large-scale social housing to the north and east overlook it. It is utilised by the non-resident creative class as lounge space in the day to be later reappropriated as the primary territory of the neighbourhood's often disaffected and vulnerable young people. It is a space where anti-social and criminal behaviour is directed and contained – to the relief of the adjacent neighbourhood. As such, Spa Fields represents a place of exchange and conflict – poorly planned and neglected, it is unable to absorb all of the pressures of the local area and its environmental deterioration has steadily accelerated.

The recent revision of Planning Policy Guidance PPG 17 maintains the neo-romantic, open space typology of Street, Square and Park – a typology based on location, capacity and to a certain extent character. In variance to this, Islington Greenspace has attempted to define, develop and manage open space according to the social and spatial needs of the neighbourhood. Within the framework of the National Strategy for Neighbourhood Renewal we have aimed to develop a 'mixed use' designation of neighbourhood space.

With limited resources, often in an opportunist manner and via interesting coalitions, open space public participation has been undertaken. The results of this have been employed to develop appropriate types or subtypes of open space to reflect or address current usage patterns and identified social-spatial requirements. This approach does not require a classification system, as each open space programme will be unique, based on the requirements of its physical locality/social constituency. An organic unwritten diversification policy emerges across the open space network, and a new design code reorders existing space where it is not robust enough to deliver the identified programme.

Following participatory exercises at Spa Fields, a particular focus on the needs of young people and other local user subgroups has defined physical interventions, proposed spatial reorganisation and enhanced cross-sector service delivery,[20] without diminishing the enjoyment of other user groups. By layering and overlapping functions within the open space it is intended to achieve a critical intensity of use. Spa Fields Open Space has been reprogrammed to provide mixed use open space; green space, sports space, youth space, lounge space, but most importantly a space of multi-agency service delivery assisting neighbourhood renewal. Spa Fields has been defined by its users needs rather than by planning formula.'

20
Meaning the coordination of the efforts of the police/healthcare/youth agencies/ social services, in an effort to achieve the joined-up thinking espoused by the present Labour Government.

A couple of people from Fluid, teaching at London Metropolitan University: Steve McAdam and Pippa Gueterbock

'A live project is always more exciting for students and teachers as you have to deal with real people, real sites, real costs. These all challenge, inspire and test. The Youth Shelters presented a challenge which was embraced from the start, with all of the high highs and low lows that you'd expect from a project involving students, 'delinquent youth', a real schedule, an architecture school with its own agenda, a Local Authority (with its own agenda), a youth outreach group (with its own agenda), a vocal community and NDC board (an agenda, just not sure what), alongside all the paraphernalia of professional practice and project delivery.

Diploma Unit 5 have long been concerned with participatory urban design, and the value of combining deep consultation and architecture. Past projects have been live, often of an urban scale, and have sometimes had important knock-on effects (assistance in winning £25 million SRB funding for Finsbury Park and tuning of conditions for the new Arsenal scheme). This project's scale and depth were of a different nature due to its specific role and client ambitions, offering a different learning experience for the students than that of the large-scale projects. This was not just about the value of participatory design but about construction and the complexities that surround realisation, particularly where youth are involved. The unusual Rural Studio-inspired [21] procurement process of having students carry out the majority of the consultation, design and construction work meant the costs of the shelters were kept to a minimum, allowing high quality and innovative designs to be produced. The projects also represent a method of seeding wider area regeneration, ownership and social cohesion.

Instead of knowledge capital and creative energy being locked up in the halls of academe, projects like this allow the university, and its students, to contribute to improving the lot of local neighbourhoods while valuable learning experience is gained from direct engagement, placing social values high on the agenda of new urban professionals. These situations offer what Cecil Handyside has described as a Chinese Contract – a win-win situation where both parties best interests are in supporting those of the other.'

Some architecture students [22] from said university, one of whom later joins Fluid and two of whom provide accounts for this chapter:

1 — *Pannos Papassotirou*

'Participatory design constitutes interaction between various groups in order to achieve a common goal. In our experience with

21
The Rural Studio was founded by Samuel Mockbee at Auburn University, USA. Mockbee took his students out to the depths of Alabama where they designed and constructed buildings for the rural underclass. This empowering educational and architectural model still continues. See A. O. Dean, *Rural Studio: Samuel Mockbee and an architecture of decency*, New York: Princeton Architectural Press, 2002.

22
London Metropolitan University. In addition to those who have written here, these students are: Documentary: Jeff Forbes; Shelters: Ezlina Adnan, Chrysi Charalampaki, Az Effroni, Asua-Shirley Ellimah, Chryssoula Ouzouni, Lee Turner.

the design of the youth shelter we had to deal with four main groups. In such a project we have to take into account various clients and their need and aspirations.

I tend to think that the challenge we were facing was a bureaucratic experience as much as it was a technical and artistic one. As a student one wouldn't normally feel that being a talented designer would necessarily include management skills or even, I must say, diplomatic skills.

We encountered problems from different directions. For instance, the youth workers felt that locating the shelter beside the existing hut (an area already colonised by local young people and used for certain youth outreach projects) might not be the best option whilst we (the students) felt it highly appropriate. At the same time the Islington Greenspaces Department felt that a shift of interest inside the park itself would open up other pockets for use (which could be beneficial or otherwise). On the other hand EC1 New Deal was pushing for a positioning that wouldn't affect the current status or trigger any unwanted tensions inside the community. The youths themselves wanted the shelter to be in a place that would maximise their sense of fun and enjoyment, disregarding any effect that this might have on the park or other park users.

20.08 – Pannos Papassotirou (facing the camera, with Az Effroni).

My biggest dilemma was in the choice of an effective model of political engagement that I would feel comfortable with. Should I choose the path of constant consultation between all the groups, disregarding the potential waste of time and money that could be caused by an ongoing discussion that tries by definition to marshal sometimes totally opposing views? Or should I work with a small group of representative people, modelled on the 'local office' approach, where a small number of people shape the answers and plan the strategic moves?

I would say that compromise between forces is the ideal but that it sometimes limits one's creative impulses. On the other hand too much democracy is never bad, so maybe somewhere in the middle is the answer. As a group we did sometimes take decisions that no one else would know about, but we knew that this was the only way forward. At the same time there were days that we would spend trying to pull together different and conflicting ideas.

In terms of how all this process was useful or could be called a student project, I would say that all of the skills I have acquired during four years at the university and one year of working experience were all called upon in this project. It is most satisfying to dream and realise at the same time. With this project we definitely 'Dreamed for Real'.'

20.09 – Alisdair Nelson (seated) with Lee Turner.

'The Clerkenwell Detached Youth Project (CDYP) open design sessions were both rewarding and frustrating – the turnout was pretty inconsistent and opinion would vary wildly from week to week, but some key criteria emerged as did major design constraints that we'd have to take on board. One regular Wednesday-nighter nicknamed Cheech – a vociferous and enigmatic 10-year-old – would glance over the latest design and describe in detail how he would take it apart with fireman's bolt cutters or a sledge hammer.

The shelter would have to be tough. There could be nothing that could be cut, prised, levered, smashed or burnt. We would like to have clung to the idea that because this was for them, because they were involved and consulted that this would instil a sense of ownership and protectiveness. But Clive Jackson (Director, CDYP) wanted to know 'What happens if they drive a flaming scooter with a full tank of petrol into it? Can it resist anti-tank rounds, grenade attack?'

Initially there were four schemes – Scheme 2 (*Zorro*) was picked to go ahead without delay but was not the preferred choice of CDYP, nor was it favoured by the young people themselves. Greenspace (LB Islington) emerged from the shadows as our client and went on to unilaterally decide where the second shelter (CU) would be sited – a grass verge in the park about as far as you could possibly get from the hut. We felt disenfranchised. A further blow came when our photovoltaic-powered lighting was deemed inappropriate for the CU scheme, given its location, and was handed to the *Zorro* scheme.

After a major manufacturing hiccup, and delay after delay, the Manchester-based company we had entrusted with the steel and aluminium fabrication finally delivered the partially assembled modules on Monday 16 June. By this time Jamie Dean was no doubt looking for ways to write off the £4k he had stumped up and vowing never to work with students again – so you can imagine the elation when that truck came round the corner with the four huge gleaming rotundas strapped to the back of it.

The final assembly of CU took place off-site in the Greenspace yard a stone's throw from the hut and the *Zorro* scheme and was not without its problems, including an unscheduled visit to the local hospital's A&E on the first morning. The Great British summer had arrived for that week and it was amazing to see the park transform – the area around the hut seemed shadowy and deserted and all the action was on the other side – hundreds of lunchtime sandwich-eaters, and young people catching the last rays in the evening. We didn't see much of 'our' youth on the first few days apart from Cheech and a couple of mates who stopped by and offered to sell me a bike, but CDYP maintained a very helpful presence. On the fourth day we managed to get the things onto the site with the help of a kamikaze forklift driver. The sight of these four very large shiny things sitting haphazardly on the grass elicited much curiosity from passers-by – mainly dog-walkers, elderly people and the odd 'character' – 'huge fucking monstrosity' is the one remark that sticks in my mind.

The following morning we found the security fencing flattened (a difficult operation), and some vicious damage to the shelter, a low point indeed, though perversely this prompted a much-needed reconnection with the young people. We had no clue who had done the damage – always easy to blame young people – but that evening CDYP spread the word again about the shelter and who it was supposedly for, and after that we had no further problems with vandalism. Whether this was down to the talk with Elsworth, the CDYP youth outreach worker, or the fact that after that we left nothing vulnerable out overnight, we'll never know for sure, but we suspected the former was true; this did much to encourage us to finish.

After a marathon effort on the Saturday we were done apart from a few nuts to tighten. We returned Sunday afternoon, spanner in hand but couldn't do much as the thing was actually being USED!! It was a sight straight from the 3D models and collages we had used to visualise the final design – young people perched on the floor or lounging back on the seats into the aluminium curve. They had a few comments to make of course: the consensus was that if you sat here, or there, when it rained you'd get wet (you would), it needed a table in the middle, why didn't it have a proper roof...

I think they secretly liked it though.'

A few young people from 8 to 18 years of age, not all of them local
The students visited the hut weekly to discuss plans and ideas with the young people. It was not always the same group, as this was not a formalised youth club but a drop-in set. 'Meetings' were very informal-looking to the kids, but they were in fact well-planned with CDYP in order to gather the right information. Many of the young people had never seen an architectural drawing before, or understood the terms, so communication and design had to be simplified, but nonetheless be engaging and active.

20.10 – 'Spa Boyz' and 'Girlz' are taken on the London Eye as part of the engagement to inspire them.

'All we want is that thing in Wilmington [Square]. A bandstand's what we want. Where's the pen?'

Discussions were about where the shelter should be sited and why (territory, overlooking, etc.); what it should do (shelter; light and heat if possible); and what materials they should use. The young people were very clear about certain aspects of the design:

> We can do anything after time. We can get through anything if you give us enough time. That will not stop anyone... big pair of fireman's bolt cutters – just smash through that. That one looks good. This one looks like it'll just take a sledgehammer.

20.11 – Some of the young people helping with construction.

The students went away after each session, worked on the designs and brought back ideas to discuss with young people who did not mince their words: 'That things ain't gonna keep us warm or anything... This is all mad! All the metal's gonna make us freezing.' 'That – that'll only fit about three people in there. It'll be like two little armies trying to kill each other! We all wanna be talking together.' When designs were agreed and construction began, the young people were encouraged to visit the site and help the students in construction where possible. The site compounds, which would have probably been victims of burglary under other circumstances, were generally left well alone... 'Respect'.

A survey of sorts... (with 'Spa Boyz')
1 Where did you play when you were little?
   'Used to play around Kings Square playing footie.'
   'Used to build Lego in my house and Scalectrix.'

2 What do you get up to now?
   'Not much – hang around here, smoke weed...'
   'Half Moon Crescent, Barnsbury.'
   'Spa Park and smoke cannabis, play football and tennis, and congregate with friends to the rear of the set.'
   'A youth club one night a week, 7.15 – 9.45 at Percy Circus wc1.'

3 How much time do you spend in Spa Fields Park?
   'About 23 hours a day. Sometimes we crash out in the bushes. Take an hour out, like to walk around.'

4 Why do you come here (Spa Fields Park)?
   'The police are scared to come in here.'

5 What would you like to see here?
   'Astroturf football pitch, tennis court revamped, less 'alkis', and acres of skunk plants.'
   'A running track. What we'd like is that hut there to be ours, to have our key we can get in there. People won't be scared of us anymore, as we'll be in there smoking pot.'

Clerkenwell Detached Youth Project (CDYP) practises detached youth work, a non-centralised, on-the-streets approach to youth work that usually involves youth workers going to spots or 'plots' in the Spa area to talk to and mentor young people. Outreach work takes place mostly at the weekend and after school hours, and requires CDYP to offer support, advice and let the young people know about activities and education, as well as possible training or job opportunities that may interest them.

Carrying out this type of work on the street when young people are in groups on the street can be challenging, as often they are suspicious of adults and authority figures. Some of the young people have anti-social behaviour charges against them, others may need advice about getting support for abuse. In all cases CDYP aim to outreach young people to involve them in activities that are engaging, educational and fun.

It is imperative that CDYP workers have the trust and confidence of the young people in order for them to act as this conduit of information and support. Without this their job is more difficult; however, the Youth Shelters project was instrumental in earning this.

1 — Jacqueline Mallon

According to Jackie, the value of the process of engagement was most important because young people felt 'respected enough to be asked to be involved'. This in turn meant that they respected the shelters due to a strong sense of ownership: 'This had not just been imposed on them – this is their shelter, and not an alien entity brought in.'

The process also benefited their youth work relations. First, the shelters are 'a testimony to what we [CDYP] are doing; visual proof of what we are doing on the street'. Second, 'respect is a big thing on the street; it's held in high esteem', and the process earned mutual respect between the young people and CDYP workers.

In practical terms, the shelters have given a focal point for activities:

> During the construction the kids came to it every day even if they weren't involved in the consultation or construction. On completion, they provided consistency, as activities could be arranged around them. Before the shelters, kids would have to wait around the 'Hut' until staff arrived to unlock it for them. Other times CDYP workers would have to go out looking for them on the streets to bring them into activities.

Overall, Jackie believes that the shelters had a positive impact on youth work, and a reduction in anti-social behaviour, since the kids 'had a place to go'. This was verified by 2003 Turner Prize Winner, Grayson Perry, famed for depicting scenes of Clerkenwell's 'misspent youth' in his ceramic work. A resident of nearby Wilmington Square, Perry noticed the difference that the shelters made:

> These boys are so menacing when they ride around terrorising everyone, but since the council put up the little hut for them to hang around in near Spa Green Fields, they seem to have calmed them down.

Six months later:

> 'A change in park opening times has significantly restricted access to the shelters.' Now managed by an agency on behalf of the council, 'the park closes at dusk, which in winter can be as early as 4pm, meaning that the shelters are out of bounds at just the time when they would be used the most. The effect that this has had on the young people is not just a sense they are "back to square one" but is also one of betrayal. Many of them see the closure of the park as the shelters "being given with the one hand, and taken away with the other".' [23]

23
Glendales, the agents charged with the upkeep of the park on behalf of Islington Council, had the park gates reinstalled. These are closed at nightfall. This is, apparently, standard practice for Islington's parks. However, the local perception is that the space has been 'taken away' at night.

2 — Elsworth Samuel

Like Jackie, Elsworth felt that the overall impact of the shelters was positive, and that the sense of ownership – 'the kids had said "this is for us!"' – and respect was of key importance in their relationships with the young people. He described how having two shelters was useful in allowing CDYP to work with more than one group at a time:

> Kids from the different areas of Spa, Wilmington Square and the Osirus Estate had come to the park together, which had had positive outcomes, [whereas] usually they would be plotting around the estates, eventually being moved on to the streets.

Six months later:

Elsworth bemoaned the negative impacts of the early park closing. The trust that had been built up with the young people has been affected and they fear they may 'get punched in the teeth again'. Youth workers are building up relationships again now and are looking forward to the late closing hours of the park in summer time. 'That should help restore things a bit.'

A reader in Urban Policy at London Metropolitan University:

Stephen Thake
See 'Place' (p.254)

A well-known and highly respected engineer:

Alan Conisbee of Alan Conisbee & Associates

'To the Spa Fields Boys, the youth shelter was to be a stage on which they could act out rites of passage, let out frustrations and stamp ownership. So, how do you engineer a structure which blends the transience of theatre with the robustness of the 'rumpus room' and whose ability to be dismantled (for planning-political reasons) can be controlled, while absorbing the destructive intent of vandalism?

The oblique arrangement of the three partitions on the *Zorro* scheme immediately offered an opportunity to achieve an inherent stability of form – simply through adding weight to the structure. Thus, by bolting the wall frames to a heavy platform, by infilling them with rendered masonry and steel sheeting and by tying them together at the top with a stiff roof, the essential elements of the shelter were united to create a whole that can hardly be shifted.

CU is composed of inherently unstable forms, being precisely balanced at the bases of their curved frames – to the extent that, standing alone, they roll backwards when somebody takes a seat. Temporary permanence is therefore achieved by connecting frames in opposition – either straining away from each other or by an oblique connection side by side. Single railway sleepers undersail the pivot-points to provide the simplest of foundations.

Under the rules of demountability, a concrete base slab was disallowed. A steel frame decked in timber planking would have been expensive and labour-intensive to construct and the shelter would have lost its monolithic quality. For *Zorro* the use of cut-down railway sleepers as benches triggered the idea of a raft of sleepers for its foundations. Here, an upper layer of sleepers running side to side is simply screwed down on top of a base layer of sleepers running lengthwise and levelled-up on a sand/cement bed. The materials are cheap, simple to install, easily trimmed to shape but heavy. The wall frames are bolted down right through both layers of sleepers – just two bolts per wall, but the effect is that nothing can move without activating the mass of the whole. Rather like the mystery of the pyramids, the key to disassembly lies hidden from view.'

A quantity surveyor:

Richard Dobson of Dobson, White and Boulcott

'The measurement of value in a building project has many dimensions. In intrinsic terms of course, it is quite simple. The sum of the cost ingredients (the project budget) is the most obvious marker of value. It can be easily assembled, understood and readily compared against available benchmarks and with other similar projects.

Extending the context of financial value, however, soon introduces a greater degree of subjectivity. The financial worth of a project is unlikely to be its cost or project budget. The completed scheme will have a financial value dependent on market prices, which in turn are dependent upon all the familiar economic and market forces relevant to that project. Location, supply, demand, market confidence, interest rates, competition and many others all have a bearing on the ultimate market value of the finished project.

In the context of a self-build youth shelter, these 'normal' measures of value become marginalised. Yes of course, one can monitor the labour and material content and cost of designing, producing and assembling the shelter. Similarly, one could place a market value on the finished project, assuming of course that such a market existed. One could then set these measures against the perceived norms which are likely to be the most comparable off the peg products or solutions available on the market. A judgement of comparative value could therefore be made in these terms if required and if appropriate.

To do this alone would be to ignore the added value of a participatory design and construct project. How does one measure the learning experience of such a project, the value of the skills acquired, the experience of working within a team in competition with others, the benefits imparted over a lifetime of future projects and of course the simple satisfaction of creating and producing the project oneself rather than merely selecting and procuring in isolation? Such added values are quite simply immeasurable. But they cannot and should not be discounted or ignored.'

Ken Worpole

Ken Worpole was assembling material for a research project on children, young people and public space for Groundwork when we met him to discuss the Spa Fields Youth Shelters. The research is now published [24] and has been referred to liberally throughout this chapter. We were inspired and enthused by his work, and found that we shared many ideas and worries. We extended the collaboration through design reviews and by forwarding details of the Youth Shelter projects, which are referred to in his publication.

Products
Having immersed themselves in the area and familiarised themselves with the not always coherent wishes of their user and client

24
Worpole, 2003.

groups, the students produced detailed designs for the two shelters. They could not have been more different in concept and execution save, perhaps, for the shared use of green oak sleepers. They were both elegant schemes; one a zigzag, high-energy compilation of a restless nature (*Zorro*), the other a smooth, gentle and complete cocoon (CU). There is no doubt that both schemes had aesthetic merit, and it is fair to say that the kids (both pre- and post-14 years of age) were as wowed by their looks as their offer of use. Both exceeded, by a huge margin, the offer of an off-the-peg solution. Yet, is it possible that the stamp of design authenticity, of resolute and measured, even agonised, decisions provided things so perfect in themselves that they intimidated their users – even if only for a short space of time? What, finally, judged those design moves – was it an interpretation of needs or an imposition of taste? Did the users speak through the design, or did the design do all the talking? In essence, which served, which was server?

All year we had spoken about the ultimately provisional state of design. The final product, after all, is only a snapshot, a point on a line that Cedric Price once so eloquently described as the cycle of 'use, abuse, refuse and reuse'. But when does use become abuse, and the results of abuse, refuse? Within this cycle where does ownership really begin and design really end?

In their perfect state, which both schemes sought to sustain, graffiti and vandalism were to be contained through the use of strong forms and robust materials. They were not to be compromised when the young people made their inevitable marks. But local (especially youth) 'ownership' was part of the aim. Squaring this with the projection of a particular aesthetic proved problematic, even where the form of the scheme has been evolved through local discussion. On the other hand, if design, as both act and product, is to retain an inherent value, it is only reasonable that the designer can make their mark too. As always, it's a question of balance, of judgement, of the nuances as well as the signatures.

Zorro

Zorro was the first shelter to be completed. It is formed of a steel frame that describes three zigzag walls each finished with a different material (rendered blockwork, perforated aluminium and painted sheet steel). The frame is set into a base of green oak railway sleepers, two layers deep, the lower layer perpendicular to the upper layer and bolted together to form a heavy and stable raft. The profiled sheet steel roof deck is finished internally in perforated metal, which encloses the 8-watt strip lights that are powered (for about two hours each evening) by the photovoltaic installation on the roof. The whole ensemble is about the composition and use of different, not quite reconciled yet nevertheless highly judged components. The benches and walls are arranged to provide both focused social space and places to be on your own. The plinth stands high enough off the ground to be a kind of seat in its own right.

20.12 – *Zorro* under construction.
20.13 – Student construction drawing.

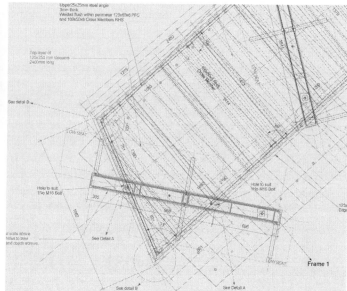

Zorro's presence at night was particularly impressive. The strip lighting, diffused by the perforated metal sheeting, gave the structure a muted glow intense enough to affirm the youthful geometry of the roof structure yet soft enough to afford privacy. When the photovoltaic lighting was knocked out, and the perforated metal

20.14 – *Zorro* lit at night (with photovoltaic panels visible on the roof).

wall and ceiling cladding knocked about, by a rival gang, within a week or so of handover, we all felt pretty miserable. The perforated metal could be, and was, 'sorted', but it was impossible to rewire the hundreds of stems that ran from the pholtovoltaic panels to the light circuits. The impressive night presence was short-lived.

20.15 (left) – *Zorro*, two weeks old and vandalised (apparently by a jealous local group.
20.16 (middle) – *Zorro*, one month old after being 'customised' by the Spa Boyz.
20.17 (right) – *Zorro*, nine months on, having been 'customised' by the council.

Since then the shelter has gone through two further incarnations. First, the youth claimed it as their own via a graffiti and paint job. This happened in various iterations until something not unakin to a Basquiat presence had been formed. Though the painting (in silver and black) of the beautiful green oak sleepers was hard to live with, the walls were always fair game. In time, the students could have got used to it.

The second incarnation was, in a sense, more curious. The council moved in, and painted everything (irrespective of material) either green (the kind of green that only local authorities can produce) or black. It seemed a considerable setback – but at least it looked, well, clean? Less amusing, however, was the fact that around the time of the re-rebranding of the shelter, the management of the park was handed over to Glendales who re-erected the park gates (which are closed at nightfall). This was something that had not happened at Spa Fields Park for many years.

Where the project had aimed to merge youth and public space, both disappeared in a puff of local authority magic.

CU

CU was completed at the twelfth hour, after the students' work had been handed in, and just before the summer exhibition at the university. It is formed of a bent tubular steel frame, supporting a floor and benches of green oak railway sleepers which, as well as describing the surfaces for inhabitation, provide additional ballast. Curved sheets of aluminium form the 'walls' and 'roof'. The shelter is made up of four sets of curved frames; three being arranged orthogonally, and the fourth turned away as if breaking from the pack. The ensemble recalls that of lounge furniture, one sofa and two easy chairs.

Sited in the more open, eastern part of the park, CU is akin to a pavilion and sits next to a footpath that bisects the small park. Its presence is more exposed, but also more 'proud' – there is little about it that is hidden. The site is not an area of the park that was used by the Spa boys and girls before CU's construction and, indeed, there were dire warnings that the shelter would not be well received by them as it was outside their usual patch. Happily these forebodings proved ill founded, and the shelter, though exposed to the usual amounts of dubbing and graffiti, remains solidly intact. An informal seal of approval has been given by the Spa kids – they think it 'looks really cool' and is 'mental'.

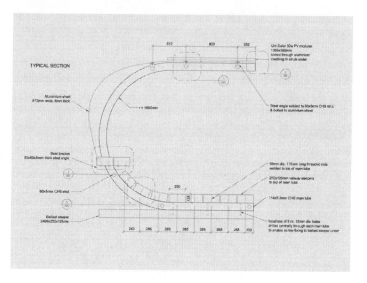

20.18 (above) – Initial sketch.
20.19 (right) – Student construction drawings.

As this shelter lies outside the typical youth domain, it is used by all manner of people. Coffee-drinking dog-walkers, sandwich-scoffing office workers and youth alike make use of it, albeit in radically different ways. There is something rather pleasing about this as, after all, why should particular things be designed for highly sifted age groups?

The structure appears to be at ease with itself, with its current status and with its projected role as signpost to a proposed youth centre 20 or 30 metres to the south.

But only time will finally tell whether the shelters worked. Youth grow up fast, to be replaced by other youths. If these successive generations appreciate and enjoy what was done for an earlier cohort, it will all have been worthwhile.

Meanwhile, the by-products of the scheme remain uncounted, and possibly will always remain immeasurable. On the downside, in the rush to design and build the schemes, little thought had been given to maintenance and management. The rusting bolt connections at the base of CU, for instance where steel bolts had to be drilled through the main tubes to overcome the damage caused by a local, who diligently stomped all over the welded galvanised steel threaded rods, are one defect, but hardly the fault of the students. It is also possible that, in drawing attention to the park as an asset, the shelters fostered negative feelings amongst local people. The withdrawal of public space when the park was subsequently closed in the evenings, though only for a few hours per day, plays to fears that are deeply felt in the area, fears that public assets will continue to be privatised.

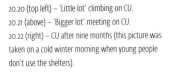

20.20 (top left) – 'Little lot' climbing on CU.
20.21 (above) – 'Bigger lot' meeting on CU.
20.22 (right) – CU after nine months (this picture was taken on a cold winter morning when young people don't use the shelters).

On the plus side it has been claimed that the shelters helped to 'calm local youths down'. Local youth workers say that they enhanced CDYP's street cred, and therefore the effectiveness of the youth outreach programme. It is also possible that they helped instigate a bottom-up use of and reprogramming of the park, as claimed by the Greenspace man, and may have helped broker better relations between the youth and the adults of the EC1 area as suggested by the engineer. Pippa's running of a forthcoming workshop at MADE (Midlands Architecture and the Designed Environment – a regional architecture centre), who plan to run their own youth shelter projects under the banner, 'Your place or mine' (...small world) may ensure knowledge transfer and the possibility of building on the shared experiences recounted here. This chapter, itself a by-product of the project, may make a difference to someone, somewhere.

Only time will tell.

Index